DAILY LIFE IN

MAYA
CIVILIZATION

Recent Titles in
The Greenwood Press "Daily Life Through History" Series

The Hellenistic Age: From Alexander to Cleopatra
James Allan Evans

Imperial Russia
Greta Bucher

The Greenwood Encyclopedia of Daily Life in America, Four Volumes
Randall M. Miller, general editor

Civilians in Wartime Twentieth-Century Europe
Nicholas Atkin, editor

Ancient Egyptians, Second Edition
Bob Brier and Hoyt Hobbs

Civilians in Wartime Latin America: From the Wars of Independence
to the Central American Civil Wars
Pedro Santoni, editor

Science and Technology in Modern European Life
Guillaume de Syon

Cooking in Europe, 1650–1850
Ivan P. Day

Victorian England, Second Edition
Sally Mitchell

The Ancient Greeks, Second Edition
Robert Garland

Chaucer's England, Second Edition
Jeffrey L. Forgeng and Will McLean

The Holocaust, Second Edition
Eve Nussbaum Soumerai and Carol D. Schulz

DAILY LIFE IN

MAYA CIVILIZATION

Second Edition

ROBERT J. SHARER

The Greenwood Press "Daily Life Through History" Series

GREENWOOD PRESS
Westport, Connecticut • London

Library of Congress Cataloging-in-Publication Data

Sharer, Robert J.
  Daily life in Maya civilization / Robert J. Sharer. — 2nd ed.
      p. cm. — (The Greenwood Press "Daily life through history"
  series, ISSN 1080–4749)
  Includes bibliographical references and index.
  ISBN 978–0–313–35129–7 (alk. paper)
 1. Mayas—History.   2. Mayas—Social life and customs.   3. Mayas—
Antiquities.   4. Central America—Antiquities.   I. Title.
  F1435.S54   2009
  972.81'016—dc22   2009000194

British Library Cataloguing in Publication Data is available.

Library of Congress Catalog Card Number: 2009000194
ISBN: 978–0–313–35129–7
ISSN: 1080–4749

First published in 2009

Greenwood Press, 88 Post Road West, Westport, CT 06881
An imprint of Greenwood Publishing Group, Inc.
www.greenwood.com

Printed in the United States of America

The paper used in this book complies with the
Permanent Paper Standard issued by the National
Information Standards Organization (Z39.48–1984).

10   9   8   7   6   5   4   3   2   1

For
Dan and Kate,
Michael and Kathleen,
Lisa and John

CONTENTS

ILLUSTRATIONS

All illustrations are by the author unless otherwise credited.

PREFACE

The Maya people created one of the most brilliant and successful of all ancient civilizations. This book presents a reconstruction of this civilization, based on a range of information from a variety of sources. The resulting reconstruction includes everything from established facts to data-based hypotheses, along with some informed speculations. This edition presents as much as possible of the latest findings about ancient Maya civilization, although future discoveries will certainly modify what is written here.

The book draws upon the author's personal experience of more than 40 years of research in the Maya area, primarily directing archaeological excavations at Maya sites in El Salvador, Guatemala, and Honduras but also including a study of a traditional Maya community in the highlands of Guatemala. It also draws on the investigations of scores of other researchers. As the pace of Maya research continues to increase, there is now an unprecedented amount of new information about Maya civilization. This comes from a variety of different fields, including archaeology, ethnohistory, ethnography, linguistics, epigraphy, and many other disciplines.

To continually cite this vast literature within the text would be disruptive for most readers. Instead, the referencing system used in the first edition has been continued and expanded in this edition: a listing of the principal sources of information for the subjects covered is included at the end of each chapter. These citations provide a sample of available sources, chosen to provide a range of accessible and current published works, along with some of the most significant older contributions, listed by author's name and year of publication. The full citations are in the Bibliography at the end of the book.

NEW TO THE SECOND EDITION

There has been considerable progress in our understanding of Maya civilization since the first edition of this book was published, in 1996. Our increased understanding stems from new decipherments of Maya writing, which has greatly expanded our knowledge of Maya history, and new archaeological research, which has produced far more information about the lives of the common people. Since the first edition, several important archaeological sites have been discovered, and research at these sites is already adding important new information about the Maya past.

This new edition presents more information about Early Maya civilization, a period that saw the genesis of social and economic distinctions, the first Maya kings and city-states, and the origins of writing. The beautifully preserved murals at the newly discovered site of San Bartolo (ca. 100 B.C.E.) provide new information about early Maya cosmology and kingship. Recent research at other lowland sites such as Blackman Eddy, Nakbe, and El Mirador, along with new data from the highland site of Kaminaljuyu and the Pacific coastal site of La Blanca, also illustrates these developments.

Newly deciphered texts have revolutionized our knowledge of political history during the Middle or "Classic" period of Maya civilization, including details about the lives of individual rulers and their reigns and about specific historical events (such as the founding of new kingdoms, alliances, royal marriages, and wars). Historical accounts, combined with archaeological research at capitals like Calakmul, Cancuen, Copan, El Peru-Waka, Nakum, and Tikal, reveal expansions and changes over the extent of this complex period and bring the careers of individual kings and king-makers to life. In the first edition, most Maya kings were referred to by nicknames in use at the time. Now, because of advances in the decipherment of Maya inscriptions, most of the Classic period rulers discussed in chapters 5 and 6 are referred to by their actual names.

Decipherments of Maya texts have revolutionized our understanding of Maya political organization, life at royal courts, religious rituals, and the underlying cosmological beliefs that guided people's lives. Newly discovered murals at Calakmul depicting activities of common people, accompanied by hieroglyphic captions, provide unique insights into everyday life and, for the first time, indicate that literacy may have been far more widespread within Maya society than previously believed.

Far more information is now available about daily life in general, including the lives of both Maya kings and commoners. Excavations at a number of smaller rural sites, such as Cerén, El Salvador, and K'axob and San Lorenzo, both in Belize, have led to a far greater understanding of how individual communities were organized and linked to larger economic, social, and political networks across the Maya area.

While the basic organizational structure of the second edition follows that of the first edition, every chapter has been updated, and most have been substantially expanded by new material. Twelve new illustrations have been added throughout the book. There is also an entirely new chapter devoted to the changes that occurred at the end of Middle Maya civilization (chapter 6), which set the stage for Late Maya civilization. To make room for some of this additional material, chapter 12 of the 1996 edition ("Arts and Crafts") has been dropped, and much of its coverage has been incorporated into expanded discussions of the ancient Maya economy (chapter 8) and society (chapter 9). Finally, reflecting the increase in information available about the ancient Maya, the number of entries in the Bibliography is more than double that in the first edition, and there are new references to DVDs and Web sites.

As in the first edition, the book opens by placing the ancient Maya within the context of today's world (chapters 1 and 2). Chapters 3–7 then describe the development of Maya civilization within its varied environmental settings, from the origins of village life and agriculture through three major developmental periods of Early, Middle, and Late Maya civilization, which span almost 3,000 years. This leads to a topical examination of Maya civilization in the second half of the book (chapters 8–12), with descriptions of the ancient economy (subsistence and trade), social and political systems, religion, cosmology, and writing. The book closes with an updated discussion of the meaning of Maya civilization in the modern world and how the achievements and failures of the Maya past can benefit people today (chapter 13).

ACKNOWLEDGMENTS

This second edition could not have been written without the help of many individuals, and it is impossible to acknowledge all of these people in this brief space. Suffice it to say that this book has benefited from the research and writings of scores of archaeologists and other Maya scholars, as well as from many discussions with both colleagues and students about the Maya past and present. I do want to specifically thank my colleagues who have provided illustrations used in this book: Arlen and Diane Chase, Arthur Demarest, Richard Hansen, Simon Martin, Jerry Sabloff, and Payson Sheets. Most especially, I want to acknowledge the help and support of my wife and colleague, Loa Traxler, who has assisted me in countless ways to prepare this book.

I would also like to thank all the people at Greenwood Publishing Group for their assistance, especially my editor at Greenwood, Mariah Gumpert, who helped me bring the manuscript into publishable form, and Bridget Austiguy-Preschel, production coordinator. But, above all, this book owes its greatest debt to the Maya people, past and present, whose brilliant achievements, perseverance, and courage are an inspiration for all of us in today's world.

NAMES, PRONUNCIATIONS, AND ABBREVIATIONS

The word *Maya* is both a noun that refers to the Maya people, past and present, and an adjective, as in *Maya history*. However, it is customary to use the term *Mayan* when referring to Mayan languages, as in *Yucatec Mayan*.

The names of some Maya cities, such as Chichen Itza and Mayapan, were recorded during the Spanish Conquest. In the highlands, the invading Spaniards had allies from Central Mexico, so many place names were translated into Nahuatl, the language of these Mexican warriors. As a result, *Q'umarkaj*, the K'iche Maya capital, was given its Nahuatl name, *Utatlan*. Many earlier Maya cities were abandoned by the Conquest era, so their names were unrecorded by Europeans. When the ruins of theses cities were rediscovered, they were often given fanciful Spanish or Mayan names, such as El Mirador ("the lookout"), Piedras Negras ("black stones"), Uaxactun ('eight stone"), or Tikal (probably from *ti ak'al*, "at the waterhole"). Today, the original names of many Maya cities are being rediscovered by the decipherment of Maya texts. As a result, we now know that the city renamed Palenque ("palisade") by the Spaniards was called *Lakamha'* ("Great Water") by the Maya people who lived there.

The English equivalents for Mayan vowels are:

a as in father

e as in let

i as in machine

o as in forty

u as in rule (but pronounced as an English w before another vowel, as in *wo*).

Long vowels are represented by doubled letters, as in *Xook*.

Consonants are also pronounced as in Spanish, with some important differences:

ch as in *ch*ur*ch* (Mayan *chaak*)

k as in *k*een (Mayan *kan*)

h (soft) as in *h*is (Mayan *baah*)

j (hard h) as in Ba*ch* (Mayan *ajaw*)

ts as in nigh*ts* (Mayan *ts'ak*)

x as *sh* in *sh*e (Mayan *Yaxchilan*)

Stress is generally on the final syllable in Mayan languages (CalakMUL), so accents are not used in spellings of Mayan words.

The abbreviation B.C.E. is used to designate dates "Before the Common Era" (e.g., 1200 B.C.E.); dates in the current era are given without designations (1200). Abbreviations and English equivalents for metric measurements are as follows: 1 meter (m) = 39.37 inches or 3.28 feet; 1 kilometer (km) = 0.62 mile; 1 square kilometer (square km) = 0.38 square miles.

CHRONOLOGY OF MAYA CIVILIZATION

Most dates are approximate.

EARLY AND MIDDLE PRECLASSIC (1500–400 B.C.E.)

Beginnings of early Maya civilization (earliest polities)

900–600 B.C.E.	Early polity at La Blanca on Pacific plain
900–600 B.C.E.	Early polity at Kaminaljuyu in highlands
800–600 B.C.E.	Early polity at Nakbe in lowlands

LATE PRECLASSIC (400 B.C.E.-250)

Early Maya civilization (first states)

400–200 B.C.E.	Earliest carved monuments in southern Maya area
200 B.C.E.–200	Apogee of Kaminaljuyu (highlands) and El Mirador (lowlands)
100 B.C.E.	San Bartolo murals (scenes of deities and royal inauguration)
100 B.C.E.–200	Earliest Long Count dates in southern area
1–100	Tikal dynastic founder (Yax Ehb Xook)
1–200	Earliest Long Count dates on Pacific coastal plain
200–250	Decline of El Mirador
250–400	Decline of southern Maya and Ilopango volcanic eruption

EARLY CLASSIC (250–600)

Beginning of middle Maya civilization (expansion of lowland states)

292	Earliest lowland Long Count date on Tikal Stela 29
359	Yaxchilan dynastic founder (Yopaat Balam)
378	Tikal takeover led by Siyaj K'ak'
379	Yax Nuun Ayiin installed as fifteenth Tikal king by Siyaj K'ak'
426	Copan dynastic founder (K'inich Yax K'uk' Mo')
431	Palenque dynastic founder (K'uk' Balam)
511–?	Earliest known woman ruler (Lady of Tikal)
562	Conquest of Tikal by Calakmul-Caracol alliance
583–604	Reign of Lady Yohl Ik'nal (woman ruler of Palenque)

LATE CLASSIC (600–800)

Middle Maya civilization (apogee of southern lowland states)

611	Palenque sacked by Calakmul
636–686	Apogee of Calakmul alliance under Yuknoom the Great
648	Petexbatun kingdom founded by Balaj Chan K'awiil from Tikal
659	Balaj Chan K'awiil defeated by Calakmul; becomes Calakmul ally
672	Petexbatun kingdom defeated by Tikal under Nuun Ujol Chaak
677 & 679	Tikal defeated by Calakmul-Petexbatun alliance
682	Refounding of dynasty at Naranjo by Lady Six Sky from Petexbatun
695	Defeat of Calakmul by Tikal under Jasaw Chan K'awiil
711	Defeat and capture of Palenque ruler by Tonina
736	Calakmul king Wamaw K'awiil visits Quirigua (alliance against Copan?)
738	Copan king captured and sacrificed by Quirigua
743 & 744	El Peru-Waka and Naranjo defeated by Tikal; Calakmul alliance broken
756	Copan recovery, with dedication of Hieroglyphic Stairway
761	Fall of Petexbatun capital of Dos Pilas; capital moved to Aguateca
800	Aguateca conquered, burned, and abandoned

TERMINAL CLASSIC (800–900/1100)

End of middle Maya civilization (decline of southern lowland states; apogee of northern states)

800–950	Apogee of Puuc states
808	Yaxchilan conquest of Piedras Negras
822	U Kit Took (failed Copan king)
849	Seibal K'atun ending with Calakmul, Tikal, and Motul de San José rulers
859	Latest dated monument at Oxkintok (northern lowlands)
889	Last dated stela in former Tikal kingdom
900–1100	Apogee of Chichen Itza
909	Last dated stela at Tonina

POSTCLASSIC (900/1100–1524)

Late Maya civilization (final states in northern lowlands and highlands)

1100	Chichen Itza sacked
1185	Mayapan becomes new capital in the north
1225–1250	Founding of K'iche Maya state in the highlands
1275–1475	Expansion of K'iche Maya state (capital at Utatlan)
1441	Mayapan sacked; begin rule by petty states in the north
1475–1500	Expansion of Kaqchikel Maya state (capital at Iximche)
1502–1524	First contacts with Spaniards
1524–1697	Spanish Conquest
1524–1527	Conquest of the Southern Maya, led by Pedro de Alvarado
1527–1546	Conquest of the Northern Maya, led by the Montejos (Elder and Younger)
1697	Conquest of last independent Maya state (Tayasal), by Martin de Ursua

1

THE MAYA OF PAST AND PRESENT

Several million descendants of a great civilization live today in southern Mexico, Guatemala, Belize, and Honduras. These people are the Maya, and the great civilization of their ancestors flourished for well over 2,000 years until 1524, when the Spanish began a brutal conquest of their lands. During that span, a succession of independent kingdoms rose and fell across the varied landscape of the Maya homeland. The Maya lived in villages, towns, and cities supported by a rich array of crops and the bounty from forests, rivers, lakes, and seashores. The largest cities were the capitals of the many Maya kingdoms spread across the landscape. In each of these cities, there were elaborate temples, palaces, carved monuments, roadways, plazas, markets, and the houses of their inhabitants. In times of peace, these cities prospered from a network of trade that linked the Maya kingdoms. In times of war, famous Maya kings led their people in the defense of their kingdoms or the conquest of their enemies. Captured warriors were often adopted by the families of the winners, but the most important captives, nobles and even kings, were sometimes sacrificed in religious ceremonies that celebrated each victory.

The achievements of Maya rulers have been rediscovered as scholars decipher the complexities of Maya writing, mathematics, and calendars, used to record dynastic histories along with myths and religious beliefs. Although the Maya kings and kingdoms have vanished, archaeology has revealed the many achievements of Maya civilization. Archaeological research has identified the plants the Maya domesticated and made more bountiful, such as maize (corn), squashes, chili peppers, and cacao (chocolate). It has also found skillfully woven textiles, precious carved jades, great painted murals and sculptures, networks of causeways and reservoirs, and beautifully proportioned palaces, temples, and other buildings rendered in a variety of styles.

We know far more about the lives of the elite members of ancient Maya society than the lives of the much more numerous common people. Most archaeological research has been aimed at elite palaces, temples, tombs, and ball courts and at the elaborate artifacts produced for the elite—carved jades, painted pottery, mirrors, and scepters. Maya historical inscriptions are even more biased toward the elite. These texts record the reigns of kings and their dealings with elite subordinates but seldom mention other members of Maya society.

The history of our Western culture is familiar to most students, with its roots in the ancient civilizations of Egypt and Mesopotamia and in the Classical civilizations of Greece and Rome. But the accomplishments of Maya civilization are not well known to most people. Treatments of American history have traditionally begun in 1492, with the "discovery" of what Europeans called the New World. Far less attention is paid to the peoples who had occupied both North and South America for thousands of years before the Europeans' arrival. So it is not surprising that most students are far less familiar with the peoples of the Americas and the history of their societies, including Maya civilization, all of which developed without any contacts with Europe or the rest of the Old World.

DISCOVERY AND CONQUEST BY EUROPEANS

Imagine the surprise and wonder of the peoples of both the Old World and the Americas when they discovered that there were entirely separate and unknown peoples elsewhere in the world. For Europeans of 500 years ago, the realization that there was an entire New World across the Atlantic Ocean and that it was inhabited by a variety of societies came as a complete surprise. Even more unexpected was the discovery that in two regions of the Americas—Mesoamerica (what is now most of Mexico and upper Central America) and the Andean area of South America—there were civilizations as sophisticated as those of the Old World. In both Mesoamerica and the Andes, many thousands of people lived in cities as large as or larger than those of Europe, with writing, metallurgy, stone architecture, painting, and sculpture.

These were the Inca of the Andes and both the Aztec and Maya civilizations of Mesoamerica. Bernal Díaz de Castillo, a soldier in the conquering army of Hernán Cortés, recalled the awestruck reaction of the first Europeans to see the great Aztec capital of Tenochtitlan from the mountain pass overlooking the Valley of Mexico in 1519: "When we saw so many cities and villages built in the water...and the straight and level causeway going towards Mexico, we were amazed....And some of our soldiers even asked whether the things we saw were not a dream...." (Diaz de Castillo 1956: 190–191; orig. 1632)

Both Cortés and Bernal Diaz de Castillo were from Spain, the European nation that sponsored the voyages of Columbus and led the discoveries of the great civilizations of the Inca, Aztec, and Maya. As a result, Spain deserves much of the credit and much of the blame for what followed. The history of the conquest and colonization of the New World was written by the victors. We seldom learn of these events from the defeated peoples of the Americas. The victorious Europeans described their heroic struggles in the New World, colonizing a new land against all odds. Yet, to the peoples already living in the Americas, this was an invasion of *their* lands and homes. Little do we know of the heroic struggles made by the peoples of the Americas to defend themselves against these strangers from the east who were interested only in the spoils of conquest and the exploitation of colonization.

For the great civilizations of Mesoamerica and the Andes, the end came relatively quickly. Within a few decades of the first European discoveries in the New World, civilizations that represented thousands of years of tradition were conquered and destroyed by plundering armies from Spain. In the Andes of South America, Francisco Pizzaro led the conquest of the Inca Empire. In Mesoamerica, Cortés led the destruction of the Aztec civilization of central Mexico. One of Cortes' lieutenants, Pedro de Alvarado, led the first conquest of Maya civilization in the highlands of Guatemala, while the Montejos, father and son, led the subjugation of the northern Maya civilization in the Yucatan Peninsula (described in chapter 7). The toll from these and other conquests of New World societies is hard to imagine today, even though our modern methods of mass destruction are far more efficient than those of five centuries ago. Nonetheless, it is clear that the combination of European conquest and alien Old World diseases caused the deaths of tens of millions of native peoples in the Americas.

The Spaniards were not the only Europeans who wanted to subjugate and colonize the New World. Portugal, England, and France competed with Spain to dominate the Americas. But Spain remained the primary power in what was to become Latin America. Because firearms and cannons could kill and destroy far more efficiently than the spears and arrows used by the peoples of the Americas, the Europeans had a significant advantage in any conflict. In fact, the very concept of warfare was different in the Americas, where gaining prestige by humbling your enemies and taking captives was more important than killing them. Warfare as practiced by the Spaniards and other Europeans meant killing as many of your enemies as possible and often destroying their cities and farms, as well. Such total warfare was unknown in the Americas, and this gave the Europeans another advantage.

Equally unknown to the peoples of the Americas were the epidemic diseases of the Old World. Without any natural immunity to measles, chicken pox, smallpox, and other illnesses, many more people in the Americas died from disease than by force of arms. Although they defended their homes, their cities, and their independence with great skill and valor, their resistance was undermined by a host of new diseases against which they had no defense. One by one, the greatly weakened peoples of the Americas were defeated, subjugated, and, in some cases, exterminated by armies and colonists from Europe.

The conquest of the Americas was far ranging. Whole cities, such as the Aztec capital of Tenochtitlan, were demolished to make way for new European settlements. The achievements of the indigenous civilizations were belittled and their religious beliefs condemned as pagan. Their human sacrifices were violent and cruel, but some early accounts were exaggerated to justify European atrocities. Such distortions continue today, such as the film *Apocalypto,* which falsely depicts the Maya as bloodthirsty savages who practiced human sacrifice on a genocidal scale. It is also well to remember that the horrors of human sacrifice were not limited to the peoples of the Americas. Europeans of the sixteenth century burned people alive at the stake and used many cruel methods of torture and execution even as they were condemning the "pagan" sacrifices of the Aztec and Maya.

Beyond the physical destruction, the ultimate means of subduing the peoples of the Americas was to proclaim that they were not able to develop civilization on their own, thus attacking their sense of pride and identity. A myth was created to justify European domination of "inferior" peoples. According to this myth, the "savages" of the Americas did not develop civilized practices such as writing, mathematics, or the arts of painting and sculpture. Rather, it was claimed, all things Europeans considered civilized had actually originated in the Old World. How did civilization come to the Americas? The answer came from imagining "long-lost" voyagers from the Old World who supposedly had arrived in the Americas before Columbus and who had taught the "savages" the ways of civilization. Thus, the Aztec, Inca, and Maya were "explained" as offshoots of forgotten colonists from Egypt or Greece or Rome or (depending on who was making up the story) a host of other places such as Carthage, Phoenicia, Israel, Babylon, India, China, and Japan. Human sacrifice and other "pagan practices" were explained as "corruptions" that developed in the Americas after the seeds of civilization were planted from across the seas.

There is no evidence to support these mythical "explanations." But, unfortunately, the core of this false myth can still be found in many popular books and magazine articles and especially on the Internet. What actually happened, what the archaeological evidence clearly shows, is that the evolution of civilization in the Americas was driven entirely by the descendants of peoples who had originally settled the Americas during the last Ice Age and took place completely independent of the process that gave rise to civilizations in the Old World.

The origins and growth of civilization in the Americas is an amazing story documented by archaeological research. This book will show that we can learn about the achievements of Maya civilization without resorting to fanciful accounts of Old World origins. Maya civilization was shaped by the efforts of the Maya themselves, along with what they learned from neighboring peoples of Mexico and Central America. It was not the result of a mythical Old World colonization. It was the result of growth processes that occur in all societies, including our own.

ETHNOHISTORY

Information from archaeology and pre-Columbian Maya texts is complemented by other written documents. After the Conquest, the Spaniards taught Maya scribes to use the Spanish alphabet to write their own languages. This allowed the Maya to transcribe many of their older documents, histories, prophecies, myths, rituals, and the like. Although only four pre-Columbian Maya books are known today, many additional colonial-period transcriptions have survived. These documents were often recopied over the years, but they provide an invaluable source of information about ancient Maya society.

The most important transcriptions come from Yucatan and the Maya highlands. From Yucatan we have several of the *Books of Chilam Balam* ("Books of the Jaguar Shaman"). These were kept by local religious leaders in many towns of Yucatan. Of those that have survived, the most important are the *Books of Chilam Balam* of the towns of Mani, Tizimin, Chumayel, Kaua, Ixil, and Tusik. They include historical chronicles known as the *U K'ahlay K'atunob*, the "count of the k'atuns" (the Maya period of 20 360-day years), which reconcile past events with prophecy and the Maya belief in the cyclic nature of history. Also from Yucatan we have a variety of colonial Spanish compilations of information about the Maya. The most important are Bishop Diego de Landa's *Relación de las cosas de Yucatán* (a sixteenth-century compendium that describes many facets of Maya life) and the *Diccionario de Motul*, a colonial dictionary of the Yucatec Mayan language.

From the highlands of Guatemala we have the history of the K'iche Maya recorded in the *Popol Vuh* ("Book of the Mat"). The outstanding surviving Maya literary work, it preserves the mythology and the traditional history of one of the most powerful peoples of the highlands (see chapter 7). The elegance and style of the *Popol Vuh* is sad evidence of the loss the Maya and the rest of the world have suffered through the destruction of most of the original Maya books during the Conquest and the colonial period. Also from the highlands come the *Annals of the Kaqchikels,* a shorter history of the Kaqchikel state.

These and related documents are priceless sources of information about Maya language, history, social and political institutions, religion, and other aspects of their vanished ways of life. For example, from documents we know that Mayan languages in colonial times had well-developed vocabularies for personal names, hereditary and occupational titles, and titles of place of origin. Mayan languages did not distinguish gender by pronouns, as does English, but they did so in personal titles and kinship terms. Some of the earliest colonial dictionaries were the most comprehensive; these preserve terms that have been lost in the spoken Mayan languages since the colonial era. Studies of these preserved vocabularies tell a great deal about ancient Maya kinship terminology and organization, numerical systems, botanical and zoological nomenclatures, and color and directional terms.

Of course, the Maya of today also preserve many of their ancient traditions. Thus, the Maya themselves can teach us much about their past. Overall, our understanding of ancient Maya society is based on many kinds of research: archaeology, ethnohistory, ethnography, and epigraphy (decipherment of Maya writing).

CONTINUITY AND CHANGE SINCE THE CONQUEST

Maya civilization may have ended with the Spanish Conquest, but the Maya people have survived oppression over the past 500 years down to the present day. The Maya way of life has greatly changed over this span. Many institutions that had governed Maya society were replaced by a Spanish colonial civil and religious administration. The old Maya elite class—rulers, nobles, priests, and military leaders—was all but destroyed, its few survivors stripped of their former wealth and power. Conversion to Christianity was used to justify the Conquest and to help control the new subjects of the Spanish Crown. Many methods, including the cruel Spanish Inquisition, were used to crush any vestiges of old Maya ritual and belief.

Many of the intellectual achievements of Maya civilization were also lost. The arts of painting, sculpture, metallurgy, and feather work disappeared from Maya society. Native Maya books (called codices) were burned, and the use of Maya writing soon vanished. A great deal of knowledge has been lost as a result, including information about Maya history, religion (beliefs, deities, and rituals), medicine, and commerce.

The Maya economy was altered forever. New markets and methods of transport replaced much of the network of trade routes that had tied the Maya area together. New technologies, new products, and new demands replaced the old. Not all changes were violent, of course. The Maya readily accepted much of the new European technology, as iron and steel tools quickly replaced those of flint and obsidian. Yet some family-based crafts—weaving, basketry, and pottery making—continue today essentially unchanged from the past. A scaled-down version of Maya-controlled trade has also persisted. Locally produced food and crafts, together with imported essentials, continue to be bought and sold in town and village markets to this day.

Figure 1.1 Maya market in the highlands of Guatemala.

Figure 1.2 Maya woman weaving on the traditional Maya belt loom.

But these changes, whether forced or voluntary, began a cycle of damage to the environment that continues to this day. The landscape was ravaged by the colonizers for valuable resources—especially gold and silver. The best agricultural lands were seized and plantations established by new landowners from Spain, who introduced new crops grown for export, such as bananas, coffee, and sugar cane. Moreover, the labor used to work the new mines and plantations was recruited, usually by force, from the conquered peoples. Over the centuries, hundreds of thousands died from the abuses of a forced labor system that almost amounted to slavery. These abuses of native peoples began a cycle of exploitation that continues to this day.

Yet, even after centuries of exploitation and change, important aspects of the traditional Maya way of life have survived. In many areas, the traditions of family and community have continued with little change. The institutions of marriage and kinship that governed family life have persisted because they were out of the reach of Spanish administrators. In places far from Spanish officials, the Maya kept their traditions alive, from one generation to the next. Realizing this, the Spaniards tried to forcibly resettle Maya communities in areas where they could be more easily controlled, closer to their colonial towns and cities. But forcible resettlement was not applied everywhere and was seldom successful. In the face of threats from Spanish authorities, some Maya families—even entire communities—"voted with their feet" and moved farther away from European settlements. In other cases, as long as the Maya accepted Christianity and paid the required taxes and labor obligations to the Spanish crown, they were allowed to govern their own affairs.

Several dozen related Mayan languages are still spoken today. These languages, and the remnants of Maya religion, have been more resistant to change than any other aspect of Maya civilization. This is because Mayan language and religion reinforce the traditions of family and community life. Even today, in the face of prolonged efforts by European missionaries to change their religion, many traditional beliefs and rituals concerned with the family and agriculture continue. Mayan languages persist because they are often the first-learned or only language spoken in the traditional Maya family. Some knowledge of Spanish is necessary to deal with the non-Maya world, but, even in today's world of instant electronic communication, several million people continue to speak a Mayan language.

THE DESTRUCTION OF THE MAYA HERITAGE

The modern world has had profound effects on traditional Maya culture. Traditions that have survived over some 500 years of European conquest, colonization, and exploitation are now changing or even disappearing because of economic, political, and social changes originating far beyond the Maya world. But this is not the only heritage that is disappearing.

The Maya past is disappearing even faster. The ruins of hundreds of ancient Maya cities are being looted and destroyed by illegal digging for jade, painted pottery, and sculpture that can be sold on a thriving antiquities market. The remains of cities that have lain undisturbed for a thousand years, including many never seen by the Spanish *conquistadores,* have been pillaged and destroyed for a few objects that have commercial value.

Most of the information in this book comes from investigations of Maya sites by archaeologists, along with epigraphers (experts in reading ancient Maya writing), art historians, and other scholars. These ruins and all other remains from the past ranging from the smallest bit of broken pottery to the ruins of the largest temple or city are sources of archaeological evidence. Like pieces of a jigsaw puzzle, that evidence reveals a picture only when its parts are found and put into place. The plundering of archaeological sites destroys many of the individual pieces; just as important, it destroys the patterns and associations of those pieces so that the total picture can never be reassembled. A looted Maya site is like a jigsaw puzzle that has had most of its pieces destroyed. But archaeological sites are far more than jigsaw puzzles; each one is part of a *nonrenewable resource*—a unique representative of past Maya society. As each site is destroyed by looting, the Maya of today lose another portion of their heritage, and the world loses another portion of the evidence that could allow us to better understand Maya civilization. Once destroyed, this evidence is gone forever.

Can this wanton destruction be stopped? The contemporary countries in which Maya sites are located—Mexico, Guatemala, Belize, Honduras, and El Salvador—all have laws against looting archaeological sites. It is illegal to import looted materials into the United States and many other countries. But no nation has the resources to police all of its archaeological sites or to prevent all antiquity smuggling. The only solution to looting is economic. Looting continues because Maya jade, painted pottery, and sculpture can be sold for huge amounts of money. The solution, therefore, is to decrease the demand for new-looted objects—looting will be stopped only if collectors and dealers refuse to buy these objects.

Today interest and progress in understanding in Maya civilization are at an all-time high. It is tragically ironic that our present world is also utterly destroying the archaeological resources that allow us to reconstruct the Maya past.

FURTHER READING

Barrera Vásquez 1980; Chiappelli 1976; Christenson 2003; Díaz del Castillo 1956; Edmunson 1982, 1986; England 2003; Farriss 1984; Fischer and Brown 1996; Grube 2001; Hanks and Rice 1989; Innes 1969; Jones 1989, 1998; Marcus 1992a; Martin and Grube 2008; Meyer 1977; Montejo 1999; Recinos and Goetz 1953; Sharer and Traxler 2006; Stephens 1962 [1841], 1963 [1843]; Sullivan 1989; Tozzer 1941; Warren and Jackson 2002.

2

UNDERSTANDING THE MAYA PAST

In this chapter we consider (1) basic concepts underlying the study of past societies such as the Maya; (2) how archaeologists find and interpret evidence from the past to reconstruct such civilizations; (3) the environment of the Maya homeland, and (4) the chronology used to understand the development of Maya civilization.

THE GROWTH OF CIVILIZATIONS

We begin by defining certain basic concepts. *Civilization* is a term often used to refer to complex and sophisticated cultural developments. Civilization implies the development of cities, as well as large-scale public architecture, writing, organized religion, far-flung trade, art, and other achievements. *Cities* are large concentrated settlements of people who specialize in non-food-producing activities. Although city dwellers may have gardens or farm plots outside the city, a proportion of them specialize in manufacturing, trade, religion, or politics and live by exchanging goods and services with an agricultural hinterland that produces food.

Civilizations are associated with a particular kind of political and economic system known as the *state*. The first states to develop in various parts of the world are called *preindustrial states*. These were characterized by full-time craft specializations, complex social stratification (i.e., societies divided into two or more classes, including an elite upper class), and a centralized political authority (such as a "king"). The centralized authority is usually supported and perpetuated by institutions, such as official religions, administrative bureaucracies, laws, courts, palace guards, and armies. But preindustrial states were very different from the modern *industrial states* that developed with the Industrial Revolution. Preindustrial states did not have machine-based mass production of goods, rapid communication, and efficient transport—all of which are typical of modern industrial states. Preindustrial states relied on human and animal power, rather than the far greater energy available from steam, electric, internal combustion, and nuclear power. Thus, the size and economic output of preindustrial states was far less than that of industrial states such as our own.

The terms *polity* or *kingdom* will be used to refer to each independent preindustrial state. For much of their history, Maya polities were small in scale; that is, each independent state controlled a relatively limited territory, measuring only several hundred square kilometers, with a population measured in tens of thousands of people. But, as with preindustrial states elsewhere in the world, some larger polities developed over time as measured by both population and territory. Some of the most aggressive and successful Maya states controlled large territories with populations of hundreds of thousands of people and also exerted authority over one or more smaller kingdoms.

Archaeologists can recognize the beginnings and development of pre-industrial states from clues left in ruins of ancient cities. Most preindustrial states developed from somewhat less complex societies called *chiefdoms*. These are complex societies managed by an elite group under one ultimate authority or chief. But, unlike the rulers of states, chiefs have little coercive or political power. They rule by controlling religion and wealth; that is, their ability to control their subjects comes from religious beliefs and from the tribute they collect as a result of those beliefs. In such societies, people believe that the chief has supernatural abilities and connections that can be used to help them or harm others. To ensure that this supernatural power is used for good purposes, people offer tribute—food, goods, or labor service. The chief, in turn, can dispense some of this tribute to others to show favor or expend it on feasts for his subjects, which, of course, helps maintain their loyalty to him.

ARCHAEOLOGY AND RECONSTRUCTING THE PAST

The study of past civilizations is a special concern of the field of archaeology (the science of studying past societies through their material remains). Archaeologists have developed methods to recover the material remains from preindustrial states, chiefdoms, and all other past societies. These remains are known as the *archaeological record*, which includes *artifacts* (small portable items that can be moved or traded far and near) and permanent *features* (roads, buildings, fields, canals, temples, palaces, and settlements). Any concentration of artifacts and features defines an *archaeological site*; thus, a site can range from a small hunting camp consisting of the remains of a cooking fire and a few hunting tools to an entire city covering many square kilometers.

Artifacts and features are not the only remains used by archaeologists to reconstruct the past. Clues to ancient environmental conditions can help archaeologists determine the natural resources that were used and traded. Plant and animal remains reveal the foods and other resources that supported an ancient society. For most preindustrial states, some of the best clues are found in recovered written records, because writing systems were often used to record the political and economic affairs of rulers and administrators. Later we will see examples of these "royal" records from Maya states.

Most ancient societies existed before writing systems were invented (prehistoric societies). But, regardless of the time period, archaeologists base their interpretations not on individual artifacts or features but on the larger patterns that can be seen in studying the forms and distributions of many such remains. For example, they study the patterns of archaeological sites as they are distributed across the landscape and the patterns of connections between sites (routes used for movements of trade goods, people, and ideas). By mapping sites and connections, archaeologists can detect hierarchies of sites based on size and location. These patterns, known as *settlement hierarchies*, allow archaeologists to reconstruct the size and complexity of ancient societies.

To understand how this is done, we can use an example based on our modern (industrial) nation-state. If we look at a map of one of our states, such as Indiana, we see that its largest city, Indianapolis, is near the center. Indianapolis is both the political and the economic capital of the state and the hub of road and other communication and transportation networks that radiate out to the rest of the state. In the territory surrounding the capital are a series of secondary political centers—the county seats. Each of these counties has even smaller political units—townships—along with cities, towns, and villages. Settlements at each level include clusters of dwellings and other buildings serving a variety of functions, along with dwellings dispersed over the countryside. The map of Indiana, therefore, reflects a political settlement hierarchy arranged on at least four levels—one capital, a number of second-level centers (county seats), even more third-level centers (townships), and far more fourth-level centers (the remaining cities, towns, and villages). Of course, a settlement hierarchy based on economic or other criteria would have a different composition.

This is similar to what archaeologists reconstruct by mapping distributions of ancient settlements and their connections. The resulting patterns reflect political, economic, and other organizations within ancient societies. In most cases, finding a past settlement hierarchy with four or more levels indicates a society organized as a preindustrial state. A prehistoric settlement hierarchy with three levels often indicates a chiefdom organization. A settlement hierarchy of fewer than three levels may indicate a society with a less complex and smaller-scale organization than a chiefdom.

Many preindustrial states increased in size through time, by natural population increase or by successful conquests of other states and territories. Such expansions were accompanied by changes in the political and economic organization to accommodate and control more people. In some cases, these changes can be recognized in the archaeological record, such as with the addition of new levels to the organizational hierarchy or the expansion in the territory controlled by a preindustrial state.

Thus, the size and complexity of settlement patterns can be an important clue toward understanding how an ancient society was organized and how it changed over time. But archaeologists do not rely on just one source of evidence to reconstruct the past. Whenever possible, they test their conclusions by looking for multiple lines of evidence. To test their interpretations of a specific settlement pattern, they may excavate sites from each level of the hierarchy to see if further clues can be found to support or change their conclusions.

THE MAYA HOMELAND

The Maya homeland is part of Mesoamerica, a large area interconnected by numerous trade routes that spread from northern Mexico well into Central America. During the pre-Columbian era (before roughly 1500 and the arrival of Europeans), the Maya and their Mesoamerican neighbors developed agriculture, permanently settled villages, and, eventually, states with cities, monumental architecture, calendrical systems, writing, and the other characteristics of civilization.

The settlement hierarchies that constituted Maya civilization were dispersed over a rich and varied environment. Indeed, the homeland of past Maya civilization and of Maya people of today shows great environmental diversity. The Maya area covers about 324,000 square kilometers in southeastern Mexico (including the Yucatan Peninsula), and northwestern Central America (Guatemala, Belize, and western Honduras and El Salvador).

The Maya area is divided into three environmental zones: the Pacific coastal plain to the south, the highlands in the center, and the lowlands to the north. Considerable variation exists in the environmental conditions within each zone, so each is further divided into subzones. But the boundaries of each of the major zones and their subdivisions are not precise, since they define subtle environmental changes or transitions in landform, elevation, climate, and soils.

The environment of the Maya area is marked by contrasts. The terrain varies from rugged mountains to level plains. Altitude differences create cool temperate climates in the highland and hot tropical conditions in the Pacific coastal plain and the lowlands. Rainfall variations produce other contrasts. In some areas of both the highlands and the lowlands, there are dry, desert-like environments, as well as areas of heavy rainfall that produce dense rain forests. Surface water is easily available in places adjacent to rivers, lakes, and *cenotes* (sinkholes or natural wells), but in other areas the Maya had to make great efforts to gain and store water by constructing

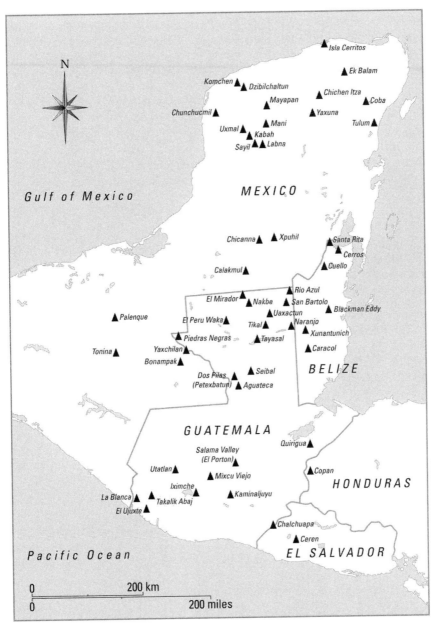

Figure 2.1 Map of the Maya area with locations of major archaeological sites.

wells, reservoirs, and canals. Plentiful harvests of food came from regions with rich volcanic or alluvial soils, but areas with far poorer soils required far greater efforts to support agriculture.

Certain environmental conditions have changed over time. Some shifts have been gradual, such as a long-term trend toward decreasing rainfall in some lowland areas. Other changes have been sudden and violent, such as frequent earthquakes and volcanic eruptions in the highlands. But humans have caused the most drastic environmental changes. At times in the past, the Maya were too successful in exploiting their environment. The result was unchecked population growth that led to overuse of agricultural lands and the destruction of forests. In areas where the soil and forest resources had been exhausted, people had no choice but to look for new and relatively undamaged areas to settle. Over time we can see patterns of exploitation, growth, overexploitation, and migration that reflect a process of combined human and natural environmental change. Of course, this process is not unique to the past; the same thing is happening today in the Maya area and in many other parts of the world.

At this point, we will briefly describe the environmental conditions in each of the three major zones of the Maya area. Later, we will describe how each zone contributed to the development of Maya civilization.

The Pacific Coastal Plain

A fertile plain stretches along the Pacific coast from southern Mexico well into Central America (southern Guatemala and western El Salvador). It is cut by many south-trending rivers that flow from the chain of volcanoes that divides the coastal plain from the highlands to the north. Several subzones along the plain blend into each other with increasing elevation from the Pacific coast to the volcano slopes to the north.

The Pacific coastal plain has a tropical climate with average annual temperatures between 77° and 95°F. Temperatures become cooler with increasing altitude toward the north. As in most parts of the Maya area, there are two seasons each year, with a dry period generally from January to April and a rainy season from about May to December. The Pacific coastal plain has some of the heaviest rainfall in the Maya area. The western portion averages more than 120 inches of rain each year. The remainder receives more than 80 inches of rainfall annually. Although much of the coastal plain is deforested today, in some areas relic stands of rain forest can still be found. As elevations increase, remnants of rain forest are gradually replaced by mixed oak and pine forest more typical of the highlands.

Some of the earliest permanent settlements in the Maya area are found among the mangrove swamps and lagoons near the coast. This fertile environment has long provided a great variety of food resources. Rich habitats for land animals, birds, and both salt- and freshwater creatures are close together, making it possible for people to hunt and gather wild food without moving great distances. Since the availability of these food sources does not vary greatly from year to year, small groups can settle down and live permanently in one place. With good soils nearby, such as the rich silt deposits along rivers, this environment also supported agriculture to produce even more food, allowing populations to thrive and grow.

The coastal plain forms a natural corridor for trade and migrations between Mexico and Central America, Products from the coast, such as dried fish and salt from evaporated seawater, were traded far and wide. Further inland, the coastal plain became a prime location for growing cacao (chocolate), a product that was traded throughout Mesoamerica. Today, agribusiness dominates the coastal plain, producing sugar cane, cotton, and cattle.

The Highlands

The greatest diversity of environmental conditions is found in the Maya highlands, and many environmental subdivisions can be defined for this mountainous area. The most obvious is marked by a great east-west rift that splits the zone into the southern highlands, highly populated today and dominated by recent volcanic activity, and the northern highlands, less populated and without volcanic activity. Both have elevations generally above 760 meters. The climate is temperate and spring-like all year, although far cooler conditions are found in the highest mountain regions, at elevations between 2,200 and 3,000 meters. Temperatures may average below 60° in the highest mountains but approach tropical conditions in the lower highland margins. Most areas have a dry season from January to April, followed by a rainy season from about May to December. Rainfall is generally less than on the Pacific plain, averaging 200–300 centimeters each year. Far less rain falls in areas sheltered from the prevailing easterly trade winds, such as the central Motagua Valley. The rainy season becomes more intense and lasts longer in the north. On the northern margins, annual rainfall averages more than 120 inches, enough to support highland rain forests.

A belt of recent volcanoes stretches from Mexico through Guatemala and into Central America and forms the boundary between the Pacific Plain and the highlands. North of this line are rugged volcanic highlands, surfaced by thick lava and ash deposits. Deep valleys have been cut into these deposits by the many rivers that rise in the highlands and flow outward to the sea. The largest of these valleys allow tropical conditions to penetrate well into the highlands. Some rivers in the southern highlands flow northward to become part of the Motagua River, which drains eastward into the Caribbean through the continental rift. The western highlands are drained by the Grijalva River, which flows westward into the Gulf of Mexico through Chiapas, in Mexico. The many interior valleys and basins of the highlands possess ideal climates and fertile soils, as well as natural routes of communication. Some highland basins contain lakes, such as the famous Lake Atitlan in central Guatemala.

Just north of the rift that divides the southern from the northern highlands are the highest mountains in the Maya area. These often rise above 3,000 meters. In the west are the Chiapas highlands and the Cuchumatanes Mountains of northwestern Guatemala. In the east, the Sierra de las Minas extends almost to the Caribbean. These mountains are rich in mineral resources, and the Maya acquired jade and serpentine from outcrops and riverbeds in the Sierra de las Minas.

The highlands contain many resources used and traded for thousands of years by the Maya. There are several sources for obsidian (volcanic glass), mined to make sharp cutting tools. Grinding stones (known as manos and metates) used to prepare maize and other seed crops were made from volcanic basalts in the southern highlands.

Further north, the rugged northern highland ranges blend into lower limestone formations. These form dramatic landscapes of karst (limestone) hills, where rivers disappear under porous mountainsides only to reappear miles away. There are numerous underground caverns, waterfalls, and sinkholes. The sources for the greatest river of the Maya lowlands, the Usumacinta, lie in the northern highlands. Many of the interior valleys have fertile soils. These, combined with plentiful rainfall and cool temperatures, make the basins of the Alta Verapaz, in central Guatemala, a prime area for modern coffee cultivation.

People living in the highlands have always been plagued by earthquakes and volcanic eruptions. Although the Maya did not record these events, they are detectable from archaeological evidence. A massive volcanic eruption about 400 created a caldera (collapse basin) and left behind Lake Ilopango, near San Salvador. This catastrophic eruption destroyed all life within 20 to 30 kilometers of the eruption. The huge cloud of volcanic ash fell over a widespread area, rendering everything within about 100 kilometers of the volcano uninhabitable for one or two centuries. Even far smaller volcanic eruptions disrupt people's lives. Archaeological excavations at Cerén, El Salvador, have revealed an entire village and its fields that were instantaneously buried by ash from a nearby volcanic vent around 600. During the 500 years since the Spanish Conquest, a succession of major quakes has been recorded. Earthquakes destroyed the colonial capital of Antigua in the eighteenth century, and in 1918 another all but destroyed Guatemala City. More recently, a rupture of the Motagua fault took more than 24,000 lives in 1976.

Despite the danger of earthquakes and volcanic eruptions, large numbers of people have inhabited the highlands for thousands of years, cultivating their fertile volcanic soils. Most highlands basins and valleys contain many remains of pre-Columbian Maya settlements. The largest and most important is the city of Kaminaljuyu in the Valley of Guatemala, although much of the site has been destroyed by modern Guatemala City.

Thousands of years of human activity have drastically changed the highland environment. The original highland forest was a mixture of evergreen and deciduous trees. In remote areas and at the highest elevations, relatively undisturbed stands of oak, laurel, sweetgum, dogwood, and pine can still be found. Lower valleys support varied semitropical vegetation.

Although highway construction, logging operations, petroleum exploitation, and hydroelectric power plants have disturbed even remote areas, there is a variety of wild animal life, especially in the less-populated northern highlands. Mountain forests are the home for howler and spider monkeys, kinkajous, coatimundis, weasels, foxes, peccaries, and armadillos. Birds are plentiful, including hawks, macaws, and parrots. The largest, the Harpy Eagle, can also be seen. In a few high and remote forests, the rare quetzal bird is still found. It was sacred to the Maya; kings adorned their headdresses with its long, brilliant-green tail feathers.

The Lowlands

The transition between the highlands and the lowlands is gradual. The rain forest of the karst region of the northern highlands continues northward into the lower elevations that extend over northern Guatemala, Belize, and the Yucatan Peninsula of Mexico. The lowlands generally lie below 760 meters in elevation and have a warm tropical climate. Although they are not as mountainous as the highlands, many lowland areas are hilly. Rainfall, drainage, soils, and seasonal cycles all create variations in the environment. Until the twentieth century, most of the lowland area was covered by forest. The ancient Maya adapted the lowland environment and made it very productive. Extensive areas of good soils were cultivated to produce a host of useful crops. Wild plants and animals provided food, clothing, shelter, and medicine. The underlying limestone was easily quarried with stone tools (the Maya had no hard metals) and was used as a durable building material. By burning limestone and mixing it with water and sand, they made plaster, which they used to cover and protect their buildings and to pave their plazas and causeways. They also mined chert, or flint, which was chipped into a variety of cutting, chopping, and scraping tools. With such resources and others imported from the highlands, the lowlands became the productive heartland of Maya civilization.

The rainy season in the lowlands extends from about May through January but is longer in the south and shorter in the north. Most of the region averages 80 to 120 inches of rain each year. In areas of highest rainfall, the dry season may be limited to only a month or two (usually between March and May), but some rain may fall even during these periods. To the north, rainfall averages less than 80 inches a year, but the driest areas in northwestern Yucatan often receives fewer than 20 inches of rain annually. Temperatures average in the 77° 90°F range typical of hot tropical climates, with generally cooler days in the wet season and highs rising well above 100°F in the dry season.

The lowlands can be subdivided into southern and northern areas. The southern lowlands feature broken karst terrain and both surface and subsurface drainage (caverns). Many large rivers emerge into the lowlands from the highlands to the south, the largest being the Usumacinta that flows northwestward to the Gulf of Mexico. North of the Usumacinta rainfall decreases and the landscape becomes less rugged, and there are more lakes and seasonal swamps (*bajos*). In the center of the southern lowlands of Guatemala is a shallow basin known as El Petén. It contains about 14 freshwater lakes. The largest, Lake Petén Itza, is some 32 kilometers long and 3.2 kilometers wide. These lakes and rivers gave the Maya steady sources of water and canoe transport. To the east, along the Belize-Guatemala border, is a rugged highland outcrop called the Maya Mountains, with peaks as high as 200 meters.

In the northern Petén, a large region, the Mirador Basin, is studded with bajos. Further north, decreasing rainfall creates a gradual transition from the tropical forests of the Petén to the bush lands of the Yucatan Peninsula. The northern lowlands form a low and flat landscape that spreads across the northern half of the Yucatan Peninsula. The soil is usually not more than a few inches deep, in contrast to Petén soils, which may be up to 1 meter thick. There are extensive outcroppings of underlying limestone in the northern lowlands. The only major variations in elevation are the low Puuc hills in northwest Yucatan, with ridges about 300 feet high.

The porous limestone of the northern lowlands allows very little surface drainage, so availability of water has long been a critical factor in the location of settlements. There are only a few lakes, such as those around the site of Coba in northeastern Yucatan, and there are far fewer rivers and streams. The only inland water sources during the long dry season are sinkholes or cenotes (from the Yucatec Mayan word *dz'onot*). Cenotes are found throughout the area, especially in the extreme north. Their depth varies. Near the north coast, the subterranean water is only a few meters below the ground, but as one goes southward, cenote depth increases to a hundred or more meters.

In undisturbed areas, the tropical forest is the most obvious feature of the lowland landscape. The tallest trees, including mahogany and ceiba (the sacred "tree of life" for the Maya) form an upper forest canopy, 40–70 meters high. A variety of other trees often form a second canopy, 20–45 meters in height. And a lower layer may be present, between 12 and 20 meters above the ground. In the drier areas of central and western Yucatan the forest is stunted, but there is an extension of the southern high forest into the somewhat wetter northeastern corner of Yucatan. Many trees support other plants, bromeliads, orchids, strangler vines, and lianas. Ferns, young trees, and many large-leafed plants grow in the deep shade of the forest floor.

A variety of animals live in the lowland forest, including many species found elsewhere in the Maya area. But today the carnivores, ocelots, jaguarundis, and jaguars (the largest New World cat and symbol of Maya kings) have become rare due to overhunting. In the past, the Maya hunted other animals for food: agoutis and pacas (large rodents), tapirs, deer, and rabbits. Both howler and spider monkeys abound. There are parrots, macaws, woodpeckers, toucans, and edible birds, including curassows, chachalacas, doves, quail, and the ocellated turkey. Reptiles and amphibians are also abundant. The rivers and lakes of the southern region provide fish and edible snails. Along coastal margins of the lowlands, there are shellfish, fish, sea birds, sea turtles, and manatees.

THE CHRONOLOGY OF CHANGE

The varied environments of the Maya area became the settings for many closely related Maya language and cultural groups. Although these groups lived in areas with distinctive local environments, each was in contact with its neighbors. These connections provided food items and goods unavailable locally, access to new ideas, and even marriage partners. Networks of trade and social interaction, tribute collection, competition, and open warfare stimulated growth and prevented any one area from being isolated from others.

A variety of societies and cultural traditions developed from the time of the earliest migrations into the Americas to the arrival of European colonists, in the sixteenth century. The Maya people formed one of these distinctive cultures, united by a series of languages descended from a common ancestral tongue and the sharing of a number of common cultural traditions. We will briefly define the chronology of major trends that led to Maya civilization before considering these developments in more detail in the following chapters.

Hunters and Gatherers (ca. 40/20,000–6000 B.C.E.)

Between 20,000 and 40,000 years ago, during the last ice age, the earliest peoples from Asia gradually moved into the Americas. Evidence from archaeology, human genetics, and linguistics all point to eastern Asia as the original homeland for Native American peoples. The archaeological evidence from Siberia indicates that human groups occupied the Asian side of the land bridge by 30,000 years ago, and the stone tools of these peoples are closely related to the earliest stone tools found in Alaska. The linguistic and molecular genetic evidence points to the same origin and indicates that there were several separate movements of peoples into the Americas from Siberia. Mitochondrial DNA (mtDNA) evidence suggests that the ultimate origins of most Native American populations lie in the southeastern region of Siberia. The latest to arrive were Inuit hunting societies that expanded eastward from the Arctic coast of Siberia.

The Americas were occupied gradually by small bands of people who moved southward from Alaska. Groups that depended on hunting moved by land, following game and other food sources. Others relied on seacoast resources and probably gradually moved down the Pacific coast using canoes or similar watercraft. In time, a variety of bands roamed over much of the Americas, relying on simple tools of wood and chipped stone for their hunting and gathering of wild food.

Over time, changes appeared among these early hunting and gathering bands. People invented new tools and new techniques for finding food and other resources. Fluted Clovis spear points were invented in the Americas by about 10,000 B.C.E. These were far more effective for hunting large game animals such as mammoths. Examples of these spear points have been found throughout the Americas, including sites in the Maya highlands and lowlands. Mammoth bones have been found associated with hunting and butchering tools in Central Mexico and in Yucatan. Although animals of all sizes were hunted, big-game species became extinct at the end of the Ice Age. As the climate gradually became warmer, new subsistence strategies were developed. Populations also slowly expanded in some areas, and this led to increasing competition for food sources.

Increased competition meant that bands often had to rely on smaller territories to acquire their food. At the same time, population growth created the need to increase the amount of food harvested from the landscape. One way of succeeding under these conditions was for people to became more efficient and specialized in hunting and gathering food. As a result, some groups became adept at following herds of animals such as bison or caribou during their yearly migrations. Other groups began to rely more and more on the seasonal growth cycles of a few very productive food plants. Some plants, supplemented by hunting or fishing, produced enough food to feed a group of people throughout the year, provided that their seeds could be safely stored during the nongrowing season. Some plants produced more food if people nurtured them by encouraging them to grow in the best soils, removing weeds, and watering them when no rainfall was available. Nurturing plants not only increased yields but also required people to spend more time in the area where the plants grew.

Measures like these to increase the food supply and to reduce seasonal movements of people were the first steps leading to two fundamental and interrelated changes that paved the way for civilization. The first was the change from a nomadic way of life to settlement in permanent villages. The second involved the domestication of certain plant and animal species. These two fundamental changes happened almost at the same time but completely independently, in both the Old World and the Americas.

Sedentary Life and Agriculture (ca. 6000–1500 B.C.E.)

The gradual shift to these new ways of life began about 8,000 years ago in the Americas. The beginnings of sedentary life and agriculture define the Archaic period (ca. 6000–1500 B.C.E.). The earliest known permanent settlements in Mesoamerica appeared along the Pacific coast. Rich shore and lagoon food resources in such environments could support year-round settled life. At about the same time, the increasing nurturing of productive food plants led to the gradual domestication of manioc, potatoes, and a variety of other crops in South America and of maize, squash, beans, and other plant species in Mesoamerica. Permanent settlements and stable sources of food supported larger populations and became the twin foundations for all the civilizations of the Americas.

In the Maya area, the coastal margins were exploited long before permanent settlements appeared. The availability of land animals, birds, and aquatic creatures made it possible to hunt and gather wild food within a day's walk of a home base. Thus, small groups could begin to live permanently in one place. The addition of agriculture, made possible by clearing and planting fertile silts along rivers, gave this environment an early edge in producing food surpluses. This, in turn, allowed populations to prosper and grow. Along the Caribbean coast of the lowlands, the many rivers gave access to the lowlands to the west, and agricultural settlements eventually spread into the interior along these riverine avenues.

The early cultural development in the Maya highlands seems to have lagged somewhat behind those of the coasts, although the traces of early occupation probably lie undiscovered beneath deep volcanic and alluvial deposits. In time, however, the abundance of natural resources allowed the occupants of the highlands to catch up, especially in the southern part of the area.

Early Maya Civilization (ca. 1500 B.C.E.–250)

The rise of the first civilizations took place during what is usually called the Preclassic period throughout Mesoamerica. These developed in several different regions, such as the Gulf Coast lowlands of Mexico, the highlands of the Valley of Mexico and the Valley of Oaxaca, and the Maya area. These earliest civilizations saw the first large civic and ceremonial centers that served as the capitals of chiefdoms and, somewhat later, the first states. These early capitals are characterized by large-scale architecture, carved stone monuments, imported goods from distant lands, and the beginnings of writing. These traits reflect new developments within society, such as social stratification, seen in distinctions between an upper class elite and a lower class nonelite, and the growth of complex religious, economic, and political institutions. We will look at some of these developments in our next chapter.

These first civilizations established a basic cultural pattern that was followed by later civilizations in Mesoamerica. Although some early civilizations declined, others became larger and more complex. By this time, writing became more common and was often used to proclaim the achievements of rulers to boost their power and authority. The capitals of new polities and the commerce they fostered grew beyond previous levels, and populations reached their highest peak in some areas. Overall, these developments laid the foundations for the even larger and populous civilizations still to come.

The highlands and the adjacent Pacific plain supported some of the earliest development of Maya civilization. During much of the pre-Columbian era, there were major population centers located in the largest and richest highland valleys. Adjacent regions were dominated by important but less powerful centers. Most grew prosperous from the production and trade of highland resources such as obsidian, jade, and other minerals. On the adjacent Pacific coastal plain, a series of settlements grew as centers of marketing, ceremonial, and political activity. These early centers prospered from the production and trade of goods produced locally (such as cacao and salt) and by controlling important trade routes that passed along the Pacific plain from Mexico to Central America.

Most of the interior portions of the lowlands to the north were colonized by village agriculturalists after about 1500 B.C.E. But development was rapid thereafter, culminating in the appearance of the first polity capitals by about 800 B.C.E. and an explosion of growth soon thereafter, including the construction of the largest temples ever built by the Maya. Early Maya civilization in the lowlands laid the essential foundations for the greatest achievements of the Middle Maya civilization that followed.

In many ways, Maya civilization in the southern area peaked during the early period, from about 1000 B.C.E. to 200. Although it remained an important area for agricultural production and trade throughout the pre-Columbian era, by the second century both the Pacific plain and much of the highlands had become secondary to the major centers of Maya civilization in the lowlands to the north.

Middle Maya Civilization (ca. 250–900/1100)

Over a span of about 600 years, from about 250 to 900, Maya civilization reached its peak in the southern lowlands. This corresponds to what is often called the Classic period in Mesoamerica, or Middle Maya civilization. During the Classic period, more powerful and more complex polities developed, marked by further population increase, and new and even larger capitals were built. These Classic polities competed with each other to control even larger territories and more resources. The most successful non-Maya polities during this period had their capitals at the cities of Teotihuacan, in the Valley of Mexico, and Monte Alban, in the Valley of Oaxaca.

For convenience, we can divide Middle Maya civilization into three periods, the Early Classic (ca. 250–600), the Late Classic (ca. 600–800), and the Terminal Classic (ca. 800–900 and extending as late as 1100 in Yucatan). Over this span, the southern lowlands were the undisputed center of development for Maya civilization. Population levels reached an all-time high, as did the competition between polities. The southern lowlands were long dominated by the rivalry between the two largest and greatest cities, Tikal and Calakmul, which involved many adjacent and allied centers. Other important cities arose throughout the lowlands, such as those along the Usumacinta River. At the same time, there were large centers in the northern lowlands. Trade and other contacts with the highlands remained strong, and powerful highland polities continued to develop during this era.

The Terminal Classic was a time of transition. Between 800 and 900, most of the polities in the southern lowland area went into a severe decline, from which they never recovered. The great populations that sustained the many powerful lowland cities slowly but surely dwindled away, as more and more people moved to new and more prosperous locales. The two areas that received most of these new populations and benefited most from these changes were the northern lowlands and the highlands. Thus, in northern Yucatan, the changes of the Terminal Classic period produced a peak of prosperity that lasted another century or more, to as late as 1100. In western Yucatan, a series of cities dominated for a time. But the greatest and most powerful northern Maya city was in the heart of the peninsula, at Chichen Itza, which dominated the Terminal Classic of the north.

Late Maya Civilization (ca. 1100–1500)

The final centuries before European intervention, between about 1100 and 1500, saw the last great era of Maya civilization. This span is usually called the Postclassic throughout Mesoamerica. The Postclassic is marked by declines in some areas. But, in other areas, population continued to grow, cities and commerce expanded, and competition and warfare increased. These areas saw the development of the most complex and powerful states in the Americas prior to European colonization. The most well known are the Toltec in central Mexico, succeeded by the Mexica, or Aztec, prior to the Spanish Conquest.

Late Maya civilization saw some polities flourish and even reach their peak of development. In northern Yucatan, Chichen Itza was succeeded by a new and prosperous capital, Mayapan, which in turn was replaced by many small and squabbling states. In fact, Yucatan was a house divided against itself on the eve of the Spanish Conquest. In the highlands, population growth, invasions, and warfare caused settlement to shift away from valley floors to more defensible hilltops. Eventually, a major conquest state arose, that of the K'iche Maya. Its chief rivals, the Kakchiquel Maya, checked the K'iche conquests. But the highlands were never unified, and, like the Maya of Yucatan, the highland Maya also presented a fragmented political landscape to their Spanish Conquerors.

With this introduction in mind, we will be able to take a closer look at the foundations of Maya civilization (chapter 3) and at the successive stages of Early, Middle, and Late Maya civilization (chapters 4–7).

Mayan Languages and Groups Today

About 4 million descendants of the ancient Maya live in the Maya area today. These people continue to speak one of the 28 closely related languages that make up the Mayan family of languages. Although most of these people also speak Spanish (the official language of Mexico, Guatemala, El Salvador, and Honduras) or English (the official language of Belize), their native language continues to define them as Maya people, holders of a proud cultural tradition.

The various Mayan languages are similar because they are descended from one ancestral language spoken thousands of years ago. Scholars who study the process of language divergence estimate that the ancestral Mayan language was spoken earlier than 2000 B.C.E., or about the time the Maya first settled in permanent communities. After this time, the ancestral language began to separate into three major subgroups, Southern Mayan, Yucatecan, and Huastecan. These subgroups became distinct during the era of Early Maya civilization (ca. 2000 B.C.E.-100). Although the process of divergence has continued to the present, producing the many language differences of today, most Mayan languages have remained in contact with other variations, and they often blend into other versions just like the environmental zones of the Maya area.

Using comparisons among languages today, scholars can reconstruct aspects of the ancestral Mayan language. In such cases, the meanings of reconstructed words can tell us about early Maya society and culture. For example, the ancestral Mayan language had a rich vocabulary for weaving and farming, indicating that these were important activities. Maize agriculture, in particular, had separate words for generic maize, the green ear, the mature ear, the cob, three stages of maize flour, maize dough, the tortilla, a maize drink, and the maize grinding stone.

Similar research has been used to identify the languages spoken in the lowlands during the era of Middle Maya civilization. This has long been a debated issue, because much of this vast region was depopulated when Europeans arrived. Evidence from hieroglyphic texts indicates that a language belonging to the Southern Mayan subgroup, known as Ch'olan, was the language recorded by Classic period inscriptions throughout the lowlands.

FURTHER READING

Ashmore and Sharer 2005; Demarest 2004; Grube 2001; Helms 1975; Houston, Robertson, and Stu11art 1996; Jones and Kautz 1981; Kaufman 1974; Marcus 1992b; Richards 2003; Sabloff 1994; Sharer and Traxler 2006; Wolf 1959.

3

THE FOUNDATIONS OF MAYA CIVILIZATION

Maya civilization did not develop in isolation, for the Maya were part of the wider cultural area of Mesoamerica. Both the Maya and the other civilizations of Mesoamerica developed together over a span of several thousand years.

THE ORIGINS OF SETTLED LIFE AND AGRICULTURE (ca. 6000–1500 B.C.E.)

Between about 12,000 and 8000 years ago, the archaeological evidence shows a shift away from nomadic hunting and gathering in several regions of the Americas. In areas with especially plentiful resources, migratory bands of people needed to move only short distances to find enough food to survive throughout the year. Thus, they could spend more time living in one place, establishing a home base from which they could forage all or most of the year. Archaeology shows that some of the earliest known year-round settlements appeared in seacoast environments with concentrations of abundant shore and lagoon food resources. These rich environments, combined with an efficient food-collecting technology, gave rise to the beginnings of permanent village life. One of the earliest examples comes from the site of Monte Verde in Chile, where a small year round settlement dates to about 12,000 years ago.

Archaeology provides evidence for the beginnings of agriculture during the Archaic period (ca. 6000–1500 B.C.E.). Although the origins of agriculture are by no means completely documented, it appears that settling down was accompanied by increasing reliance on a select few foods. At least some of these were plant species that could be easily stored and that possessed a genetic makeup that allowed people to improve their natural yields. Genetic changes occurred as people selected seeds that kept well in storage or those that produced more food when planted. This gradually led to the domestication of a variety of species and to a greater reliance on agriculture.

Agriculture developed further as people learned more about the reproductive cycles of plants, when and where to plant their seeds, and how to protect and nourish them as they grew. Species that responded well to this manipulation include maize (corn), chili peppers, squash, beans, and a few other plants in highland Mesoamerica and manioc, potatoes, and a several other crops in South America. Over time, domestication and agriculture resulted in an increased and more reliable supply of food. This led to population increase and the expansion of permanent village life into less abundant areas, some still occupied by migratory bands. Over the centuries, the consequences of these developments can be seen in expanded population concentrations that came to be the foundations of all the civilizations of the Americas. Two broad traditions for these developments can be seen in Mesoamerica, one in the highlands, the other along the coastal lowlands.

Highland Mexico

Recent research shows that teosinte (*Zea mexicana*) was the wild ancestor of maize, and that maize probably originated in the Balsas River region of Guerrero, Mexico. Remains of domesticated maize have been found in the Valley of Oaxaca in highland Mexico that date to over 6,000 years ago. By 3000 B.C.E., maize cultivation had spread to coastal Chiapas and eastward into the Maya area and beyond (Belize and Lake Yojoa, Honduras), probably following trade routes. Maize quickly became the staff of life for peoples throughout Mesoamerica because of its great productivity, ease of storage, and nutritional benefits. However, reliance on maize agriculture developed gradually in the highlands, extending over several thousand years. The best growing methods and the more productive strains had to be perfected before agriculture could support a group of people year-round. As a result, permanent village life emerged gradually in the highlands, where archaeology has revealed this process in the Valley of Oaxaca, the Valley of Mexico, and the more marginal Tehuacan Valley.

In the Valley of Oaxaca, excavations have documented a sequence for the transition from nomadic hunting and gathering to settled agricultural villages that began about 6000 B.C.E. The earliest crop to be domesticated in Oaxaca appears to have been squash, followed by the maize. As in other highland areas, the development of settled communities and agriculture in the Valley of Oaxaca was a long, slow process, extending over several thousand years. Permanent villages did not emerge until the end of the Archaic, about 2000 B.C.E. The sequence was similar in the Valley of Mexico, where permanent settlements were also found by about the same time as in Oaxaca. Excavations in the nearby Tehuacan Valley reveal a 10,000-year sequence of gradual change from hunting and gathering to agriculture based on maize, beans, squash, and other crops. The semi-arid conditions in the Tehuacan Valley were right for a gradual increasing reliance on maize and other domesticated food plants and for the good preservation of plant remains that allowed archaeology to document the process.

The Maya Archaic Period (ca. 6000–1500 B.C.E.)

The evidence from the Archaic period is scarce in most other Meso-american areas, and we know less about the origins of settled communities and agriculture in the Maya homeland. In many parts of the Maya highlands, most Archaic period sites are deeply buried under later volcanic or alluvial deposits. Archaic occupation has been detected by finding distinctive chipped-stone hunting tools. Hunters and gatherers occupied Santa Marta cave, in Chiapas, Mexico, until about 3500 B.C.E. After a gap of some 2,000 years, sometime around 1300 B.C.E. the cave was reoccupied by farming people. Archaeologists in the southern highlands of Guatemala have found over 100 pre-agricultural sites, marked by chipped-stone tools. These early hunting and gathering sites span about 10,000 years, from about 11,000 to 1200 B.C.E.

Archaic period occupation has also been detected on both the Pacific and Caribbean coasts. Along the Caribbean coastal lowlands of Belize, a long sequence of human exploitation has been reconstructed, mostly from stone tools. The earliest peoples on the Pacific and Caribbean coasts lived by both hunting and gathering the plentiful resources of the sea, lagoons, rivers, and swamps. On the Pacific coast of Chiapas, excavations have found evidence of year-round occupation by seashore foragers dating to about 5500–3500 B.C.E. The principal food sources were plentiful supplies of clams and shrimp, especially in the dry season, when inland plant and animal resources were scarce.

Given developments elsewhere in Mesoamerica, we can assume that the earliest peoples in the Maya area underwent a long, slow development, adapting agricultural methods and crops to a variety of local conditions. Because of the environmental diversity of the Maya area (see chapter 2), it is probable that human groups took a long time to adapt successfully to the conditions in each region. On the coasts, settled villages apparently developed by relying more on plentiful wild food resources than on agriculture. In the highlands, with far fewer concentrations of wild food resources, settled life was possible only when agriculture became productive enough to support a group of people all year in one place.

Figure 3.1 Pottery often signals permanent settlements.

The earliest evidence for the beginnings of settled villages from the Maya homeland dates to the end of the Archaic. This evidence comes from the Pacific coast, where people used a kind of pottery that dates to ca. 1700–1500 B.C.E. Pottery is one of the best markers for permanent village life, because people who move from place to place seldom make and use fragile clay containers. The Pacific coast villages were supported by seashore and lagoon fishing and gathering, following the pattern seen elsewhere in Mesoamerica. The year-round availability of plentiful fish, shellfish, turtles, sea birds, reptiles, and other species made it possible for these early villagers to live permanently in one place. They also did some farming of manioc and maize. (Manioc is a lowland root crop originally from South America, but maize is a highland crop that had been adapted to lowland conditions by this time.)

The Maya Early Preclassic Period (ca. 1500–1000 B.C.E.)

Village life along the Pacific coast continued to expand for about 500 years, dated by the use of more elaborately decorated pottery. By ca. 1500–1200 B.C.E., settled populations had increased and people had spread further inland from the coast. Although hunting and gathering continued as more of the Pacific plain and highlands were settled, agriculture became far more important because it could support the ever-growing numbers of people. Maize was especially crucial, for, of all the domesticated crops developed in the Americas, it is the most productive.

On the Caribbean coast of Belize, there is evidence for a similar growth of village life based on seashore fishing and gathering, supplemented by agriculture. Recent evidence reveals that the transition from nomadic hunting and gathering to settled village life and agriculture began as coastal peoples expanded inland, in this case, up the rivers into the Maya lowlands. The earliest appearance of maize pollen in lowland lake cores dates to about 3400 B.C.E., with evidence for forest clearing and expanded cultivation by ca. 2500 B.C.E. For several thousand years, lowland farmers practiced seasonal slash-and-burn agriculture (swiddening) without permanent settlements. The evidence for permanent settlement, pottery, first appears in the Maya lowlands by about 1100 B.C.E. These earliest pottery-using settlements appear in several different lowland regions, the result of the gradual settling down as crops and growing methods became more productive. Thereafter, village life based on maize agriculture spread rapidly throughout the lowlands.

Populations were low, compared to levels reached in later periods, and there were still uncleared areas without settled occupation. But changes were taking place in these village societies. Trade brought contacts between villages and even distant areas, including the Maya highlands, and this allowed the exchange of ideas as well as products. Most important, the combination of settled villages and agriculture had the potential to support far more people than had been possible with hunting and gathering. As a result, populations began to expand throughout the Maya area. To accommodate the increasing numbers of people, new kinds of authority developed in the economic, political, and religious organizations of Maya society. These became the seeds for the growth of Maya civilization.

THE EARLY NEIGHBORS OF THE MAYA

By 2000 B.C.E., agricultural villages were established in most areas of Mesoamerica, providing the foundation for further population growth and increasingly complex societies. Radiocarbon dates from remnants of palisades and burned buildings indicates that, by about 1800 B.C.E., raiding and warfare were present in the Valley of Oaxaca. This was probably the result of increased competition for resources. Warfare escalated in Oaxaca until by the end of the Preclassic era the entire valley had been consolidated under the authority of a single capital at Monte Albán.

Evidence for warfare in the Maya area is somewhat later in time. However, its consequences—especially in the consolidation of settlement and authority—were essential to the development of more complex societies among the Maya and throughout Mesoamerica.

Population growth produced only more competition and warfare. Populations expanded rapidly in some coastal settlements once maize cultivation was added to an abundant wild-food inventory. This created needs for new products and spurred the production of new commodities. By the beginning of the Early Preclassic period (ca. 1500 b.c.e.), people throughout Mesoamerica were making a variety of pottery and other goods and trading these items with other communities. Growth of trade also spurred the development of larger and more complex societies.

Some people produced more food and other commodities or controlled some goods by being more successful in trading with other groups. These economic successes gave these early entrepreneurs greater status and prestige. Larger and more complex societies began with the emergence of these kinds of social and economic differences, especially when some individuals gained authority over other members of their communities as a result.

Evidence for the beginnings of these social and economic distinctions comes from several regions of Mesoamerica. Some of the earliest indications date to ca. 1650–1500 b.c.e. on the Pacific coastal plain of Chiapas, Mexico. Differences in house size, craft specialization, appearance of status symbols, and burial practices all point to inequalities within a settled agricultural society. Although these early villages were egalitarian, where the only social differences were based on age and gender, other distinctions may have begun by this time. Excavation of a burial of a small child revealed that she wore a mica mirror, a symbol of elevated status that may have been inherited from generation to generation within her family. Clustered settlement patterns reflect a two-tiered hierarchy in which larger villages controlled several smaller hamlets. One of these larger settlements, composed of houses built of pole and thatch, included a single building larger than the others. This may have been a community building or the residence of a village headman or chief—in which case it would indicate the appearance of higher status within the community. Interestingly, this larger building underwent at least nine successive renovations over time, indicating the importance attached to its location and its connections with the ancestral past.

We can better understand these developments by looking at some neighbors of the Maya in the Early and Middle Preclassic periods, since trade interconnected all these village agriculturalists throughout Mesoamerica. The most important of these neighboring societies were the Olmec, in the coastal lowlands of the Gulf of Mexico, and several societies in the highlands of Mexico. The development of larger and increasingly complex societies in both regions provides important lessons for better understanding the origins of Maya civilization.

The Olmec occupied a humid lowland region along the Gulf coast of Mexico, adapting to a tropical environment very similar to that of the lowland Maya. The Olmec rose and fell during the Early and Middle Preclassic periods. Civilization in the Valley of Oaxaca rose at the same time but continued to grow and expand, like that of the Maya, into the Classic period. Early Oaxacan civilization developed a writing system used for political purposes, very much like the Maya. Both had trade and other contacts with the early Maya and with each other.

There is evidence in both the Olmec and the Oaxacan societies of a growing elite that managed many aspects of society. The origins and development of the ruling elite class and understanding the basis of their power to manage their societies helps explain the origins of civilization itself. In fact, the core of all early Mesoamerican civilizations, including the Maya, lies in the characteristics of their ruling elite.

Olmec Civilization (ca. 1500–400 B.C.E.)

Olmec civilization grew out of an early village tradition similar to that of the Pacific and Caribbean coasts of the Maya area. Dating to the Early Preclassic period, early village foundations have been found at two key Olmec sites, La Venta and San Lorenzo. Both of these sites became major Olmec capitals by the Middle Preclassic period.

La Venta is located on a low hill or "island" surrounded by lowland swamp. Study of ancient settlement at La Venta shows the growth in complexity of Olmec society. Like that of the lowland Maya, Olmec agriculture was adapted to use the wet, swampy environment to support large populations and complex social and political organization.

Olmec farmers grew maize and other crops on the fertile natural river levees in the swampy terrain surrounding La Venta. Other foods came from plentiful resources acquired by fishing, gathering, and hunting. People lived on both the levees and the main island. Permanent occupation began at the end of the Archaic and continued through the Early and Middle Preclassic (ca. 2,000–400 B.C.E.). Population size increased substantially during this span. By the Middle Preclassic (ca. 800–400 B.C.E.), there was a three-level site hierarchy, headed by the main center on La Venta Island. This indicates that La Venta was the capital of a large and powerful polity with a variety of economic, social, political, and religious distinctions.

The best evidence of Olmec political organization and religious beliefs comes from ritual artifacts and monumental stone sculpture. These reflect a religious basis for the power held by Olmec rulers (a term that refers to the leaders of both chiefdoms and preindustrial states), a belief that the rituals the rulers conducted guaranteed people success in agriculture and other essential activities. Olmec rulers also gained economic power from managing agriculture, from which they received food tribute, and from control over trade networks. These networks provided Olmec rulers with a variety of rare and precious materials, including jade (used for ornaments) and magnetite (used for mirrors). Items of jade and magnetite were

Figure 3.2 Stela 2 from the Olmec site of
La Venta, Mexico, with a carved portrait of
an Olmec ruler holding a scepter (Middle
Preclassic).

displayed as symbols of the ruler's special powers and authority. When a
ruler died, these status symbols were buried with him, along with other
offerings and even human sacrifices, all to better serve him in the next
world.

The most famous objects from La Venta and other Olmec sites are huge
carved stone monuments, often weighing several tons each. Most were
made from basalt, a hard volcanic rock that was moved many miles by
water (on huge log rafts) and over land (on log rollers pulled by gangs of
men). These carved monuments appear by the end of the Early Preclassic
and continued throughout the Middle Preclassic. They display carved
portraits of Olmec rulers adorned with status symbols and insignia of
office, such as mirrors and scepters. These Olmec monuments included
colossal portrait heads of rulers, carved in the round, upright stones with
full standing portraits carved in relief carved on one side, and rectangular
stones with seated portraits, usually carved on three or four sides.

Carved and plain stone monuments appear in many regions of Mesoamerica during the Preclassic period, reflecting the connections between

ruling elites in these rapidly developing societies. Colossal carved heads also appear on the Pacific coast of the Maya area, but not in the Maya lowlands. Upright stones called "stelae" and rectangular or round flat stones called "altars" (probably used as seats or thrones for rulers) are found throughout the Maya area from the Middle Preclassic on. Different Mesoamerican societies also share motifs carved on Preclassic monuments. For example, carved portrayals of rulers seated in a monster mouth, symbolizing a cave at the entrance to the underworld, are found in the Mexican highlands and on both Olmec and Maya monuments. Carved emblems that indicate either names or titles identify some Olmec rulers. Portraits of Maya rulers are identified by hieroglyphs for their names and titles. After a ruler's death, both the Olmec and Maya followed the custom of defacing or breaking that ruler's monuments, probably to cancel the supernatural power believed to dwell within the stone.

Early Civilizations in Highland Mexico (ca. 1500–400 B.C.E.)

Many other societies thrived at the same time as the Olmec. These included complex societies (chiefdoms) in the Mexican highlands, especially those in the Valley of Oaxaca and the Valley of Mexico. Trade between the Gulf coast and these highland regions added to the wealth and authority of local elites. The Olmec imported obsidian for cutting tools from central Mexico and from the Maya highlands. Trade in prestige goods was probably managed directly by elites for their use. These included jade from the middle Motagua Valley, in Guatemala, imported by elites in both the Mexican highlands and on the Gulf coast. Magnetite (used to fashion ceremonial mirrors) was exported by elites in the Valley of Oaxaca, and fine kaolin clay (used to make distinctive white ware pottery and figurines) came from near Chalcatzingo, in the highlands of central Mexico. Other perishable commodities were undoubtedly traded also, although no direct evidence has survived. In addition to material goods, these economic networks were avenues for social, political, and religious interaction. These contacts communicated information and new ideas, which accelerated cultural development throughout Mesoamerica.

Excavations at Chalcatzingo and in the Valley of Mexico just to the north show local sociopolitical developments that paralleled those on the Gulf coast. Although these areas were in contact, both the Olmec and Chalcatzingo asserted their distinct identity in several ways. The civic and ceremonial core of Chalcatzingo was laid out in a north-south pattern and displayed sculptures commemorating rulership in the northern half of the site. This was the exact opposite of the Olmec pattern at La Venta, where rulership monuments are displayed in the southern half of the site. The authority of Chalcatzingo's rulers was reinforced by depictions carved on a secluded cliff face overlooking the site, while the Olmec used freestanding sculptured monuments in a more public setting. Some of

Chalcatzingo's carvings incorporated elements similar to those on Olmec monuments, indicating that both societies shared motifs and ideological meanings, probably communicated by long-established trade contacts. But the way these carved elements were used, and their meanings, also varied from one region to another.

Versions of far older basic concepts shared by all Mesoamerican societies were also communicated by these trade routes. Some of these are revealed by the use of similar symbols for the major earth and sky deities found on pottery throughout Mesoamerica dating to ca. 1200–900 B.C.E. These symbols probably reflect religious concepts that helped motivate and unify societies, as well as justifying the power of local ruling elites. Religion became a major means to integrate societies, even as socioeconomic distinctions were separating rulers from the ruled.

One of the best examples of the development of early Mesoamerican civilization comes from the Valley of Oaxaca, in southern Mexico. In this highland valley, the first clues of social and economic divisions and of chiefdom organizations also appear by the Early Preclassic. By the Middle Preclassic, the valley appears to have been divided between several rival chiefdoms, each with a capital. Here each ruler lived in a palace close to temples and civic structures, separated from the houses of the rest of the population. The temples were used to worship agricultural deities that controlled vital forces such as rain and lightening. Middle Preclassic Oaxaca pottery was decorated with designs of "fire serpents" and "were-jaguars," These were powerful and ancient religious symbols used throughout Mesoamerica at this time, used as emblems for elite families.

Elites began to advertise their authority and accomplishments using carved stone monuments in the Valley of Oaxaca by ca. 1000 B.C.E. By ca. 700–500 B.C.E., these monuments were carved with simple glyphs to record dates or personal names. These stones displayed portrayals of captives and sacrifices. This contrasts with carved motifs at Olmec sites along the Gulf coast. Whereas Olmec rulers reinforced their authority with personal portraits that linked them to earth and sky deities, early Oaxacan rulers asserted their authority with carved stones that recorded their successes in leading raids and taking captives. Later, Maya rulers reinforced their authority by using both of these themes in their public displays of power.

Research in the Valley of Oaxaca reveals distinct local patterns of gender-associated ritual activity. Before ca. 700 B.C.E., women used fired-clay figurines to conduct ancestor-veneration rites in their households. Men conducted rituals in specialized men's houses away from residences, using lime probably mixed with ritual plants such as tobacco. By ca. 700–500 B.C.E., the earlier rituals conducted in households and in men's houses disappeared as elite leaders began to monopolize ritual activity. Internal social distinctions became more pronounced, and large-scale public buildings appeared as the elite class monopolized wealth and labor.

Figure 3.3 Carved portrait of a war captive from the site of Monte Alban in the Valley of Oaxaca, Mexico (note glyphs to left of head).

Overall, archaeological evidence indicates that there was an interrelated developmental process throughout Mesoamerica. In the Valley of Oaxaca and elsewhere, competition and warfare encouraged the consolidation of settlements and increased the authority of elite leaders. Success in war meant that defeated territories were incorporated into the realms of the victors. In time, warfare gave rise to more complex and efficient organizations to maintain control over these larger territories and their populations.

INTERACTION AND THE DEVELOPMENT
OF CIVILIZATION

By the end of the Middle Preclassic, the Olmec had declined because of competition from other polities and internal problems. Oaxacan civilization went on to develop into a powerful and unified state. In addition to the Olmec and Oaxaca, there were similar developments in other Mesoamerican areas at about the same time. The central Mexican highlands and both the Maya highlands and Pacific coastal plain soon supported even more complex preindustrial states. These developments were stimulated by contacts between all of these regions, especially by trade in status goods used by rulers and in everyday items such as cutting tools of obsidian (volcanic glass).

Residents of each polity made or acquired local products to exchange for the products in other regions. Thus, a region with valuable mineral resources to trade not only marketed them in other regions but obtained from its foreign contacts information about new agricultural practices, or improvements in pottery making, or new religious customs. Some of these exchanges of ideas undoubtedly helped rulers to find better ways to unify their subjects, more efficient ways of organizing their economy, or new and more powerful symbols to reinforce their authority. Indeed, the Mesoamerican trade network exposed everyone to new products and ideas. Knowledge of new crops or better farming methods resulted in increased food supplies, which in turn led to increased populations. New natural resources, crafts, and markets increased prosperity and created the need for a variety of specialists to make goods and middlemen to trade them. As societies became larger and more complex, the rulers in each polity consolidated their economic, political, and religious power. These Middle Preclassic developments spurred further growth of civilization in later times.

The Maya, located in a diverse and rich environment at a crossroads between southern Mesoamerica and Central America, were perfectly situated to prosper from their natural wealth and to learn from their neighbors. By adapting new ideas to their customs, the Maya developed a distinctive and brilliant civilization that would thrive for some 2,000 years.

THE FABRIC OF MAYA CIVILIZATION

The development of Maya civilization can be understood by considering a series of underlying factors. The interplay of Maya ideology, ecology, economy, political organization, and warfare created the unique characteristics of Maya civilization.

Ideology

To understand Maya civilization, we need to understand how the Maya viewed their world. Generally speaking, the Maya believed that supernatural powers, spirits, gods, and invisible forces controlled all aspects of life and governed their world. The ever-present powers of the supernatural guided the ways the Maya adapted to their environment, the ways they organized their society, their trade, warfare, and all aspects of their culture and daily life.

Every member of Maya society—rulers, other elites, the common people (farmers and a variety of occupational specialists)—believed that they had to keep the world an ordered place. If a person failed his or her duties, this threatened that order. Accidents, illness, or death were seen as punishments for transgressions by the supernatural powers that governed the universe. These powers could be visible as celestial objects, such as the sun, moon, and stars. Invisible powers were inside all things, animals, mountains, and other places such as caves (believed to be entries to the underworld). The Maya believed that knowledge of these things was revealed to religious specialists—shamans and priests—who held special powers to communicate with the supernatural.

Maya rulers were both political and religious leaders. As king and high priest of their polities, responsible for the prosperity, health, and security of their subjects, rulers were connected to important supernaturals and enjoyed greater wealth, prestige, and power as a result. Rulers and their elite allies directed public activities, including tribute collection, temple construction, trade, warfare, and the spectacular public rituals believed to ensure supernatural favor. But if a polity fell on hard times, it could be blamed on the ruler for failing to keep the supernatural powers happy. We will provide a fuller discussion of Maya religion and cosmology in chapter 11.

Ecology

The term *ecology* refers to the relationships between societies and their environments. As we have seen, environmental diversity was critical to the development of Maya civilization. The ways in which Maya society adapted to its environment determined how much food was produced and the size, growth, health, and nutritional status of Maya populations. The earliest means for acquiring food—hunting and gathering—can support only a limited number of people, usually in a nonsettled lifestyle. Although hunting continued to provide animal protein for the Maya, the growth of their civilization depended on large permanently settled populations, supported by agriculture.

The earliest Maya farmers harvested rich and naturally replenished riverbank soils. This technique has the potential to support fairly large numbers of people in a concentrated area. In colonizing new forest areas, Maya farmers used swiddening, that is, clearing, burning, and planting a field for two to three years until its soil is exhausted. Swiddening cannot support large numbers of people, and it keeps them dispersed over the landscape. But it is adaptable to many conditions and requires a smaller investment of time and energy to produce food.

Ancient Maya farmers practiced other methods that produced more food and supported more people. While these methods usually required more work initially, they produced more food and allowed people to concentrate in larger settlements. For example, Maya households could produce a variety of foods in garden plots next to each house, with the soil constantly replenished by refuse from the household. Household gardens

continue to be important in Maya communities today. Ancient agricultural terraces have been found in both the Maya highlands, where they
are sometimes still used, and in hilly portions of the lowlands, where the
Maya converted sloping land to highly productive fields. No longer used
today except in experimental areas, manmade islands of fertile soil built
up from swamps and drained by canals on all sides (raised fields) were
extremely productive, because the canals provided rich muck that was
scooped up to renew the fields. The remains of Maya raised-fields have
been found and studied in several southern lowland areas.

Each farming method had different potentials for supporting people.
The most favored areas and most efficient methods produced the greatest amounts of food to support population growth. Population growth in
turn led to development of more productive farming methods, more labor
to produce goods, services, and infrastructure (e.g., buildings, roads, reservoirs), and increased competition for land and other resources. This is
discussed more fully in chapter 8.

Trade

The Maya economy fostered the production and distribution of goods,
using a network of trade routes and markets that extended throughout
Mesoamerica. One axis of this network connected the Maya with central
Mexico to the northwest and with Central America to the southeast. This
axis consisted of many routes: those in the south, which ran along the
Pacific coastal plain, those in the southern lowlands (using river canoes
for transport wherever possible), and those to the north, which followed
the Yucatan coast (traders also used canoes wherever possible). The other
axis comprised overland routes that ran north and south, interconnecting
Yucatan, the lowlands, the highlands, and the Pacific plain.

Goods and services were exchanged in centralized markets. These
allowed people in one village to specialize in one product (such as pottery) and to exchange it for other necessities brought from elsewhere. This
created an economic interdependence that unified the entire Maya area.

This economic system was crucial to the development of Maya civilization. While parts of the system were maintained without elite control,
elites undoubtedly managed some of the most important trade networks
and markets. It is usually assumed that the state was at least minimally
involved in promoting trade, such as maintaining routes and providing
facilities for markets. Cities that controlled access to essential goods or to
important trade routes or that held important markets had an advantage
over other settlements. Of course, the elites who controlled these favored
settlements enjoyed more wealth, prestige, and power as a result. Rulers
and the elite class directly boosted their prestige and authority by controlling status goods, such as jade and feathers, that symbolized their special
powers. Trade and markets are discussed more fully in chapter 8.

Social and Political Organization

The ways a society is organized ultimately determines its destiny. Social organization establishes the bonds that tie a society together and the means for harnessing human energy for a variety of purposes. Political organization determines how rulers and other elites wield power. While united by social ties, the Maya were always politically divided into many individual polities. The fortunes of each independent kingdom varied over time. Some polities increased their power and prestige by forming alliances with other kingdoms. Others expanded by conquest—although few such military expansions were long-lived. Many factors contributed to the success or failures of each polity: location, environment, access to trade, organizational efficiency, prestige, military success, and the abilities and lifespan of individual rulers. These last factors often proved critical, for the Maya believed that the successes or failures of their rulers reflected supernatural favor or disfavor.

Although they were never politically unified, these Maya polities were dependent on one another. No kingdom could succeed without cooperating with other polities. Cooperation made possible the trade and distribution of goods. Alliances between polities allowed smaller kingdoms to resist aggression from more powerful states. This interdependence is reflected in the episodes of growth and decline seen in Maya history. In the lowlands we can see three cycles of this growth and decline for most of the polities in the area. Maya society and government are the subject of chapters 9 and 10.

Competition and Warfare

Warfare, or violent confrontations between polities, was part of the fabric of Maya civilization. But Maya warfare had different rules and purposes from what we think of as warfare in our modern world. Indeed, warfare played a role in the origins of Maya civilization itself. As populations grew and farmers colonized more of the landscape, competition for land and other resources increased. Competition could be lessened by the development of more productive methods of food production or by attempts to control more people by attracting them to markets or to spectacular religious ceremonies. The more people a ruler could control, the more power he could gain from their labor and the goods they produced. Yet, competition often led to violence, as one polity sought to take over the resources of others.

By the Middle Preclassic, Maya polities were raiding each other for tribute and captives, to be used as labor and for ritual sacrifices (as part of important religious ceremonies). Tribute meant more wealth for the victorious ruler and his people. Captives meant more labor and advertised the dominance of one polity over another. The prestige of victorious rulers was enhanced, while defeated rivals were diminished or even eliminated by sacrifice. By the Classic period, warfare intensified, so that alliances and conflicts between kingdoms not only brought tribute, captives, and prestige but also were used to control lands, resources, and entire populations of defeated polities.

Success in war depends on well-organized and well-trained warriors. By the Classic period, specialized warriors were part of Maya society (along with other specialists). As the threat of warfare increased, the organization of power changed. Success in attacking an enemy or defending a city often depends on placing all authority in the hands of one person (the ruler). Thus, over time, warfare gave greater power to Maya kings and reinforced their authority at the head of a hierarchy of command.

Polities with larger and better-organized populations and better ways of making decisions had a better chance to defeat and dominate those with fewer people and poorer organization. But even successful conquerors eventually reach a limit to their resources and capabilities. The Maya political and military organizations were not capable of large-scale conquest, nor could they administer ever-larger territories and populations in the wake of conquest.

The expansion of powerful polities by warfare was also influenced by alliances. Strong and successful states used alliances to confront their most powerful rivals to see which could dominate center stage. But successful kingdoms could also be checked by alliances of lesser powers. See In chapter 10 we discuss alliances and warfare.

The following chapter discusses how these factors contributed to the rapid growth of the first episode of Maya civilization between about 1000 B.C.E and 250 (the Middle and Late Preclassic periods).

FURTHER READING

Clark, Carneiro, and de los Angeles Montaño in press; Dillehay 2000; Drennen and Uribe 1987; Flannery and Marcus 1983; Grove 1984; Grove and Joyce 1999; Hirth 1984; Pool 2007; Sharer and Grove 1989; Turner and Harrison 1983.

4

EARLY MAYA CIVILIZATION

The first blooming of Maya civilization took place within the southern portion of the Maya homeland, the Pacific coast and highlands, and in the lowlands to the north. These developments date to the Middle Preclassic (ca. 1500–400 B.C.E.), and the Late Preclassic (ca. 400 B.C.E.–250).

THE ORIGINS OF STATES IN THE MIDDLE PRECLASSIC (ca. 1500–400 B.C.E.)

By the Middle Preclassic a series of complex chiefdom societies linked by trading relationships had developed in many regions of Mesoamerica. The most important route between Mexico and Central America was on the Pacific coastal plain. The Maya living on the coastal plain were especially important in keeping this coastal trade route open and prosperous.

The first states developed from these chiefdoms during the Middle Preclassic and define the appearance of Early Maya civilization. By this time there were growing populations, increases in the size and number of settlements, and expansions into new areas throughout the Maya homeland. Archaeologists have identified several indicators of emerging states in the Middle Preclassic period. Maya society became more complex as status and role distinctions became more numerous and well defined by economic and ideological changes. These distinctions and the increasing power of elite leaders is reflected by the appearance of large-scale public works, carved monuments, and warfare. These changes were spurred by population growth and by new economic opportunities—increased food production, expansion of trade, and the rise of craft specialization, which in turn spurred further growth. So, by the Middle Preclassic, an emerging elite class had mobilized resources within a host of developing polities dispersed across the Maya area. By the Late Preclassic, many of these polities were headed by a single ruler who monopolized available resources, wealth, and power, aided and abetted by the remainder of the elites that controlled most of the balance of resources.

Economic changes resulted in an expansion in the production and distribution of goods. A variety of items that identify and reinforce elevated status make their appearance in the archaeological record—mirrors, masks, bloodletters, scepters, and the like, made from rare materials (such as jade). These status goods were usually embellished with religious motifs or symbols, which created and maintained authority and defined the distinctions between elite and nonelite members of Maya society.

There was an increase in long-distance trade of these prestige goods as the demand for these items produced a need to secure their supply. The elite created their wealth and elevated status by controlling critical segments of the economy. These included the acquisition, production, and distribution of prestige goods, long-distance trade for both prestige items and some critical utilitarian goods, the collection of tribute from their subjects, and the redistribution of goods through feasts, gift giving, and markets. Elite rulers also controlled corvée labor—the obligation for subjects to work for a set period every year for the king. From earliest times, Maya rulers used corvée labor for the construction and maintenance of monumental public works and for the manufacture of status goods produced by specialized craftsmen.

The most conspicuous products of corvée labor were large platforms built of either stone or adobe (sun-baked earth) that were far larger than everyday constructions, for they supported temples and elite palaces. The rapid expansion of these public works—monumental constructions that required the mobilization of resources and large labor forces—reflects the growth of elite authority and its reinforcement by ideological changes. Constructions in the earliest Archaic period villages were confined to small features—houses, hearths, and storage pits—built by individuals or families. Of course, family-built houses continued in use during later times, but, by the Middle Preclassic, larger towns and cities became dominated by plazas, causeways, canals, reservoirs, and huge adobe-plastered or masonry-faced "pyramids" (platforms) that supported buildings of wood, adobe, and thatch. Large numbers of people were needed to build and maintain these monumental constructions, mobilized by elite authority. The organization of labor to construct public works also institutionalized status and role hierarchies. This gave rulers more effective control over their subjects. Maya rulers created monumental public works, and these public works also created and reinforced the power of Maya rulers.

Initially, the motivation for corvée labor probably came from a desire to promote the common good for all society. This was based on obvious connections such as that between digging irrigation canals and improving food and water supplies or on faith-based connections between constructing temples and gaining supernatural protection. Of course, once these kinds of facilities were constructed, management of their use likely became a source of power for the elite. Early on, therefore, rulers acquired great power by controlling temples because these provided access to the gods. They also gained power by controlling canals or other water sources because these furnished the water critical for growing food and even meant the difference between life and death during the annual dry season.

The Maya believed that corvée labor obligations, beyond serving practical benefits, were part of the order of things as ordained by the gods. Working for the elite was believed to please the gods and to ensure supernatural protection. These beliefs allowed elite rulers to expand their subject's labor and tribute. In time, corvée labor was used to build and maintain facilities with less obvious practical benefits, such as royal palaces, and to provide the elite with rare and costly foodstuffs, gifts, and other perquisites. The palaces of early Maya rulers and their elite kin were far larger than the houses of their subjects. When they died, rulers were buried with symbols of their authority in specially prepared tombs that were often located under temples, also built by their subjects. These efforts were motivated by an elite-sponsored religious system, which held that, like temples, royal palaces and tombs pleased the gods. As elite demands increased, more coercive measures may have become necessary to acquire labor. But a reinforcing ideology continued its essential role, especially in justifying the disparity in wealth and power between the elite and the nonelite classes.

Thus, the economic dimensions of elite power were intertwined with Maya ideology. Religious beliefs motivated and mobilized Preclassic society and increased the authority of elite leaders. Shared Mesoamerican supernatural symbols that first appeared on Early Preclassic pottery and monuments became more common in the Middle Preclassic. These represented the critical needs of society for water (rain deities), food (maize deities), and protection (lightning and earth deities). The belief that rulers could placate and even control these deities was a critical source of power. Rulers conducted rituals to bring plentiful rain and maize and to protect against storms, earthquakes, and other natural disasters.

Another labor requirement for Maya commoners was the hauling of large stones for monuments that glorified the achievements of their rulers. Carved stone monuments are a vivid marker of elite power backed by religious beliefs. The use of monuments in the highlands of Mexico, on the Gulf coast, and in the Maya area expanded the Middle Preclassic period. Many are plain but probably once had painted motifs, and a few are carved with symbols of supernatural power recognized throughout Mesoamerica. For

Figure 4.1 Rubbing of a boulder sculpture from Chalchuapa, El Salvador, depicting a local ruler with scepter and winged-cape costume (Middle Preclassic).

example, a Middle Preclassic carved boulder at Chalchuapa, El Salvador, has four figures. The two largest represent local rulers who were portrayed with powerful symbols, including costumes, headdresses, and scepters very similar to those found on carvings at Chalcatzingo, in the Mexican highlands, and at La Venta, in the Gulf coast lowlands.

By the end of the Middle Preclassic (ca. 500–400 B.C.E.), Maya rulers began to dedicate stelae carved with their portraits as public testimonials to their political legitimacy and personal achievements. These portrayed rulers in positions of authority, as warriors or personifications of gods (wearing masks and headdresses of deities). By adding carved texts, rulers could record their place in time, their relationships to sacred ancestors, and their achievements. Large public plazas were constructed for these royal monuments at some of the earliest polity capitals. This allowed the power of past rulers to continue to inspire awe and respect in their subjects and demonstrated the living king's right to rule by his connections to his royal ancestors. The appearance of these public monuments marks the beginnings of the institution of dynastic kingship in Maya society. Their presence also identifies polity capitals that administered a hierarchy of subordinate centers.

Warfare also played an important role in the development of Maya states. The archaeological evidence points to its Preclassic beginnings as occasional small-scale raids between polities. These eliminated rivals and secured needed goods and labor. Ritual captive sacrifices reinforced the ideological foundations of elite authority. Successful attacks or defenses against enemy raids strengthened the power of Maya rulers and streamlined lines of command and control. Indeed, warfare helped determine the winners and losers among competing Maya polities.

The Middle Preclassic in the Southern Area

Archaeological research on the Pacific plain shows that between ca. 1000 and 750 B.C.E., settlement expanded inland from the coast, accompanied by major social changes. There was rapid growth in population, site hierarchies became more complex, and social stratification increased. Some of the most dramatic changes occurred at the site of La Blanca, the capital of a Middle Preclassic polity in southwestern Guatemala. From about 900 to 600 B.C.E., La Blanca controlled a territory of about 300 square kilometers and headed a three-tier site hierarchy that included 2 secondary centers and some 60 smaller hamlets. La Blanca's monumental constructions reflect a huge mobilization of labor over a span of about three centuries, including one of the largest temple platforms in Mesoamerica built during this time (24 meters high).

Populations and numbers of sites continued to increase during this period. Further east on the coastal plain of Guatemala, research has identified a string of five sites dating to ca. 800–600 B.C.E. These are all about 35 kilometers from the sea and are spaced about 10 kilometers apart at about the same elevation. All are within the same environmental zone paralleling the coast, intermediate between coast and highlands, and possessing especially fertile soils with good rainfall. By the later Middle Preclassic (ca. 600–400 B.C.E.), the number of sites in this environmental zone more than doubled to 12, site sizes increased, and a more complex site-size hierarchy developed. Site locations show that, although two-thirds of the population continued to occupy elevations above 100 meters, the remaining one-third of settlement had expanded back toward the coast (elevations below 100 meters).

Similar growth can be seen elsewhere in the southern Maya area. Some of the best evidence for these developments in the highlands comes from the Salama Valley, located north of the Motagua River. This fertile valley is at a crossroads of routes serving both the southern highlands and the lowlands to the north. People in the Salama Valley maintained trade connections with other Mesoamerican areas, and there was steady population growth throughout the Preclassic. Large adobe temple platforms, elaborate elite residences, and tombs appeared ca. 800–500 B.C.E. The tombs of several rulers were excavated from beneath one temple platform, probably members of a dynastic succession. The largest tomb was a stone stone-lined crypt dating to about 500 B.C.E.; it contained the bones of an adult male buried face up. Status goods of jade and shell, a carved stone scepter, and three trophy heads accompanied this ruler in his tomb. But the best indication of his power were the remains of at least 12 human sacrifices found around the crypt, some bound, others dismembered, and all buried face down, presumably to serve the dead ruler in the Maya underworld.

The trophy heads and sacrifices in this tomb are also evidence for warfare, a powerful factor in the development of states. Other indications of Maya warfare come from projectile points and carved depictions of rulers as warriors. Over time, successful small-scale raids to eliminate rivals and gain wealth and labor increased the power of rulers and also increased their ability to control their subjects. The Maya creation myth involved human sacrifices (discussed in chapter 11), so rulers further reinforced their authority by sacrificing their captured enemies to the gods.

Between 500 and 400 B.C.E., authority became more centralized in the Salama valley. A small settlement in the center of the valley, known as El Portón, was transformed into the political and religious capital of the entire valley. Large adobe platforms supported temples and palaces constructed of timber and thatch. A sequence of paired stelae and altars was placed in front of one low platform, perhaps the house or shrine of the ruling family. The earliest and largest monument, a carved stone stela with a now-eroded scene and a column of glyphs and numerals, may commemorate the ruler who founded this local capital. It dates to about 400 B.C.E. Its glyphs are an early form of later Maya writing—one of the earliest examples of Maya writing yet discovered.

El Portón was a capital of a prosperous chiefdom by the end of the Middle Preclassic. At the same time, Kaminaljuyu ("place of the ancient ones"), a far larger highland polity capital, developed just to the south of the Salama Valley. Also located on the north-south routes that connected the Pacific coast with the Maya lowlands, Kaminaljuyu rapidly developed on the shores of a small lake in the Valley of Guatemala.

The beginnings of monumental architecture, carved stone monuments, and sociopolitical stratification dates to about 900–600 B.C.E. in the Valley of Guatemala. By ca. 600 B.C.E., Kaminaljuyu consolidated the valley under its authority and grew dramatically, supported by the first in a series of enormous irrigation canals that brought water from the lake to fields south of the city. Constructed by elite-directed labor, canals allowed for irrigation to increase food production, furthered population growth, and reinforced centralized power for Kaminaljuyu's rulers. Carved portraits on stone monuments indicate that a succession of rulers reigned at Kaminaljuyu with considerable wealth and authority based on religious

Figure 4.2 Eroded glyphs from a stela at El Portón in the highland Salama Valley, Guatemala, among the earliest evidence for Maya writing, dating to ca. 400 B.C.E.

Figure 4.3 Stela 11, Kaminaljuyu, Guatemala, showing a Preclassic ruler with an elaborate god mask and headdress holding an axe ("decapitator") (ca. 400–200 B.C.E.).

sanctions and success in taking captives by warfare, in addition to water management.

The Middle Preclassic Lowlands

Further north in the lowlands, rapid population growth and the first indications of civilization appeared a few centuries after initial colonization by farming villagers (ca. 1200–800 B.C.E.). These migrants came from the coastal margins of the lowlands to the east and west and from the highlands to the south. In the northern lowlands, these earliest lowland communities were situated near cenotes. In the southern lowlands, they were on the rivers and lakes that provided fertile soils for farming, water, and canoe transport. Several such farming villages have been excavated in Belize. At the site of Cuello, settlers built low house platforms coated with lime plaster that supported pole-and-thatch houses (indicated by the pattern of postholes left in the platforms). There are the remains of hearths, human burials, maize and other foods, pottery, and stone tools, including manos and metates for grinding corn.

The origins of many southern lowland polity capitals date to between ca. 800 and 600 B.C.E. A number of these seem to have been established on hilltops commanding river valleys, lakes, or bajos. Excavations at one of these early capitals, Cival, in the eastern lowlands of Guatemala, indicate that at its founding an entire hilltop was cleared and leveled, then dedicated by the placement of an elaborate offering beneath the center of the new settlement. This ritual cache formed a symbolic representation of the Maya world, with offerings placed at each of the four directions and at the center, the location of the world tree that supports the sky.

As lowland populations grew, the number of settlements grew, and people spread from the earlier river valley and lakeside locations into interior forested regions. Expansion into this less fertile environment was made possible by swidden agriculture that allowed people to farm the heavily forested inland areas and by the digging of underground cisterns (chultunes) to trap and hold water during the rainy season.

The first monumental buildings appear throughout the lowlands during the later Middle Preclassic (ca. 600–400 B.C.E.). Excavations at Blackman Eddy, Belize, reveal an example of the sequential development of public architecture, beginning with postholes from timber-and-thatch houses and low earthen platforms dating to ca. 1100–900 B.C.E. By about 900–700 B.C.E., these were replaced by larger rectangular platforms built of limestone blocks and plaster. The first of these was associated with evidence for food processing, dedicatory feasts, and religious rituals. The next platform was decorated by plaster masks but was burned, possibly during a raid. This was replaced during the later Middle Preclassic (ca. 700–400 B.C.E.) by a much larger platform and by later expansions that continued onto the Late Preclassic period.

There is even more dramatic evidence for the transformation of low-land society at Nakbe, in the Mirador Basin (northern Petén). One of several Middle Preclassic centers in the basin, Nakbe has the earliest known masonry buildings (including a ball court), *sacbeob* (elevated roadways), and carved stone monuments in the Maya lowlands. As such, it is a prototype for later lowland Maya polity capitals. Nakbe's initial settlement (ca. 1000–800 B.C.E.) had pole-and-thatch houses, tamped clay floors, and stone retaining walls. Between ca. 800–600 B.C.E., it rapidly expanded with its first monumental masonry platforms (2 to 3 meters high), covered with mixed clay and lime plaster. Much larger terraced platforms, up to 17 meters high, were built between ca. 600 and 400 B.C.E., with more carefully shaped masonry covered by plaster. All of these platforms supported buildings of perishable materials. Carved upright stelae and altars were placed in front of these platforms. Nakbe Stela 1 is an outstanding example of Preclassic Maya sculpture depicting two masked figures facing each other.

The Middle Preclassic saw increased settlement in many other areas of the lowlands. Village agriculturalists had settled much of the northern lowlands of Yucatan by ca. 1100 B.C.E., as part of the same expansion of Maya farmers who colonized the rest of the lowlands. These initial Yucatecan populations made and used pottery very similar to that found to the south and constructed masonry platforms for their earliest public buildings, including ball courts. What we know of these developments has been learned from archaeological work at Preclassic sites such as Komchen, located in northeastern Yucatan.

THE FIRST STATES IN THE LATE PRECLASSIC (ca. 400 B.C.E.–250)

While some of the largest Middle Preclassic sites like La Blanca and Nakbe were clearly capitals of incipient states, the first clear examples of states emerged throughout the Maya area during the Late Preclassic era, marking the full bloom of Early Maya civilization. The largest manifestations of early Maya states were at Kaminaljuyu and El Mirador, but there were numerous smaller examples, as well. The best signs of this development are the growth of cities that held large numbers of people, a society stratified into elite and nonelite classes, centralized authority held by dynasties of kings, elaborate tombs, monumental buildings, carved monuments, complex rituals, a sophisticated art style, and the full development of Maya hieroglyphic writing. It is Maya writing and its use for political purposes that most clearly distinguish the peaking of Early Maya civilization during this period.

Writing in Mesoamerica originated in the Middle Preclassic period. We have already mentioned an example of Maya writing dating to ca. 400 B.C.E. on the stela at El Portón. There are more examples of Middle Preclassic writing in other parts of Mesoamerica, especially in Oaxaca.

It is not clear whether the knowledge of writing was brought to the Maya from outside or whether it has a local Maya origin. The earliest known examples are carved in stone or painted on murals inside buildings and represent a well-developed writing system. This implies that the origins of Maya writing are further back in time and that perhaps that earliest writing was on perishable wood and bark paper, rather than carved on durable stone or painted on plaster.

Whatever its origin, the knowledge of writing was quickly adapted for political purposes by Maya rulers in the emerging Late Preclassic polities of the southern Maya area and lowlands and becomes a hallmark of Early Maya civilization. A few glyphs and concepts were borrowed from other writing systems, while the rest was developed by the Maya to create the most complex writing system in the pre-Columbian New World. This was used to record the genealogies and achievements of Maya kings, a tradition of keeping political history that was to endure until the Spanish Conquest.

An important aspect of Maya writing is a calendrical system for recording dates for events. The most complex calendar used a fixed zero date, known as the Long Count (this and other systems are discussed further in chapter 12). The Long Count recorded the time elapsed from a fixed point in the past (in the year 3114 B.C.E. in our calendar), using five time units. The Maya had symbols for both numbers and time units, but we now write these dates using numbers in descending order (separated by a period). For example, the Long Count written as 8.4.6.0.3 refers to a date 8 *bak'tuns* (8 units of 144,000 days), 4 *k'atuns* (4 units of 7,200 days), 6 *tuns* (6 units of 360 days), 0 *winals* (0 units of 20 days), and 3 *k'ins* (3 units of 1 day) after the zero date in 3114 B.C.E. Maya numbers were written with dots (for the number one) and bars (for the number five).

The Long Count first appeared during Early Maya civilization to record important events in the reigns and lives of kings. The dates and other information about events such as inaugurations, conquests, and deaths, were most commonly carved on stone monuments, along with portraits of rulers. These portraits often illustrated the events recorded by the hieroglyphic text and show the king impressively costumed, with symbols of supernatural power to promote the ruler's political and religious authority. Texts are also found on buildings and on portable items such as pottery, jewelry, and utensils.

Early Maya States in the Southern Area

There were two courses of development of Early Maya civilization in the Late Preclassic. In the highlands and on the coastal plain, civilization reached its apex in the Late Preclassic and then declined. In the lowlands, after a short decline at the end of the Late Preclassic, civilization went on to even greater developments during the following episode of Middle Maya civilization.

A number of Late Preclassic political capitals of the Pacific plain and highlands have carved stone monuments; some also have Long Count dates. The earliest monuments with Long Count dates appear in the first century B.C.E., and continue in these regions for several hundred years before disappearing. This span of about 300 years defines the greatest period of development for the southern Maya area. As hosts of lavish ceremonies, the rulers of these polity capitals invested in the construction of huge temple platforms and adjacent plazas where large numbers of people could assemble. The most important polity capitals had areas for displaying carved monuments with portraits of their rulers and shrines that protected their lavish tombs. These early cities were also market centers for trading cacao, foodstuffs, pottery, highland minerals, and other products from as far as Mexico and Central America. The prosperity that flowed from this trade was assisted by alliances between the rulers of neighboring polities.

Kaminaljuyu was the largest and most powerful city in the southern highlands. Like many other sites, Kaminaljuyu was the capital of a prosperous polity and a center for ceremonial, political, and economic activities. Kaminaljuyu once covered about 4 square kilometers and contained more than 200 large earthen platforms that supported buildings of timber, plaster, and thatch. Because the site has been largely destroyed by modern Guatemala City, little is known about everyday life in the city, its administrative hierarchy, or the extent of its polity. But it is clear that, in the Late Preclassic period, Kaminaljuyu reached its peak of power and prosperity and that its irrigation system was expanded by the construction of two far larger canals. Most of its many carved monuments date to this era, including those that depict its rulers with their trappings of power and several that also have hieroglyphic texts. Examples include a fragment of a large throne, bordered with a carved mat motif, emblematic of Maya kings. Carved on its upper surface is one of the longest Preclassic texts known from the Maya area. Another carved monument depicts the succession of three Preclassic rulers, each flanked by bound, kneeling captives.

Kaminaljuyu's economy prospered from trade in jade and other highland products. Control of one of the most important obsidian quarries, El Chayal (located 19 kilometers to the northeast), made Kaminaljuyu the center of trade in essential cutting tools exported throughout the Maya area. The power and wealth of the Late Preclassic kings of Kaminaljuyu are best seen in two spectacular royal tombs. Both were found within a large earthen platform that originally supported ancestral shrines built over the tombs. The rulers' remains were found in the center of both tombs, adorned with jade and other status goods and surrounded by hundreds of pots to hold food and other offerings. Both tombs also included sacrificed companions; in one were two children and a young adult who had been placed face down in the chamber.

Other early polity capitals with similar architecture, tombs, and monuments are found throughout the highland and coastal regions. The emergence of Preclassic states on the Pacific plain was fueled by economic prosperity from the cultivation of cacao and other crops such as rubber and from control over the important coastal trade routes. The site of El Ujuxte is a good example of the capital of such a state. It was, in fact, the successor of the Middle Preclassic capital of La Blanca. El Ujuxte was a centrally planned city: its monumental structures were arranged in a grid-like pattern covering 3 square kilometers. It headed a four-tiered administrative hierarchy that included four secondary centers and dozens of smaller tertiary villages within a polity covering 600 square kilometers. Like that of Kaminaljuyu, El Ujuxte's development was marked by an increasing centralization of authority in the hands of rulers who monopolized wealth and who were backed by religious belief. There were also increased expenditures for public works and intensified food production. Unlike at Kaminaljuyu, there is archaeological evidence that El Ujuxte's elite class enjoyed increased control over the everyday economy of its subjects.

As mentioned, a number of coastal and highland sites displayed carved monuments, the earliest in the Maya area to combine written and visual records of royal events. Ruler portraits were carved in an early Maya style, ancestral to the later Classic style seen in the Maya lowlands. These carved images proclaim the ceremonial and political authority of Late Preclassic kings. The scenes relate either to warfare or to succession of rulership. Warfare themes often show weapons and human heads, taken as trophies in battle. Succession of rulership may be depicted by two standing figures facing each other. As we have seen, this motif is found on what may be the earliest lowland Maya monument discovered thus far, Nakbe Stela 1.

The site of Takalik Abaj is one of the largest Late Preclassic Maya sites with carved monuments on the coastal plain. The ruins cover a series of large terraces that support earthen platforms arranged around open courts or plazas, the settings for an array of carved stelae and "altars" (thrones). Several stelae are especially important for their carved hieroglyphs and their royal portraits of two elaborately costumed rulers facing each other, separated by texts that begin with Long Count calendrical dates. Stela 2 has a partially preserved date that equates to the first century B.C.E. The better-preserved Stela 5 has two Long Count dates, the best-preserved corresponding to 126 C.E. Both monuments are good examples of early Maya sculptural style. The presence of Maya-style dynastic monuments with Long Count dates show that Takalik Abaj was an important Late Preclassic polity capital on the southwestern fringes of the Maya area.

Monuments and carved motifs like those at Takalik Abaj and Kaminaljuyu link the southern area and the lowlands to the north. There are other connections in common political and religious institutions. Late Preclassic

Figure 4.4 Takalik Abaj, Guatemala: Stela 5 and its companion "throne stone" excavated from the base of a temple stairway (Late Preclassic). Courtesy of John Graham.

sites in both areas have monumental funerary shrines associated with tombs of rulers. Not all temples had tombs, however. Unfortunately, many Late Preclassic Maya tombs have been illegally plundered, but, when the tombs are excavated by archaeologists, they furnish vivid evidence of the prestige and exalted status enjoyed by these early Maya kings.

Early Maya States in the Lowlands

In the Maya lowlands, similar large and complex polities developed during the Late Preclassic era. Cities founded in the Middle Preclassic greatly increased in size. In addition, many new cities were founded during the Late Preclassic throughout the lowlands. As in the southern area, distinctions between commoner and elite became more pronounced. The tombs of kings contain a varied inventory of imported luxury goods: jadeite, seashells, pottery, and stingray spines, used for ritual bloodletting by the ruling class. Besides reflecting class and status differences, these goods indicate increased occupational specialization and trade contacts with other regions.

Late Preclassic architecture also reflects these trends. At the site of Tikal (to be discussed in chapter 5), a monumental temple known as the Lost World Pyramid was constructed. In addition, the first funerary shrines in the North Acropolis were built, destined to be the place of burial for most of Tikal's rulers. One Late Preclassic shrine buried beneath later

Figure 4.5 Stela 5, Takalik Abaj, Guatemala: two eroded Long Count dates using bar and dot numerals, flanked on each side by portraits of a ruler and his successor. The date on the left reads 8.4.5.17.11, corresponding to the year 126 in our calendar. Courtesy of John Graham.

buildings had walls decorated by paintings closely related to the southern Maya style.

The largest individual buildings ever constructed by the Maya date from the Late Preclassic. The largest of these are found at El Mirador, the greatest of all known Late Preclassic Maya capitals. The huge scale of architecture at El Mirador—a larger assemblage than was found at other Late Preclassic lowland sites—certainly reflects the authority of its rulers and indicates that El Mirador was much more powerful than its neighbors during the peak of Early Maya civilization.

El Mirador is north of Tikal, in the Mirador Basin adjacent to a large seasonal lake. Radiating outward from its center is a network of causeways, including one that connects El Mirador to Middle Preclassic Nakbe, some 11 kilometers to the southeast. Causeways moved people and goods and gave El Mirador political and economic control over its outlying and subordinate centers. This network connected the major centers of the Mirador

Basin and greatly facilitated communication and commerce within the region. Causeway construction and maintenance required far more labor than even the largest temples, so El Mirador's rulers clearly commanded thousands of workers and exercised considerable authority over their subjects.

Archaeological excavations show that El Mirador began in the Middle Preclassic, but most of its buildings date to the Late Preclassic. Its civic and ceremonial core covers almost a mile from east to west. The eastern group is dominated by a huge platform that supports several triadic temples. These are composed of a tall terraced platform that has three summit temples—the largest in the center, flanked by two smaller temples on each side. Huge deity masks modeled in plaster and painted in several colors decorated the facades of these temple platforms. Triadic temples are found at several other lowland sites, but there are more at El Mirador than anywhere else. A 1-kilometer-long causeway connects the eastern group with the western group, which contains even more triadic temples. One of these, El Mirador's largest temple, El Tigre, covers a surface area six times greater than Tikal's largest building. Researchers excavating a smaller triadic temple on the south side of the Tigre complex, known as Structure 34, found that debris from the collapse of its roof had sealed Late Preclassic pottery vessels still on the floor of its central temple building.

Extensive plazas flank El Mirador's massive temples, so great crowds could assemble for public ceremonies. One of these plazas has the eroded

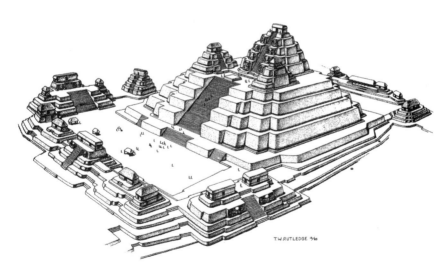

T.W. RUTLEDGE '91

Figure 4.6 El Mirador, Guatemala: Reconstructed view of a triadic temple complex known as El Tigre, one of the largest temples ever built by the Maya (Late Preclassic). Drawing by T. W. Rutledge, after Hansen 1984, 1990: ii. Courtesy of Richard Hansen, Regional Archaeological Investigation of the North Petén, Guatemala.

fragments of several stelae, carved in the distinctive Late Preclassic style seen in the highlands and on the Pacific coast, far to the south. One example retains traces of a Preclassic hieroglyphic text, but it is too eroded to decipher.

The recent discovery of well-preserved murals at the site of San Bartolo, about 60 kilometers east of El Mirador, provides important new information about Late Preclassic Maya kings in the lowlands. The murals are inside a buried building that dates to ca. 100 B.C.E. They present the earliest known version of the Maya creation myth—the origins of the four directional world trees and the central tree of life, associated with the birth of the maize god (discussed further in chapter 11). Significantly, there is also a royal inauguration scene with a painted hieroglyphic text. Most of the glyphs remain undeciphered, although there is a clear *ajaw* glyph (meaning "lord" or king).

The San Bartolo murals show that not only were Maya kings ruling in the Late Preclassic lowlands but that they were inaugurated and supported by the same rituals of earthly and supernatural power known from the Classic period. The murals may also reflect a hierarchy of political capitals in the Late Preclassic lowlands. San Bartolo is much smaller than El Mirador, and this could indicate that San Bartolo's rulers were subordinate to its huge neighbor.

Further east in Belize is an example of another small Late Preclassic center. The site of Cerros is situated on a promontory overlooking Chetumal Bay, on the Caribbean coast. A canal encircles the site, composed of raised fields, houses, ball courts, shrines, temples, and elite buildings. Cerros began as a Preclassic village like many others in the Maya lowlands. Its strategic location provided access to the sea and its resources, along with products moved by canoes up and down the Caribbean coast. Beginning about 50 B.C.E., the original village was buried under a series of monumental platforms and buildings, and Cerros was transformed into a small city to control trade on Chetumal Bay. It is likely that the closest major polity capital, Lamanai, directed this transformation. However, it is also possible that El Mirador may have held sway over both Lamanai and Cerros during the Late Preclassic.

Early states also developed further north in Yucatan during the Late Preclassic. One of these, Komchen, is located in the northwestern corner of the northern lowlands, about 20 kilometers from the coast, adjacent to the later and larger Classic city of Dzibilchaltun. Although the site was heavily looted for stone building materials, research reveals that it covers an area of 2 square kilometers and has about 1,000 buildings. At the center are five large platforms, the largest some 8 meters high, surrounding a central plaza. The site was occupied from about 700–650 B.C.E. onwards, and its population peaked during the Late Preclassic era. Komchen's location near the salt-producing Caribbean coast indicates that it prospered from commerce centered on salt and other marine resources.

POLITICAL POWER IN EARLY MAYA CIVILIZATION

Archaeology testifies to the emergence of a series of state-level polities across the Maya area in the Late Preclassic period. Each polity was headed by a capital with similar architecture, artifacts, sculpture, and writing. The origins of these attributes and the beginnings of most polity capitals date to the preceding Middle Preclassic era.

Early Maya civilization was characterized by regional differences in ways political power was reinforced and proclaimed to the public. In the southern area, both the ceremonies and symbols of political power—carved stelae with portraits of rulers and historical texts with Long Count dates—were placed in public settings. The combined written and visual records carved in stone were in open plazas to impress both subjects and visitors. They proclaimed the ruler as a successful warrior, taker of captives, and descendant of royal ancestors. These were combined with the other obvious symbols of the power of the state and its ruler—monumental temples that served as backdrops for arrays of carved monuments.

Carved stelae are much more rare in the Late Preclassic lowlands. More frequently, the symbols of political and religious power were combined and presented on huge temples emblazoned with huge painted plaster masks of the Maya gods, not Maya kings. The newly discovered San Bartolo murals testify to the supernatural basis for royal power, but these decorated a secluded building interior and were probably seen by only the king and his royal court. This is consistent with the general lack of public displays of royal images in the Preclassic lowlands. Yet the San Bartolo murals verify that royal inaugurations and other rituals performed by kings were public ceremonies that were clearly an important means for advertising and reinforcing royal power.

In time, these distinctions faded. The southern custom of displaying stelae combining royal texts and images was adopted by lowland rulers, where, during Middle Maya civilization, they could be found in every polity capital. Lowland rulers continued to sponsor the building of great sacred temples, where they performed impressive rituals that ensured the blessings of the gods. But these structures never approached Preclassic temples in size, and they became backdrops for beautifully carved records of each king's achievements in both texts and visual images.

THE DECLINE OF EARLY MAYA CIVILIZATION

Early Maya civilization experienced a severe decline between 200 and 250. This setback was more widespread in the south than in the lowlands to the north. In the lowlands, some sites survived the upheavals of this period, but the most powerful Late Preclassic polity, El Mirador, declined dramatically and was abandoned. El Mirador was probably a victim of its own success, as overpopulation and overexploitation of soil, forests, and

other resources created a crisis that could be resolved only by abandonment. Other sites were also abandoned, perhaps for the same reasons. But
then, within a century or so, the lowlands recovered as less affected regions
took up the slack. Although the greatest lowland power, El Mirador, was
gone, many Preclassic polities and newly founded capitals filled the vacuum and went on to reach their peaks of size and prosperity over the following 500 years of the Classic period.

In the southern area, the changes at the close of the Preclassic period were
more profound and enduring. Every Preclassic polity declined, and many
Preclassic capitals were completely abandoned. The most profound change
is seen in the disappearance of carved stelae with hieroglyphic texts. Although sites such as Kaminaljuyu would recover and go on to further glories in later times, the use of these carved royal records was never revived
in the south.

The decline of Early Maya civilization in the south seems to have resulted from a combination of causes. Changes in Mesoamerica and in the
Maya lowlands, together with population movements in the highlands,
disrupted the old order. Kaminaljuyu appears to have been taken over by
a new Maya group from the western highlands. Old trade routes like that
along Pacific plain declined in favor of routes through the lowlands. A final
blow to the south came from a titanic eruption of the volcano Ilopango
in central El Salvador in about 400, which caused further disruptions in
agriculture, trade, and human populations. Huge amounts of volcanic ash
buried a vast portion of the southeastern Maya area, making the growing
of crops impossible. This caused population decline and migrations, as
people were forced to flee the disaster area. The Late Preclassic center of
Chalchuapa, for example, on the edge of the heaviest ash fall zone, was
almost completely abandoned for a century or more.

These events caused disruptions that radiated throughout the Maya
area like ripples on a pond. Of course, the decline in the southern polities
led to opportunities outside the affected region. For example, the fortunes
of lowland states able to take advantage of changing trade patterns were
boosted. This reinforced the expanding prosperity and power of lowland polities and allowed them to take center stage during the following Classic era.

OVERVIEW OF EARLY MAYA CIVILIZATION

The first flowering of Maya civilization took root in the Middle Preclassic
period. The southern Maya area was especially important in this era because it lay along the routes between Mexico and Central America. It was
also a prime area for agriculture, producing local food crops and export
crops such as cacao. At the same time, Maya elites founded new capitals in the tropical forests of the lowlands to the north. Trade expanded,
as well, and, from the beginning, exchange networks linked the lowlands
and highlands, adding further fuel for population growth and increases

in wealth and power throughout the Maya area. Everywhere, population growth and access to trade goods led to increasing wealth and power for the privileged segment of society, the elite class. Thereafter, Maya society would be divided between this small but powerful elite group and a far more numerous but nearly powerless nonelite.

But the Maya area is diverse in its resources and its potential for human exploitation. Areas with good soil and rainfall, locations that controlled valuable resources, and places that were believed to possess sacred powers attracted and supported more people than less-favored locations. Favored areas grew faster, leading to the growth of the first chiefdoms, and further emphasized the distinctions between elite and nonelite segments of society. The power of the chief and his elite allies relied on the nonelite, who farmed the land or extracted the resources destined for trade and who provided the elite class with tribute in labor or food. The rulers who held power in each polity provided physical and psychological security to the populace. As war leaders, they protected their subjects from their enemies. As religious leaders they were believed to hold special powers over supernatural forces and sacred ancestors.

The places where rulers and their elite allies resided became the settings for ceremonies, craft manufacturing, markets, and other activities they sponsored or controlled. Markets furnished a variety of food, goods, and services and were an outlet for the products of each household. By sponsoring markets, craftsmen, and merchants, the elite encouraged long-distance trade and gained new sources of wealth and power. Certain rare materials, such as jade, and exotic symbols were believed to possess special powers, so these were reserved for elite use, reinforcing leaders' prestige and authority. Thus, the power held by rulers and the elite class was reinforced by the economic system.

The rapid growth of major population centers, characterized by monumental temple and funerary constructions, as well as the palaces for the elite, led to competition and conflict, as each polity attempted to gain control over more land, people, and trade routes. Sometimes the advantage went to polities that controlled scarce but vital raw materials. By controlling highland products such obsidian and jade, Kaminaljuyu became the dominant early capital in the Maya highlands. Locations along major routes gave other polities control over the transport, exchange, and redistribution of products. Several lowland sites were situated to control the portages between river routes across the base of the Yucatan Peninsula. Nakbe was perhaps the first major polity to control this strategic zone in the Middle Preclassic. By the Late Preclassic, El Mirador had taken over this role. But success was not due simply to location and economic control. Social, political, and religious activities were also crucial to the development of these Preclassic polities.

The full flowering of Early Maya civilization is defined by the first Maya states that emerged in the southern area, such as El Ujuxte and

Takalik Abaj on the Pacific coastal plain and Kaminaljuyu in the highlands. Comparable developments in the lowlands included El Mirador and numerous smaller Late Preclassic states across the Peten into Belize and further north into Yucatan. These early states were marked by increases in the size of polities, greater concentrations of power in the hands of rulers, public proclamations of this power, and the use of writing to record and verify royal achievements. The rulers of each state also advertised their power and authority by warfare and ceremonial displays, including feasts, inaugurations, and rites of succession.

Early Maya civilization began a trend that would always dominate the Maya political landscape. This was the rise of one or more major polities that would seek—and often, for a time, manage—to dominate the entire stage. Kaminaljuyu was such a polity in the highlands. In the lowlands, Nakbe may have been the first to try, but it was soon succeeded by a far larger capital, El Mirador, which dominated the lowland political landscape during the second half of the era of Early Maya civilization.

Early Maya civilization ended with a decline that saw disturbances and changes in the economic and political landscape. Old polities declined or were abandoned altogether, and new polities asserted their power. There were multiple and reinforcing causes for these changes, including environmental problems, population movements, changes in trade routes, and at least one major volcanic disaster. In the lowlands, the decline of the dominant power of El Mirador, probably due to overexploitation of local resources, led to repercussions throughout the region. In the south, most Preclassic polities failed and abandoned the use of royal stelae. Ultimately, the loss of commerce in the south probably led to an increase in lowland trade, which stimulated development in some regions and decline elsewhere, ushering in the era of Middle Maya civilization.

FURTHER READING

Bove and Heller 1989; Drennen and Uribe 1987; Feinman and Marcus 1998; Garber 2004; Grove and Joyce 1999; Grube 2001; Johnson and Earle 2001; Love, Poponoe de Hatch, and Escobedo 2002; Marcus 1992b; McAnany 2004; Sabloff 1994; Saturno 2002; Schele and Freidel 1990; Sharer and Sedat 1987; Sharer and Traxler 2006; Willey 1987.

5

MIDDLE MAYA CIVILIZATION

Early Maya civilization emerged during the later portions of the Preclassic period. At the close of the Preclassic, major changes in the economic and political landscape were followed in the southern lowlands by the apex of Maya growth and prosperity. This defines Middle Maya civilization, which dates to the Classic period (ca. 250–900).

The Classic era is divided into the Early Classic (ca. 250–600), when state-level polities expanded in the southern lowlands; the Late Classic (ca. 600–800), which saw the rise of important new polities and the peaking of population and cultural development in the southern lowlands; and the Terminal Classic (ca. 800–900/1100), which witnessed the decline of the southern lowlands and the rise of new polities in the northern lowlands of Yucatan and in the highlands.

LOWLAND STATES IN THE EARLY CLASSIC (ca. 250–600)

Middle Maya civilization began with the Early Classic period, which saw the rapid rise and dominance of two major lowland states, Calakmul and Tikal. Our information about the rise to power of all the Early Classic lowland polities comes from the combination of archaeology and the reading of Maya inscriptions. The origins of many of the capitals of these kingdoms, including both Tikal and Calakmul, lie in the Late Preclassic. El Mirador probably dominated Tikal, Calakmul, and other lowland centers at this time. But, when El Mirador declined at the end of the Preclassic, the stage was set for the expansion of Classic period states and the dynasties of their kings.

Figure 5.1 Tikal, Guatemala; to the left is Temple I, the funerary shrine of Jasaw Chan K'awiil, Tikal's twenty-sixth king, and in the center is the royal palace complex where most of Tikal's rulers lived.

The inscriptions of the Classic period give us many details about dynastic rulers and their activities—but do not even mention the common people. Two great centers of Middle Maya civilization, Tikal and Copan, have the most surviving inscriptions and the most archaeological evidence, so we know far more about their history. We know far less about the history of Tikal's great rival, Calakmul, because it has far fewer surviving texts. We can reconstruct the successes and failures of these kingdoms by combining the results of archaeological and historical research. This allows us to glimpse important events and to understand how Maya kings attempted to advance the interests of their polities.

Tikal and Its Kings

Tikal is strategically located at the confluence of trade routes in the central Petén, situated on several low ridges above wetlands (*bajos*) to its east and west. Most of its largest temples date from the Late Classic period and were built as funerary shrines for some of its greatest rulers. The largest visible buildings from the Late Preclassic and Early Classic eras are in the North Acropolis (burial place of its early kings) and the Lost World Group. Monumental causeways (*sacbeob*) radiate from the Great Plaza, with its temples and stelae, to connect Tikal's major civic-ceremonial complexes.

One of these connected complexes, immediately east of the Great Plaza, once held Tikal's main market. To the south lies the Central Acropolis, containing the palaces of Tikal's kings. Beyond lie numerous building groups scattered over an occupation area covering some 60 square kilometers, mostly on higher and better-drained terrain. An unfinished system of earthworks, consisting of a shallow moat and an interior rubble wall, was built to protect the city from both the north and the south. The area within these defensible boundaries totals some 123 square kilometers. Although difficult to estimate, Tikal's population at its peak probably numbered more than 100,000 people.

Tikal's rise is marked by a historically recorded royal dynasty—beginning with a ruler recognized by his successors as a dynastic founder who began a new line of kings (Table 5.1). This founding ruler was named Yax Ehb Xook. There were earlier rulers at Tikal, but Yax Ehb Xook earned the title of dynastic founder from later rulers, perhaps because he was an outstanding war leader or the first to proclaim Tikal's political independence. He may have come from outside Tikal. His name appears in a text at Kaminaljuyu, but there is no way to know if this mention refers to the same person. Since no monuments from his reign have survived, the only records of his rule are those made by his successors. Yax Ehb Xook reigned during the Terminal Preclassic period (about 100).

Figure 5.2 Drawing of the Leiden Plaque showing an unknown Early Classic lowland ruler standing on a captive; note the human trophy head hanging from the back of the belt (320).

Table 5.1:
Kings of Tikal (Mutul Kingdom)

Yax Ehb Xook (Founder, ca. 100)

Little-known kings (second–tenth rulers, ca. 100–307)

Siyaj Chan K'awiil I (eleventh ruler, ca. 307)

K'inich Muwaan Jol I (thirteenth ruler, ?–359)

Chak Tok Ich'aak I (fourteenth ruler, 360–378)

Yax Nuun Ayiin I (fifteenth ruler, 379–411)

Siyaj Chan K'awiil II (sixteenth ruler, 411–456)

K'an Chitam (seventeenth ruler, 458–486?)

Chak Tok Ich'aak II (eighteenth ruler, ca. 488–508)

"Lady of Tikal" (ca. 511)

Kaloomte' Balam (nineteenth ruler, ca. 527–?)

"Bird Claw" (twentieth ruler?)

Wak Chan K'awiil (twenty-first ruler, 537–562)

"Animal Skull" (twenty-second ruler, ca. 562–593)

K'inich Muwaan Jol II (twenty-third or twenty-fourth ruler, ca. 593–650)

Nuun Ujol Chaak (twenty-fifth ruler, 650–ca. 679)

Jasaw Chan K'awiil I (twenty-sixth ruler, 682–ca. 734)

Yik'in Chan K'awiil (twenty-seventh ruler, 734–ca. 766)

Unidentified king (twenty-eighth ruler, ca. 766–768)

Yax Nuun Ayiin II (twenty-ninth ruler, 768–ca. 794)

Nuun Ujol K'inich (thirtieth ruler?, ca. 800)

"Dark Sun" (thirty-first ruler?, ca. 810)

"Jewel K'awiil" (thirty-second ruler?, ca. 849)

Jasaw Chan K'awiil II (thirty-third ruler?, ca. 869)

Tikal likely emerged as an independent state by this time. A later ruler (name unknown) dedicated Stela 29, which records the earliest known lowland Long Count date, 8.12.14.8.15 (292; from now on only Gregorian dates will be used—Maya calendars are explained in chapter 12). On the front of Stela 29 is the portrait of the king wearing royal regalia and holding a double-headed serpent bar, one of the most important symbols of Maya rulers. Above him is the head of an ancestor, possibly the dynastic founder. He carries a trophy head in his hand, and another is on his belt. Stela 29 also records the royal title of Tikal's kings, the emblem glyph of the Mutal kingdom. This emblem glyph endured for some 600 years as a symbol of Tikal and the power of its kings.

Another early ruler given the nickname "Moon Zero Bird" is known from an incised jade celt (small plaque) bearing his portrait and the date of his "seating" as king in 320. This celt, known as the Leiden Plaque, shows the king in royal costume and holding the double-headed serpent bar, standing over the prone figure of a captive. Although it is often assumed the king on the Leiden Plaque ruled at Tikal, the evidence for this is inconclusive.

The eleventh and thirteenth rulers of Tikal have been identified from inscriptions, but almost nothing is known about them or their reigns. There is more secure information about the fourteenth king in the dynasty of Yax Ehb Xook. His name was Chak Tok Ich'aak, and he came to power ca. 360. The lower portion of one of his monuments, Stela 39, was discovered in one of the oldest parts of Tikal. Stela 39 records ceremonies held in the year 376, marking the end of the seventeenth k'atun (a cycle of about 20 years) in the Maya calendar. It shows Chak Tok Ich'aak standing over a bound captive, while holding a sacrificial ax decorated with jaguar markings. His royal palace has been identified from a pottery vessel excavated under its west staircase. The text on this vessel says it was used in the dedication rituals for the *k'uh nah* (sacred house) of Chak Tok Ich'aak.

By this time, other lowland polities were also expanding and dedicating monuments with portraits of their rulers. The site of Uaxactun, only a day's walk north of Tikal, commemorated its early political history with a series of six monuments between 328 and 416. Several capitals east of Tikal, including Naranjo and Yaxha, developed into local powers, as did El Peru-Waka to the west. To the southeast, protected by the Maya Mountains of Belize, the city of Caracol began its rise. To the southwest, Piedras Negras and Yaxchilan, on the Usumacinta River, began to compete for dominance over their region. And, furthest to the southeast, Copan developed into the major power on the Central American frontier.

These and most other Early Classic lowland cities were spread across the southern lowlands, each the capital of an independent kingdom. Yet, some cities began to expand at the expense of their neighbors. In Tikal's case, one by one its neighbors stopped dedicating monuments, indicating that they had been taken over. Conquered rulers were either turned into a subordinate of the victorious king or sacrificed and replaced. Tikal's power and prosperity were also increased by its trade links. By about 300, it had established commercial and diplomatic connections with the powerful city of Teotihuacan, in Central Mexico.

These connections culminated in a regime change at Tikal in 378, probably orchestrated by Teotihuacan. Tikal's texts record that Chak Tok Ich'aak died on the same day in 378 that a man named Siyaj K'ak' ("Born of Fire") arrived in Tikal. This suggests that one event caused the other—that a regime takeover resulted in the death of Tikal's king. That a violent takeover occurred is also suggested by the fact that most of Tikal's stelae dating before 378 were found broken and mutilated. The texts do not say where Siyaj K'ak' came from, but, given Tikal's already established ties with Kaminaljuyu or Teotihuacan, either city is a likely candidate.

More than a year later, a new king, Yax Nuun Ayiin (379–411) became the fifteenth ruler in Tikal's dynastic succession. The delay could reflect the time needed for Siyaj K'ak' to consolidate his control, including the incorporation of Uaxactun into the Tikal kingdom. The texts state that Yax Nuun Ayiin was installed as king by Siyaj K'ak'. The texts do not say where Yax Nuun Ayiin came from but do record that he was the son of "Spearthrower Owl," ruler of an unidentified kingdom, possibly Teotihuacan. In sum, the historical record suggests that Siyaj K'ak' commanded a force sent by a king named Spearthrower Owl to take over Tikal and to install this foreign ruler's son, Yax Nuun Ayiin, as Tikal's new king.

After these events, Tikal expanded its power further until it dominated the southern lowlands. Tikal was clearly more fully integrated into the dominant Early Classic economic and political network that included both Teotihuacan and Kaminaljuyu. The resulting increase in resources at its disposal allowed Tikal to set about to directly or indirectly impose its authority over other lowland polities. Evidence from monuments at the site of Rio Azul, located in the northeast corner of Guatemala, suggests that Tikal consolidated its power over this center during the reign of Yax Nuun Ayiin. Painted texts from the walls of several tombs at Rio Azul mention two Tikal kings, Yax Nuun Ayiin and his son and successor, Siyaj Chan K'awiil, along with a local lord nicknamed Six Sky.

Yax Nuun Ayiin died about 425 after being in power for some 47 years. Excavations at Tikal uncovered his tomb (identified from a small carved jade head forming Yax Nuun Ayiin's name glyph). Inside were the skeletal remains of the king and offerings showing close connections between the king and the Early Classic rulers of Kaminaljuyu in the highlands to the south and even beyond to the central Mexican city of Teotihuacan.

These ties indicate crucial trade and military alliances between Tikal and these other important cities. These alliances continued during the reign of Tikal's sixteenth ruler, Siyaj Chan K'awiil, the son of Yax Nuun Ayiin. Siyaj Chan K'awiil was one of Tikal's greatest kings, successful in warfare and at expanding Tikal's power. He is portrayed on Stela 31, a beautifully carved monument, discovered enshrined and buried in the temple built over Siyaj Chan K'awiil's tomb. Dedicated in 435, Stela 31 shows Siyaj Chan K'awiil in traditional Maya regalia, complete with his name glyph on a headdress held above his head. Above this is the figure of his father and celestial protector, Yax Nuun Ayiin. The text on the back records much of Tikal's Early Classic dynastic history, naming the founder, Yax Ehb Xook, as well as Chak Tok Ich'aak, Yax Nuun Ayiin, and Siyaj K'ak'.

Siyaj Chan K'awiil's tomb was excavated deep beneath the temple containing Stela 31. The tomb held offerings linked to both Teotihuacan and Kaminaljuyu. The tomb's plastered walls were painted with sacred symbols and a Long Count date equivalent to 456, marking Siyaj Chan K'awiil's death or burial.

Tikal's Early Classic history continues with Siyaj Chan K'awiil's son, the seventeenth king, known as Kan Chitam. His portrait on Stela 40 is modeled after his father's portrayal on Stela 31. During Kan Chitam's reign Tikal's power and influence continued to expand. However, we know little about Kan Chitam's successors (Rulers 18–20), except that during their reigns Tikal's fortunes began to decline.

One of the few monuments that have survived from this time is Stela 23, which commemorates the first woman known to Maya history. Her palace has been identified on the southeast edge of the city, but her name is unknown, so she is referred to as Lady of Tikal. Her badly damaged portrait is on Stela 23, and she may have reigned for a time beginning in 511. Nonetheless, she was not counted in the sequence of rulers recorded by later kings. If she ever ruled alone, her reign probably ended with her marriage to a male successor, most likely the nineteenth ruler, Kaloomte Balam.

The name of the twentieth ruler remains unknown. Stela 17 is the only surviving monument of the twenty-first ruler, Wak Chan K'awiil, whose reign marks the end of the Early Classic period at Tikal. For the next century and a half, Tikal suffered a severe decline in the wake of the triumph of Calakmul, its greatest rival. During this time, Calakmul had built an alliance with a number of lowland polities, even displacing former Tikal allies such as Naranjo and Caracol. As a result, Calakmul succeeded in nearly surrounding Tikal with allied cities. Evidence of destruction and abandonment for some 70 years (ca. 530–600) at Rio Azul indicates that this ally of Tikal was conquered by Calakmul before the major confrontation between these two Maya superpowers.

Confrontation and Defeat by Calakmul

Calakmul is one of the largest and most important of all lowland Maya cities. Like Tikal, it is located to control overland routes through the lowlands. The ruins of the city are situated on high ground above the eastern edge of a large reservoir. Calakmul's civic-ceremonial core covers about 2 square kilometers. Beyond the area of smaller residential remains covers more than 20 square kilometers. A network of canals and reservoirs surrounds much of the site and probably provided protection from attack. Its overall extent and estimated population size (ca. 50,000–100,000) are about the same as those of Tikal. Calakmul has the largest number of stelae (117) of any Maya site. Unfortunately, most are too eroded to read because of the softness of the local limestone used at Calakmul.

The origins and early history of Calakmul is not clear. In the Late Classic, it was ruled by a dynasty that used the Kan or snakehead glyph as its emblem (Table 5.2). There is evidence to suggest that the Kan dynasty

Table 5.2:
Kings of Calakmul (Kan Kingdom)

"Skyraiser" (Founder)

Yuknoom Ch'een I (?)

K'altuun Hix (ca. 520–546)

"Sky Witness" (ca. 561–572)

Yax Yopaat (572–579)

"Scroll Serpent" (579–ca. 611)

Yuknoom Ti' Chan (ca. 619)

Tajoom Uk'ab' K'ak' (622–630)

Yuknoom Head (630–636)

Yuknoom Ch'een II ("Yuknoom the Great," 636–686)

Yuknoom Yich'aak K'ak' (686–695?)

"Split Earth" (ca. 695)

Yuknoom Took' K'awiil (ca. 702–731)

Wamaw K'awiil (ca. 736)

"Ruler Y" (ca. 741)

"Great Serpent" (ca. 751)

Bolon K'awiil (ca. 771–789?)

Chan Pet (ca. 849)

Aj Took (ca. 909?)

originated in the Late Preclassic at El Mirador, after which it continued its rule at the site of Dzibanche (northeast of Calakmul), before taking over Calakmul.

Calakmul's West Group probably served as a royal palace, and the smaller East Group perhaps was used for members of the royal court and visiting dignitaries. In between is a complex that likely served as the principal market, to judge from the excavated remains of murals depicting the sellers of various products. Of the three largest temple complexes (Structures I–III), Structure II is the largest and covers an entire Late Preclassic quadrangle, including a structure with an elaborate and essentially intact stucco-decorated façade.

It was Calakmul under its king known as Sky Witness that orchestrated the stunning defeat that ended Tikal's Early Classic expansion. Archaeologists at the site of Caracol discovered the evidence that Caracol, originally an ally of Tikal, became one of Calakmul's key supporters. The text of a Caracol monument records the crucial events in a confrontation between Tikal and Caracol, after it switched its alliance to Calakmul. In 553, a new ruler named "Lord Water" came to the throne of Caracol,

Figure 5.3 Caracol, Belize: The Caana royal palace and temple complex once occupied by the kings who, as allies of Calakmul, defeated Tikal. Courtesy of Arlen and Diane Chase, Caracol Archaeological Project.

under the authority of Tikal's ruler, Wak Chan K'awiil. Three years later, Caracol switched sides, and Wak Chan K'awiil attacked Caracol to defeat the alliance of its enemies. Tikal won this first round, for the Caracol monument records the capture and sacrifice of a Caracol noble by the Tikal king in 556. But the conflict continued between Tikal and the Calakmul alliance, led by Sky Witness, and in 562 Tikal was defeated and Wak Chan K'awiil was apparently captured and sacrificed.

After this, Calakmul and its victorious allies were able to overwhelm Tikal and destroy many of the monuments of its rulers. The successors of Wak Chan K'awiil, the twenty-second through the twenty-fifth rulers of Tikal, were subordinate to Calakmul. They were probably prohibited from displaying monuments, and it is likely that the wealth once controlled by Tikal was siphoned off as tribute to the victors. Suppression of Tikal's power and fortunes continued for more than a century. Population growth at Tikal stopped, and many people in outlying areas resettled closer to the center of the city for greater security.

At the same time, the defeat of Tikal boosted the wealth and power of Calakmul and its allies. For example, Caracol experienced dramatic increases in size and prosperity. But, over the next century, Calakmul and its allies were embroiled in a series of wars that involved most of the southern Maya lowlands. Calakmul was able to exploit its newly won power, but its rulers were unable to convert their military alliance into permanent political domination of the southern lowlands. Indeed, the allied cities resisted domination and were able to maintain their independence. In addition, Tikal's defeat had created a power vacuum that was filled by the rapid expansion of other Maya cities.

LOWLAND STATES IN THE LATE CLASSIC (ca. 600–800)

Despite the rise of warfare, the Late Classic period (ca. 600–800) was a time of unprecedented expansion that saw the peak of Middle Maya civilization. We trace this period by discussing the development of several better-known Maya states in the southern lowlands, beginning with several areas that expanded in the wake of Tikal's defeat. Then we return to Tikal in the Late Classic before looking at two more distant lowland polities, Palenque and Copan.

The Petexbatun Kingdom

To the south of Tikal is a region of rivers and lakes known as the Petexbatun. A branch of the royal lineage of Tikal, escaping the defeat by Calakmul and probably seeking new access to trade routes to the south, established a new capital in the Petexbatun region at the beginning of the Late Classic period. To do so, they had to subdue a local royal family that ruled from its capital of Tamarindito. But, once in control, and drawing on their connections with the prestige of Tikal, the new Petexbatun rulers embarked on an independent and aggressive course to expand their realm, even becoming allied with Calakmul to do so.

The new Petexbatun capital was at Dos Pilas, where the founder of the new kingdom, Balaj Chan K'awiil, was inaugurated in about 648. Tikal's ploy seemed to succeed, for Calakmul was probably concerned with events elsewhere. But, some 11 years after its founding, texts at Dos Pilas record an attack and defeat by Calakmul and B'alaj Chan K'awiil's acknowledgment that he was now a vassal of the Calakmul king, Yuknoom the Great (659). In other words, after defeating Tikal's new colony, Calakmul accomplished more than a victory over Dos Pilas, for Balaj Chan K'awiil was forced to switch sides and join the Calakmul alliance. In so doing, Yuknoom the Great turned the two branches of Tikal's royal house into enemies.

Tikal avenged this setback in 672 by attacking Dos Pilas and sending Balaj Chan K'awiil into exile, regaining its control over its former vassal state for five years. But, in 677, Calakmul struck back, drove Tikal's forces from Dos Pilas, and returned B'alaj Chan K'awiil to his throne. Two years later (679), Balaj Chan K'awiil led Dos Pilas to a decisive victory over Tikal, likely with Calakmul's aid. The Dos Pilas texts vividly describe the "pools of blood" and "piles of heads" in the aftermath of Tikal's defeat.

After these victories over Tikal, Balaj Chan K'awiil and his kingdom were secure under Yuknoom the Great's protection. Although he owed his power to Calakmul's military might, like many Maya kings Balaj Chan K'awiil used marriage alliances to reinforce his position as ruler of the

Petexbatun kingdom. His principal wife was from a noble family of one of his subordinate cities. A son from this marriage, Itzamnaaj Balam, became his royal heir. A second marriage produced a daughter, Lady Six Sky, destined to cement an alliance with the Naranjo kingdom by restoring its royal dynasty.

Calakmul's command over the southern lowlands was threatened when two of its allies went to war. An old dispute was rekindled in 680 when Naranjo attacked Caracol and forced its king to flee his city. But the evidence suggests that, after its decisive victory, Calakmul retaliated, crushed Naranjo, and wiped out its royal family. Yet, instead of absorbing the Naranjo polity into its realm, Calakmul apparently ordered Lady Six Sky, the daughter of Balaj Chan K'awiil, to Naranjo to restore its dynasty. Her arrival in 682 was recorded in Naranjo's later texts, and Lady Six Sky ruled her new kingdom for the next decade. Carved stelae recorded her achievements, including crushing her war captives beneath her feet. She married an unnamed Naranjo noble, and her son, born in 688, ascended to the throne at the age of five years in 693. Lady Six Sky acted as regent until her son could rule on his own.

Meanwhile, Yuknoom the Great died after a long and successful reign. Balaj Chan K'awiil went to Calakmul in 686 to witness the inauguration of his 36-year-old successor, Yuknoom Yich'aak K'ak'. Soon afterward, Balaj

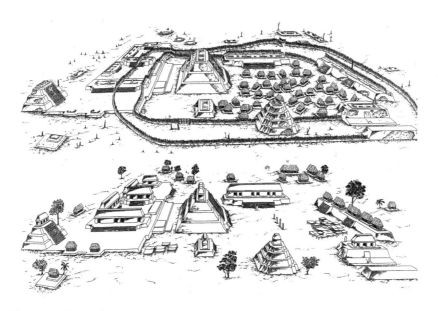

Figure 5.4 Dos Pilas, Guatemala, first capital of the Petexbatun kingdom: (below) reconstructed view from the northeast; (above) under siege with defensive walls built to defend the city, conquered ca. 760. Courtesy of Arthur Demarest, Petexbatun Archaeological Project.

Chan K'awiil died and was succeeded by his eldest son, Itzamnaaj Balam, and then by a second son, Itzamnaaj K'awiil (both half-brothers of Lady Six Sky), who continued to use warfare and marriage alliances to secure the independence of the Petexbatun kingdom.

In 735, the largest city of the region, Seibal, was defeated and its king made captive. At its height, this powerful and expansionistic state was suddenly defeated. Dos Pilas was attacked and besieged by its old enemies, the descendants of the deposed Tamarindito royal family. The capital was defended by hastily erected walls that were built over the very symbols of its kings, including a hieroglyphic staircase recording the history and conquests of the Petexbatun dynasty. Stones were ripped from its buildings, including the royal palace, to support the palisades that protected the center of the city. But revenge motivated the attackers, and in 761 Dos Pilas was overwhelmed. The victorious Tamarindito ruler could then record on his monuments how he had demolished the royal palace and the throne of the Petexbatun kings.

The survivors of the Petexbatun royal family continued to rule from a new fortified capital at Aguateca. It is not known how long the last rulers were able to hold out behind their defenses, but ultimately warfare doomed the Petexbatun kingdom. Archaeological excavations reveal that Aguateca was overwhelmed by a sudden attack around 800, after which it was burned and abandoned. Another center was located on a narrow peninsula in Lake Petexbatun, converted into an island fortress by cutting a massive moat across its base. It too was attached and abandoned. The level of violence became so high that not only were walls built to protect cities, but small settlements and agricultural fields had to be fortified, as well. In the end, warfare and the breakdown of authority led to the destruction of the Petexbatun kingdom. Much of its population fled the violence to settle in more secure and stable areas, and the region was nearly abandoned.

Yaxchilan and the Usumacinta Cities

In addition to the birth of new polities, the Late Classic saw the expansion of older powers. For example, to the west of the Petexbatun region, a string of important capitals along the great Río Usumacinta reached their apex during the Late Classic. Two of these, Piedras Negras and Yaxchilan, competed for control over the region. Yaxchilan occupied a well-defended position within a nearly closed loop of the river. From this secure base, the Yaxchilan kings ruled an independent state that controlled an important portion of the Usumacinta trade route. Its inscriptions tell of a dynastic founding in 320, and its many carved monuments and temple lintels document the conquests and deeds of a line of Classic period kings.

During the Early Classic, Yaxchilan was often overshadowed by its neighbor, Piedras Negras. But, in the Late Classic, it succeeded in challenging Piedras Negras for dominance over the Usumacinta region. Yaxchilan reached its peak of power under the aggressive leadership of a long-lived warrior king, Itzamnaaj Balam (681–742), and his successors. Itzamnaaj Balam reigned for some 61 years, during which warfare, marriage alliances, and longevity secured resources and prestige for his kingdom. He also refashioned his capital by commissioning monuments and buildings embellished with carved lintels that record a long list of captives taken in battle.

A 10-year hiatus (742–752) followed Itzamnaaj Balam's death in 742, before a new king, Bird Jaguar, took the throne. Bird Jaguar was not the designated heir, for his mother is not mentioned in Itzamnaaj Balam's texts. In fact, the designated heir apparently did not survive the 742–752 interregnum. A Piedras Negras text records that a Yaxchilan king, Yopaat Balam, visited Piedras Negras in 749. This suggests that Yopaat Balam was the legitimate successor of Itzamnaaj Balam.

But no record of Yopaat Balam survives at Yaxchilan. In fact, any mention of Yopaat Balam's reign appears to have systematically erased by Bird Jaguar. After the 10-year silence of the interregnum, the official history continues by advancing Bird Jaguar as king. Bird Jaguar's texts rewrote history to proclaim and reinforce his royal legitimacy. He did this through marriage alliances and warfare. He married an important local elite woman and three noble women from allied cities. Bird Jaguar's accounts say he spent the decade after his father's death leading raids and taking captives. Military success not only reinforced Bird Jaguar's authority but also promoted the careers of his loyal subordinate lords.

Bird Jaguar ensured the succession of his son by securing the loyalty of nobles who administered the kingdom's secondary centers. Carved lintels depict Bird Jaguar with his royal heir, Chel Te' Chan K'inich, accompanied by subordinate lords. These records were obviously intended to flatter his nobles and to solidify their allegiance to Bird Jaguar and his son. These efforts were successful, for, after Bird Jaguar's death, in 768, his son was renamed for his grandfather, Itzamnaaj Balam, and took the throne. His 30-year reign was marked by a continuing use of warfare to secure the boundaries and dependencies of the Yaxchilan kingdom. Itzamnaaj Balam's son is the last known ruler of Yaxchilan. In 808, he led a successful attack on Piedras Negras, captured its king, and ended the royal house of its oldest foe. The victory was short-lived, however, for the downfall of the Yaxchilan dynasty followed soon thereafter.

Two other Usumacinta cities, Bonampak and Piedras Negras, are also important to our understanding of Maya civilization. The smaller site of Bonampak is located about 30 kilometers south of Yaxchilan. Bonampak is famous for its beautiful murals, which are masterpieces of Classic Maya art. They cover the walls of three rooms in a small palace and record the naming of the royal heir, one of the most important rituals of Maya kings. The heir designate in this case was the young son of the Bonampak ruler,

Chan Muwaan, and the rituals took place over a two-year period (790–792), during which the king of Yaxchilan and Chan Muwaan's overlord visited Bonampak to participate in these events. There are scenes recording the presentation of the royal heir, a violent battle to gain captives for sacrifice, the display of the captives, a great procession of dancers and musicians, and the bloodletting ritual by the royal family that sealed the heir designation ceremony.

Piedras Negras is a larger city located some 40 kilometers downriver from Yaxchilan. For much of the Classic period, Piedras Negras dominated its portion of the Usumacinta region, before being conquered by Yaxchilan at the end of the Classic period. Research at Piedras Negras has yielded a number of important insights into the history and operation of Maya states. Recent investigations in the area between Piedras Negras and Yaxchilan have defined the boundary between these two kingdoms. Texts at Piedras Negras and several of its subordinate centers tell us about the operation of the kingdom's administrative hierarchy. These reveal examples where a Piedras Negras king presided over the installation of a *sajal* (subordinate lord) in charge of a secondary center. In other cases, a high-ranking *ajaw* (noble or lord) had the authority to install a *sajal*. This shows that an organizational hierarchy of *ajawab* and *sajalob* administered subdivisions of the Piedras Negras kingdom under the ultimate authority of the king.

Figure 5.5 Stela 14 from Piedras Negras, Guatemala, showing a young, newly inaugurated ruler seated in a niche, accompanied (lower left) by his mother (758).

In the mid-twentieth century, the beautifully sculptured monuments of Piedras Negras provided the first evidence that Maya texts dealt with political history. By studying an unbroken series of monuments spanning more than 200 years (608–810), the Russian-American scholar Tatiana Proskouriakoff was able to define a pattern that began with the portrait of a seated male figure associated with a date and a "seating" glyph read as "accession to power." Each of these examples was followed by monuments at five-*tun* (five-year) intervals until a new "seating" glyph appeared. The span of time between such seating motifs did not exceed a normal human lifetime, and Proskouriakoff realized that each series of monuments, together with glyphs referring to birth and death, defined the life and reign of a king. This allowed her to work out a sequence of six Piedras Negras rulers who were in power for most of the Late Classic era.

The Revitalization of Tikal

In 682, a new king became Tikal's twenty-sixth ruler (Table 5.1). The son of the twenty-fifth ruler, Jasaw Chan K'awiil had witnessed his father's victory over Dos Pilas in 672, followed by two disastrous defeats at the hands of Calakmul and Dos Pilas, in 677 and 679, respectively. The latter loss may have resulted in his father's death. In any case, once Jasaw Chan K'awiil became king, he set out to defeat Tikal's nemesis and to revive its prestige and power by both warfare and the restoration of its past glories.

Jasaw Chan K'awiil paid homage to the past by constructing a new temple that sealed the funerary shrine of his illustrious predecessor, Siyaj Chan K'awiil. Stela 31, Siyaj Chan K'awiil's great monument, was carefully placed inside the rear room of the old shrine before it was buried beneath the new temple. Jasaw Chan K'awiil also directed the reburial of the shattered remains of Stela 26, dedicated by another of his ancestors, within a new bench built inside the old funerary temple built over the tomb of Yax Nuun Ayiin.

By sanctifying these relics of Tikal's past glories, Jasaw Chan K'awiil restored the prestige of his royal dynasty. His next step was to strike back at Tikal's old enemies to reestablish Tikal's power and position within the Maya world. In 695, Jasaw Chan K'awiil attacked Naranjo. Then, later that same year, he defeated the powerful state of Calakmul and "brought down the flint and shield of Yuknoom Yich'aak K'ak," its young ruler. Some 40 days after the battle, Jasaw Chan K'awiil recorded his victory celebration at Tikal, which included the sacrifice of prisoners taken from the defeated enemy.

Jasaw Chan K'awiil died after a most successful reign of about 50 years. Never again would Calakmul, or any other kingdom, threaten Tikal's power or independence. The king was buried in a sumptuous tomb along with a wealth of offerings of jade, shell, and pottery, including an exquisite jade mosaic vase and a set of beautifully carved bones that recorded

Figure 5.6 Two jade mosaic vessels from Tikal, Guatemala; (left) from the tomb of the twenty-sixth king, Jasaw Chan K'awiil, whose portrait head decorates its lid; (right) from an unidentified tomb, either of the twenty-seventh king Yik'in Chan K'awiil, or the short-lived twenty-eighth king (Late Classic). Photograph by William Coe; Tikal Project, University of Pennsylvania Museum.

Tikal's renewed prosperity and power. Above his tomb, his son and successor, Yik'in Chan K'awiil, directed the construction of the most famous of all Tikal's buildings, now known as Temple I, as his funerary shrine.

Yik'in Chan K'awiil, the twenty-seventh Tikal ruler, was inaugurated in 734. He capped his father's success at restoring Tikal as the most powerful capital in the Maya world with triumphs over Calakmul's major allies, El Perú-Waka (743) and Naranjo (744). These victories restored Tikal's control over the east-west trade routes across the lowlands and opened a period of renewed expansion and prosperity. Yik'in Chan K'awiil ordered the construction of Tikal's largest temple, Temple IV, marking the western boundary of Tikal's civic and ceremonial center. Yik'in Chan K'awiil died about 766, although his tomb has yet to be located; it is probably beneath Temple IV. The little-known twenty-eighth ruler (766–768) has been identified with a sumptuously furnished tomb found beneath a small shrine near Temple I. The next king, named after his famous ancestor Yax Nuun Ayiin, was the twenty-ninth member of Tikal's long and illustrious dynasty. Yax Nuun Ayiin II carried on his forefathers' efforts but recorded building programs rather than wars. However, by the end of his reign (768–ca. 794), Tikal's prosperity and power were in decline. We know very little about the kings that followed. By the time of Tikal's latest known monument (869), the ancient kingdom had broken up into smaller polities, and the last members of Tikal's dynasty had disappeared from history.

Palenque and Tonina

The western Maya lowlands were a frontier region bordering non-Maya groups living on the Gulf coast and beyond. Research has been done at several of the Classic Maya cities in this region (Palenque, Tonina, and Comalcalco). Palenque's history is the best known since its texts have been studied for many years. The Palenque inscriptions deal with mythology and dynastic succession in more detail than those at any other Maya site. Thus, Palenque provides the best example of how Maya rulers used religion, myth, and history for political purposes.

Palenque was a relatively small but compact city located in the southwestern lowlands, situated against the foothills of the Chiapas highlands and overlooking the vast Gulf Coast plain. Palenque's texts tell us of a long sequence of rulers (Table 5.3). Like other Maya rulers, the Palenque kings arrayed themselves in the trappings of power, performed rituals to ensure the continuance of the world order, led raids against their neighbors, sacrificed captives, and accumulated the prestige and wealth that set them apart from the rest of society. The later rulers of Palenque also credited a founding king but did not count themselves in a numbered sequence from this ruler.

The record of Palenque's rulers begins with the inauguration, in 431, of a king named K'uk' Balam ("Quetzal Jaguar"), later to be called a founder. The next six Palenque rulers were descended from K'uk' Balam. When the last male ruler in this line died in 583 without fathering a son, the throne passed to his daughter, Lady Yohl Ik'nal. She was the last of the original royal lineage and the first woman ruler of Palenque, reigning for 20 years until her death in 604. Lady Yohl Ik'nal's son, the royal heir, was a member of his father's lineage. So, in 605, with the accession of her son, Ajen Yohl Mat, a new lineage held the throne.

A few years later, Palenque suffered a major disaster, for Calakmul sacked the city in 611. Ajen Yohl Mat survived but died about a year later. His successor was Muwaan Mat, named for the mythical progenitor of the Palenque's patron gods. With this supernatural association, the new king probably symbolized a rebirth of Palenque's ruling house for later rulers looking back at their ancestors. Three years after the accession of Muwaan

Table 5.3:
Kings of Palenque

K'uk' B'alam (Founder, 431–435)

"Casper" (435–487)

B'utz'aj Sak Chiik (487–501)

Ahkal Mo' Nahb I (501–524)

K'an Joy Chitam (529–565)

Ahkal Mo' Nahb II (565–570)

Kan Balam (572–583)

Lady Yohl Ik'nal (583–604)

Ajen Yohl Mat (605–612)

Muwaan Mat (612–615)

K'inich Janaab Pakal I (615–683)

K'inich Kan Balam I (684–702)

K'inich K'an Joy Chitam (702–ca. 720)

Ahkal Mo' Nahb III (721–ca. 736)

K'inich Janaab Pakal II (ca. 742)

K'inich Kan Balam II (ca. 751)

K'inich K'uk' Balam (764–ca. 783)

Janaab Pakal (ca. 799)

Mat, a 12-year-old boy, K'inich Janaab' Pakal, assumed the throne, in 615. His relationship with Muwaan Mat is unclear, but it appears that there had been another shift in the royal line. K'inich Janaab' Pakal and his successors went to great lengths to link their lives and reigns to parallel events in the mythical past, claiming to represent a living replication of the mythological events surrounding the creation of the world.

The Palenque texts say K'inich Janaab Pakal reigned 67 years, until his death in 683. Early in his reign, Palenque was again sacked by Calakmul. K'inich Janaab Pakal oversaw the recovery of his kingdom, and the archaeological and historical evidence indicates that under his rule Palenque became a major player in the southwestern Maya area. Its power and prestige were boosted by the political stability resulting from K'inich Janaab Pakal's long reign. (Prosperity was linked to the longevity of rulers in a number of other cases, as at Tikal under Jasaw Chan K'awiil, and Yaxchilan under Itzamnaaj Balam.)

The records left by K'inich Janaab Pakal and his successors allow us to reconstruct the dynastic sequence but also give us unique information about the supernatural world and how religious beliefs were used to support the status and power of Maya kings. The Palenque texts contain far more details about Maya creation myths than texts found at other Maya sites. These accounts gave K'inich Janaab' Pakal supernatural justification for his right to rule. His son and successor, K'inich Kan Balam, inherited the same problem of political legitimacy and further elaborated his father's claims of a supernatural basis for his reign.

According to the creation myth, three gods inherited their power from their mother, Muwaan Mat, the mother of all creation. The birth of the sons of the First Mother created a new order, the present world, and these three gods became the special patrons of Palenque's kings. K'inich Janaab Pakal's texts associate his mother, Lady Sak K'uk', with the First Mother. K'inich Janaab Pakal himself was identified with the three patron gods who inherited the right to rule over the present world from their mother. Through this religious justification, K'inich Janaab Pakal claimed a divine right to rule and his role as living replication of the creation of the present world.

Figure 5.7 Temple of the Sun, at Palenque, Mexico, part of a royal ritual complex dedicated by K'inich Kan Balam, son and successor of K'inich Janaab Pakal in 690. After Maudslay 1889–1902.

Because his father lived a long life, K'inich Kan Balam was middle-aged when he took the throne, and he reigned just over 18 years. K'inich Kan Balam's texts continued the supernatural connection made by K'inich Janaab Pakal and justified his right to rule from his divine father. His texts record a series of ceremonies performed by K'inich Kan Balam that were reenactments of the creation of the present world by the gods, his ancestors. In 687, he defeated Palenque's greatest rival, Tonina. In 690, K'inich Kan Balam installed Muwaan Jol as ruler of Moral Reforma, a former dependency of Calakmul. This expanded Palenque's power and influence northward into the rich Tabasco plain at the expense of Calakmul, the former overlords of this region.

K'inich Kan Balam died in 702. His younger brother, K'an Joy Chitam, then 57 years old, became the new ruler 53 days later. During his reign Palenque suffered its greatest setback, soon after K'an Joy Chitam had begun the construction of an addition to the splendid royal residence, the Great Palace. To secure the necessary captive sacrifices to dedicate his new palace, K'an Joy Chitam led a raid on the neighboring city of Tonina. But fate dictated otherwise, for at Tonina there is a record of K'an Joy Chitam's capture by the Tonina king. K'an Joy Chitam was held captive for a long period before eventually being repatriated, keeping Palenque in a leaderless limbo for a time.

Tonina is about 50 kilometers south of Palenque, in a transitional lowland-highland setting. Its monuments span most of the Classic period and record the history of a powerful Late Classic state. Tonina's rulers often depicted their captured enemies on their monuments, including a rare portrait of a woman captive. One of its most successful rulers, K'inich Baaknal Chaak, came to power in 688 and dedicated Tonina's Sunken Ball Court to commemorate three victories over Palenque. The ball court markers are carved torsos of six captured vassals of the Palenque ruler K'inich Kan Balam. K'inich Baaknal Chaak's successor was still a child in 711 when Tonina defeated Palenque and captured its king, K'an Joy Chitam. He is depicted on Tonina Monument 122 as a reclining figure, identified by glyphs incised on his right thigh that read "K'an Chitam Ajaw of Palenque." Monument 122 is carved in the style of Palenque rather than Tonina. In fact, it is probably the work of a master stone sculptor from Palenque sent as tribute to Tonina to carve the monument commemorating the defeat and capture of his king. With the tribute and expanded territory from this victory, Tonina replaced Palenque as the dominant power in the lower Usumacinta region.

Palenque inaugurated a new king, K'inich Ahkal Mo' Nahb, in 721. He came to the throne at age 43 and ruled for only a short time. During his reign, a military commander rose to a powerful position within the Palenque political hierarchy. This reflects the weakening of centralized royal authority, a trend seen in other Maya kingdoms toward the end of the Late Classic era. The names of three rulers after K'inich Ahkal Mo'

Nahb are recorded, but little is known of their reigns. Around 750, an elite woman from Palenque, Lady Chak Nik Ye' Xook, married a Copan lord and later became the mother of the sixteenth Copan ruler, Yax Pasaj. Tonina defeated Palenque again in about 764. Its last ruler is recorded in 799, but the fate of Palenque's dynasty after this date is unknown.

Copan and Quirigua

During the Classic period, Copan was a powerful capital that dominated the southeastern Maya region. The Copan state, together with its subordinate center at nearby Quirigua, controlled the critical Motagua River trade route and the frontier with Central America. Famous for its elaborate sculpture, Copan contained buildings and monuments that proclaimed Maya traditions in a city nearly surrounded by non-Maya people. Although it was far from the rivalries of the southern lowlands, Copan eventually appears to have been drawn into the wars between Tikal and Calakmul.

The Copan valley had been occupied since early in the Preclassic era. Later texts recall events as early as 159, so it is likely that Maya lords held sway over the valley by the end of the Late Preclassic. But all the known Copan rulers counted their succession from a king named K'inich Yax K'uk' Mo' ("Radiant Sun, First Quetzal Macaw"), given the title of founder. Archaeological evidence indicates that K'inich Yax K'uk' Mo' established centralized rule at Copan and thereby founded the Copan state.

The ruins of the capital consist of a large royal Acropolis on the south and a series of connecting plazas and structures to the north. The northern portion includes the Hieroglyphic Stairway, recording Copan's history in the longest known Maya text. It is flanked by a ball court and beyond by the Monument Plaza, the setting for the greatest grouping of Copan's stelae and altars. The Acropolis was the heart of the kingdom, holding the palaces, temples, and tombs of Copan's 16 known rulers (Table 5.4).

The Copan dynasty is summarized on an extraordinary monument set in the West Court of the Acropolis, known as Altar Q, dedicated by the sixteenth ruler, Yax Pasaj ("First Rising Sun"). The four sides of this carved stone display the portraits of 16 Copan rulers seated on thrones formed by their name glyphs. The sequence begins with K'inich Yax K'uk' Mo', whose name is in his headdress and who sits on an *ajaw* ("ruler") glyph as he hands the royal scepter to Yax Pasaj. Behind K'inich Yax K'uk' Mo' sits his son, the second ruler of Copan, followed by the rest of the successors, four to a side. The text on the upper surface of Altar Q records the inauguration of K'inich Yax K'uk' Mo' in 426 and his arrival to take the throne of Copan five months later.

No monument dedicated by a dynastic founder has survived, either at Copan or elsewhere. But tunnel excavations beneath the Acropolis have discovered the palaces and temples constructed and used at the time of

Table 5.4:
Kings of Copan

K'inich Yax K'uk' Mo' (Founder, 426–437)

K'inich Popol Hol (2nd ruler, ca. 437–?)

Ruler 3 (?)

K'altuun Hix (ca. 480)

Ruler 5 (?)

Ruler 6 (?)

Balam Nehn (7th ruler, 524–532)

Wil Yohl K'inich (8th ruler, 532–551)

Ruler 9 (551–553)

"Moon Jaguar" (10th ruler, 553–578)

K'ak' Chan Yopaat (11th ruler, 578–628)

"Smoke Imix" (12th ruler, 628–695)

Waxaklajuun Ub'aah K'awiil (13th ruler, 695–738)

K'ak' Joplaj Chan K'awiil (14th ruler, 738–749)

K'ak' Yipyaj Chan K'awiil (15th ruler, 749–ca. 761)

Yax Pasaj Chan Yopaat (16th ruler, 763-ca. 810)

Ukit Took' (ca. 822)

Figure 5.8 The two central figures on Copan Altar Q show K'inich Yax K'uk' Mo' (left), the dynastic founder inaugurated in 426, giving a royal scepter to the sixteenth king, Yax Pasaj Chan Yopaat (right), who dedicated this "throne stone" three and a half centuries later (in 776).

the dynastic founding and three hieroglyphic inscriptions dedicated by K'inich Yax K'uk' Mo's son, the second ruler. All three refer to father and son and to events of their reigns. A later text records the dedication of a building by the eighth ruler (534–551). Thus, it is certain that Altar Q refers to the sequence of actual rulers and events in the history of Copan that began with the royal founder.

Excavations in the earliest levels under the core of the Acropolis have revealed a series of beautifully decorated temples. Beneath the earliest temple is a building and tomb that may be the original house and burial place of K'inich Yax K'uk' Mo' himself. Built over this are the first of a series of temples commemorating the founder, as well as another tomb, along with a hieroglyphic text with a date in 437 and a reference to K'inich Yax K'uk' Mo'. The second tomb is probably that of K'inich Yax K'uk' Mo's queen, the mother of Ruler 2. North of the early Acropolis, excavations under the Hieroglyphic Stairway have found several other Early Classic buildings. In front of the earliest was another monument portraying both K'inich Yax K'uk' Mo' and his son. This stone and another monument found inside a slightly later building, Stela 63, refer to important ceremonies performed by K'inich Yax K'uk' Mo' and his son in 435, marking the end of a major calendrical cycle, the eighth Bak'tun.

These initial constructions form Copan's first royal complex and indicate that centralized political power began at the very time the later texts tell of the founding of the royal dynasty. The reigns of the early kings depicted on Altar Q were marked by huge building efforts. Much of the Acropolis was created during the reigns of the first eight rulers (or between 426 and 551). The general size and layout of the Acropolis seen today was established by the time of the eighth ruler, Wil Yohl K'inich (534–551). Another royal tomb discovered beneath the Acropolis may well be his. The tomb was on the west side of a courtyard, opposite a temple dedicated by Wil Yohl K'inich in 542.

The eight later kings of Copan elaborated and expanded the basic plan dating to the eighth ruler's reign. The original sacred location in the center of the Acropolis associated with the founder and his son was further commemorated by a splendid temple decorated by painted stucco masks. Named Rosalila by the archaeologist who discovered it, this temple was eventually buried completely intact by an even larger structure. A later and final temple built by the last Copan king, Yax Pasaj, completed a sequence of seven temples built on this spot dedicated to the founder of Copan's royal dynasty.

During the reign of the tenth ruler, nicknamed Moon Jaguar (553–578), most of the stelae of Copan's preceding Early Classic kings were mysteriously smashed, perhaps the result of outside intervention. After this, the eleventh ruler, K'ak' Chan Yopaat, increased Copan's power during a reign of 46 years (578–626). The Copan polity was expanded further by Smoke Imix, the twelfth ruler, whose 67-year reign was the longest of any

Copan king (628–695). These lengthy and stable reigns allowed the Copan kingdom to reach its maximum extent in area, power, and prestige. The Copan state included Quirigua, its smaller satellite center, located in the lower Motagua Valley some 50 kilometers to the north. Quirigua enabled Copan to control both this fertile valley and the "jade route" that followed the Motagua River.

Smoke Imix was buried in an elaborate tomb beneath Temple 26 and its Hieroglyphic Stairway. His son, Waxaklajuun Ubaah K'awiil, took the throne in 695. He concentrated on constructions in the site center, especially the Great Plaza north of the Acropolis, which was the setting for Copan's greatest assemblage of monuments. One of these, Stela A dating to 731, proclaims that Waxaklajuun Ubaah K'awiil's kingdom ranked with Tikal, Palenque, and Calakmul as the four greatest polities of the Maya world. The final project of his reign was the rebuilding of the Great Ball Court, in 738. But Waxaklajuun Ubaah K'awiil fell victim to the same fate as Kan Joy Chitam of Palenque, for 113 days after dedicating his new ball court he was captured by his vassal, K'ak' Tiliw Chan Yopaat of Quirigua. In this case, however, the captured king of Copan was beheaded, perhaps in a ball game ritual orchestrated by K'ak' Tiliw Chan Yopaat.

Figure 5.9 View of the ball court at Copan, Honduras, dedicated in 738 by the thirteenth king, Waxaklajuun Ubaah K'awiil, shortly before his demise at the hands of his subordinate, the ruler of Quirigua (in the background are the Hieroglyphic Stairway and Acropolis).

As a result, Copan's monopoly of power in the southeast was broken. Although Quirigua did not conquer Copan, it had gained its independence from Copan's control and enjoyed unprecedented prosperity thereafter. For the remainder of K'ak' Tiliw Chan Yopaat's 60-year reign at Quirigua, he used his newly won wealth and prestige to transform his capital by a major rebuilding effort.

Until this event, Quirigua was a minor vassal center with a population only a tenth the size of Copan's. It has long been a mystery, therefore, how Quirigua defeated its far more powerful superior and captured its king. But a brief account on Quirigua Stela I provides the likely answer. The text states that in 736, two years before Quirigua's victory, its ruler, K'ak' Tiliw Chan Yopaat, hosted the king of Calakmul, Wamaw K'awiil. This certainly suggests that during this meeting an agreement was made that secured a role for Calakmul in Copan's defeat, probably by providing the armed forces needed to overpower Copan. The motives for such support are obvious: by striking a blow against Copan, one of Tikal's oldest allies, Calakmul would have a measure of revenge against its long-term foe. As a bonus, this action may have given Calakmul crucial access to the bounty of the Motagua Valley and its trade route.

Thereafter, not only did Quirigua gain its economic and political independence, but K'ak' Tiliw Chan Yopaat now commanded his own destiny. This allowed him to direct a major rebuilding effort that transformed his capital into a fitting symbol of his newly won wealth and prestige. He sponsored the construction of several new buildings, but most of his efforts went into creating an impressive public space for new monuments that proclaimed his achievements. The new plaza laid out north of Quirigua's palace complex was the largest such public space ever designed at a Maya site. While there is archaeological evidence that the southern portion was a marketplace, most of this plaza was devoted to displaying an array of huge stelae adorned with K'ak' Tiliw's portraits, including several of the largest carved stones ever erected by the Maya. The tallest stela towers more than 7 meters above the plaza and weighs an estimated 30 tons. The huge size and the beautiful carving on these monuments, clearly visible from the Motagua River that flowed along the west side of the Great Plaza, testified that K'ak' Tiliw controlled all the resources he needed to create a new polity capital as a powerful and independent Maya king.

Meanwhile, Copan suffered a severe economic setback by losing control over the productive lands and trade of the Motagua Valley. Just as important, it lost prestige and power, because to the Maya the capture and sacrifice of a ruler signified that the gods had withdrawn their blessings from king, kingdom, and their destinies.

Almost nothing is known about Waxaklajuun Ubaah K'awiil's successor at Copan. K'ak' Tiliw Chan Yopaat claimed the title of fourteenth successor to K'inich Yax K'uk' Mo', and it is possible that he even controlled Copan for a time, installing or controlling a subordinate named K'ak' Joplaj Chan K'awiil. The damage to its power and prestige caused internal political changes at Copan. Ruling authority during this critical time apparently came from the sharing of power among the leaders of the highest-ranking elite houses who met in the *popol nah* (council house) located next to Waxaklajuun Ubaah K'awiil's former palace.

The fifteenth Copan king, K'ak' Yipyaj Chan K'awiil, re-established much of Copan's prestige and power. This was dramatically symbolized by his dedication of the famed Hieroglyphic Stairway. Part of a new temple built over a shrine to the dynasty next to the Great Ball Court, the staircase was carved with the longest known Maya inscription, some 2,200 glyphs recording Copan's royal history. Decorated with statues of Copan's most famous kings arrayed as warriors, it negated the humiliation of Quirigua's victory and proclaimed the restoration of the cosmic order by returning Copan to its former place of importance in the Maya world.

Yax Pasaj became the sixteenth ruler of Copan in 763. He dedicated two famous monuments to Copan's royal dynasty, Altar Q and Temple 16, the last temple built over the sacred center of the Acropolis established by K'inich Yax K'uk' Mo'. However, a continued weakened central authority marked Yax Pasaj's reign. Despite his predecessor's achievements, the fifteenth ruler had not been able to reverse the power held by the nobles of the ruling council. Yax Pasaj tried to keep his kingdom together by rewarding his officials with more titles and greater status, but in so doing he unwittingly increased the power of the nobles. They proclaimed their authority on elaborate carved thrones in their palaces, where they held court like lesser versions of the Copan king himself.

During the century after the victory over Copan, the rulers of Quirigua reigned supreme over the lower Motagua Valley, controlling the critical jade route between the Maya highlands and the Caribbean. The architect of Copan's defeat, K'ak' Tiliw Chan Yopaat, died in 784 after a reign of 60 years. His presumed son, Sky Xul, succeeded him and ruled for more than a decade. He commemorated his reign with three mammoth carved monuments. All are sculptural masterworks, especially Zoomorph P, which in its text recalls the founding of Quirigua under the auspices of K'inich Yax K'uk' Mo' almost 400 years earlier.

In 810, the ceremonies that marked the auspicious *k'atun* ending were held not at Copan but rather at Quirigua, where Yax Pasaj visited a reconciled Quirigua ruler, Jade Sky, Sky Xul's successor. The end of dynastic rule at both sites is reflected by Copan's last monument, Altar L. It is a poor imitation of Altar Q, showing Yax Pasaj seated opposite of a noble named Ukit Took', who attempted to be the seventeenth ruler of Copan. Altar L was never finished, and its inscription was never carved. Ukit Took' failed to rule Copan, and the last remnant of centralized authority vested in its kings disappeared. For a time, power at Copan was divided

Figure 5.10 Quirigua Zoomorph P, dedicated in 795, with a portrait of the ruler Sky Xul and texts that record the founding of Quirigua under the authority of K'inich Yax K'uk' Mo', founder of the Copan dynasty.

among the principal nobles who lived in their compounds throughout the valley, until they too lost control over their subjects.

OVERVIEW OF MIDDLE MAYA CIVILIZATION

Middle Maya civilization emerged after the decline of most of the major cities that dominated the rapid growth of Early Maya civilization. The decline was more complete in the southern area, where the tradition of erecting dated portrait monuments—and, by extension, of rule by kings, as well—ended for a time. But the royal political system survived in the lowlands and was reinforced by increased use of carved monuments proclaiming royal power. In this setting, the demise of the greatest Preclassic city, El Mirador, was followed by the rise of Tikal, Calakmul, and other cities that prospered during the heyday of Middle Maya civilization.

With Tikal's rise the thread of Maya history begins to supplement archaeological evidence, and an understanding of the developmental course of Maya civilization becomes more complete. During the Classic period, the southern lowlands saw the greatest growth in population and number of states, accompanied by the florescence of Maya art, architecture, and intellectual achievement. These developments define Middle Maya civilization, which is marked by dynastic political systems in each of the major lowland polities, focused on centralized power in the hands of individual kings.

Middle Maya civilization was also a time of increasing competition and conflict, culminating in a great rivalry between the two most powerful lowland states, Tikal and Calakmul. After initial success in the Early Classic period, Tikal was defeated by a coalition of states managed by Calakmul. But Calakmul was unable to unify its control, and the coalition eventually broke down. In the Late Classic era, Tikal revived and defeated Calakmul and its allies under the leadership of its twenty-sixth king, spawning the era of its greatest power and growth. Other powerful polities and their capitals prospered at this time. The Petexbatun kingdom used conquest to dominate its region, only to be overwhelmed by its former victims. Along the Usumacinta River, Piedras Negras enjoyed considerable success before succumbing to its longtime rival Yaxchilan, which was led to success by a series of long-lived warrior kings. In the southwest, Palenque emerged into the limelight of history under the leadership of K'inich Janaab' Pakal and his successors, only to suffer defeat at the hands of Tonina. In the southeast, Copan prospered during four centuries of royal rule by the successors of its dynastic founder. Its only setback was the breakaway of Quirigua, leading ultimately to greater power for Copan's nobility.

FURTHER READING

Andrews and Fash 2005; Bell, Canuto, and Sharer 2004; Braswell 2003; Culbert 1991; Demarest 2004; Fash 2001; Grube 2001; Houston 1998; Marcus 1992b; Martin and Grube 1995, 2008; Miller 1986; Sabloff 1994, 2003; Sabloff and Henderson 1993; Schele and Freidel 1990; Sharer and Traxler 2006; Stuart 2005; Tate 1992; Urban and Schortman 1986.

6

TRANSFORMATIONS IN MAYA CIVILIZATION

Maya civilization was transformed by profound changes during the Terminal Classic period, which began about 800. The duration of the Terminal Classic varied from one region to another. The most dramatic changes occurred in the southern lowlands with the downfall of almost all the Classic states roughly between 800 and 900. Outside the Classic heartland, transformed Maya polities continued to prosper for a time. In the northern lowlands, a number of Maya states reached their peak of power before declining within a span of about two centuries (ca. 800–1000), although the most powerful Maya state, Chichen Itza, endured until about 1100.

DOWNFALL OF THE SOUTHERN LOWLAND STATES

Archaeologists have found evidence for important changes over the southern lowlands, the area that had supported some of the greatest cities of Middle Maya civilization. The process varied from place to place, but the result was the same. A combination of overpopulation, overexploitation of an exhausted environment, and destructive warfare created massive problems for the people of the southern lowlands. Food shortages caused famine and malnutrition, which in turn made people more vulnerable to diseases. New evidence indicates there may have been a series of severe droughts in the lowlands between 800 and 900, which intensified these problems. Famine, disease, and warfare certainly killed large numbers of people, but the actual toll will never be known. The survivors had no choice but to seek a better life elsewhere. By about 800, most cities in the southern lowlands had reached their peak population. A century later, populations had fallen drastically, and most southern lowland cities were all but abandoned.

Although there are many reasons for the Terminal Classic decline, ultimately it happened because people lost faith in their kings. The deified rulers and the elite class could not solve the critical problems facing most of their subjects. So the people no longer supported a political system that had failed them. This is evident in the decline of all the things sponsored and directed by Maya kings. No more temples and palaces were built. No more monuments were carved with their portraits and the texts and dates that preserved their achievements. The elaborate prestige and ritual goods used by rulers and the elite, objects made of pottery, jade, wood, bone, and shell, all but disappeared from the southern lowlands.

This political change was not sudden. In some polities, a gradual trend away from power concentrated in the hands of kings began before 800. Increasing numbers of Maya kings had to share center stage with subordinate nobles, who held prestigious titles and lived in larger and more elaborate residences. After 800, the shifting balance of political power is evident throughout the lowlands. For most of the Classic period, Maya rulers were portrayed bearing all the trappings of supernatural and secular power, alone and aloof, except for downtrodden captives. But, during the Terminal Classic, increasing numbers of kings were portrayed with nobles, who had increased their power at the expense of their overlords.

At Copan, political change began early with the power-sharing council formed by the successors to Waxaklajuun Ubaah K'awiil. Once increased power was granted to the council of nobles, it was difficult to reverse the process. The weakening of centralized political power led to a dispersal of authority among the elite class. The downscaling of political organization managed to keep Copan going, but only for a time. Once the kings were gone, rule by a coalition of nobles soon failed, as well. The problems at Copan and elsewhere in southern lowlands eventually overwhelmed everyone, kings, nobles, and commoners alike.

In some kingdoms, the change was more rapid, brought on by warfare and conquest. At Dos Pilas and Aguateca, kings were overthrown by conquest and their cities abandoned. In other areas of the southern lowlands, the combination of overpopulation, environmental degradation (deforestation and soil exhaustion), and drought resulted in famine and disease. Evidence from lake cores indicates that rainfall shortages in the southern lowlands were more severe during the Terminal Classic than in any other period over the past 7,000 years. When these problems went unsolved, the common people responded by moving away from areas of crop failures, famine, and disease, attracted to less-affected areas and newly rising polities outside the southern lowlands. The drop in population and shift of population concentrations was a long-term process extending over a century or more, but it steadily weakened city after city until all were abandoned.

Regardless of whether their rulers failed to provide security in the face of war or food in the face of famine, the common people became disillusioned when they could not solve their problems. At Tikal and many other cities, the power of kings simply evaporated as their subjects died of malnutrition or left to find better lives in other areas. The people who quarried the stone, built the temples and palaces, and performed all the other labor to support the Classic kings had spoken. For a hundred years or more, the families of the common people drifted away from the shrinking cities of the southern lowlands. Some families stayed on and were successful because there were far fewer people to feed. A few areas, such as seacoasts and the margins of rivers and lakes, continued to support populations long after the Classic period.

TERMINAL CLASSIC ENCLAVES

As the great capitals declined between 800 and 900, some of their subordinate cities broke free and even prospered for a short time. Thus, the former dependency of Nakum took control over local trade routes and prospered as Tikal declined. When the capital of the Naranjo polity faltered, its former subordinate of Xunantunich asserted its independence. Situated on a defensible ridge overlooking a fertile floodplain, Xunantunich controlled a tributary of the Belize River and its important trade and communication link with the Caribbean. During the troubled Terminal Classic period, the newly independent rulers of Xunantunich maintained their power even though most of their subjects and resources had melted away. Unable to support a traditional royal lifestyle, they abandoned the Late Classic palace used by their predecessors, lords of a province in the Naranjo kingdom. Without large numbers of corvée labor, they concentrated on updating Xunantunich's largest and most secure structure. It was modified to serve as a royal shrine and residence, and a new stucco frieze was added to advertise the continuity of royal power. They also asserted a claim of royal legitimacy through dedicating Xunantunich's first dynastic monuments that celebrated calendrical cycle endings in 820, 830, and 849. Soon thereafter, Xunantunich fell silent and was abandoned.

Revival at Seibal

Similar strategies are found at other Terminal Classic sites, as heirs to ancient dynasties and new claimants to royal power attempted to assert their legitimacy to rule as the major polities lost power and subjects. One of the most successful was the city of Seibal, which reasserted its former dominance for several decades after the downfall of the Petexbatun kingdom. Once the largest center in the region, Seibal is situated on bluffs overlooking the Río Pasión, a major tributary of the Usumacinta River. For a time in the Terminal Classic, a revived Seibal again became a major lowland capital, boosted by its command of trade along the Rio Pasión route. Its Terminal Classic monuments, architecture, and pottery reflect trade connections with the Gulf coast and the northern Maya lowlands.

Seibal proclaimed its revived power with traditional royal monuments. Some 17 carved stelae, dating between 849 and 889, reflect Seibal's status as a major Maya capital during the twilight of the Classic period, in addition to its new trade connections. These late monuments are carved with a mixture of Classic Maya and foreign characteristics, such as a depiction of the central Mexican wind deity, Ehecatl, on one stela. The blend of styles probably represents an attempt to adopt a variety of symbols of royal power, for Seibal's rulers were traditional Maya lords trying to maintain their power by adapting to the changing conditions of the Terminal Classic.

The texts on Seibal's monuments reveal that it was revived by two surviving states in the eastern lowlands, the allied polities of Caracol and Ucanal. The goal was undoubtedly to reopen the old Pasión-Usumacinta River trade route to the Gulf of Mexico. Seibal's defensible location made it the prime choice for securing this route. Stela 11 records the refounding of Seibal as a polity capital in 830. Seibal's new founding ruler was Aj Bolon Haabtal, who named Chan Ek' Hopet of Ucanal as his overlord. In 849, Aj Bolon Haabtal activated a small temple, Structure A-3, by dedicating five carved stelae, one inside his new temple and one at the base of each of its stairways. One of these, Stela 10, depicts Aj Bolon Haabtal dressed in Maya royal regalia, holding a double-headed ceremonial bar, although wearing a nontraditional mustache. The text of Stela 10 refers to visits by the kings of Tikal, Calakmul, and Motul de San José to witness Seibal's K'atun-ending ceremonies. However, by 849, the Tikal and Calakmul rulers held only vestiges of the power and domains once possessed by these once great capitals.

Aj Bolon Haabtal ruled until 889, when Seibal's final dated stelae were erected. It is not known if he had a successor. Archaeology indicates that Seibal's late success was relatively brief, for the site was practically abandoned soon thereafter. Most of the old trans-Peten trade routes had closed down, and Seibal had lost any strategic advantage gained from its control over the Pasión-Usumacinta route. In addition, any support from Caracol and Ucanal, or any other old lowland Maya capitals, had vanished by this time.

The short-term successes enjoyed by a few enclaves of traditional Classic Maya kings were destined to fail. By 900, at Xunantunich, Seibal, and other surviving capitals across the lowlands, the façade of royal authority collapsed, and the last of these southern lowland cities were soon abandoned.

Figure 6.1 Seibal, Guatemala: A polity capital that enjoyed a brief revival in the Terminal Classic under ruler Aj Bolon Haabtal, who dedicated this temple in 849, witnessed by the rulers of Tikal, Calakmul, and Motul de San José. Courtesy of Jeremy A. Sabloff.

TRANSFORMATIONS OUTSIDE THE SOUTHERN LOWLANDS

The demise of the southern lowlands was due to many factors that began in the heartland of Middle Maya civilization and later reverberated in Yucatan. It was played out in many different ways from one polity to another and was the product of countless decisions made by king and commoner alike.

During the Terminal Classic, decline and migrations relocated Maya civilization to areas outside the southern lowlands and transformed its economic and political organization. Those who fled to safer havens in coastal areas, in the highlands, or in Yucatan created a host of changes that sparked a renewal of Maya civilization and a new era of prosperity in all these regions, especially the northern lowlands. By the end of the Terminal Classic, a reoriented society had emerged in these areas—a society that would prosper during the remainder of the pre-Columbian era and eventually suffer the ravages of the Spanish Conquest.

Although the processes of change in the Terminal Classic involved all levels of Maya society, politically the greatest changes were to the traditional institutions of dynastic kingship and centralized political organization. In the southern lowlands, the political hierarchy ruled by divine kings had disintegrated by ca. 900. But, in the northern lowlands, a modified institution of dynastic kingship enjoyed a reprieve before succumbing at the end of the Terminal Classic period. This reoriented system was based on downplaying the authority of the king and on an increasing reliance on the authority and acumen of the nobility, who often met in councils to advise the ruler.

The Maya economy had began to change in the Late Classic period as prestige goods such as jade, shell, and polychrome pottery became more widely distributed within society. A variety of occupations involved in this newly emerging economy became part of a growing mercantile-oriented middle class made up of wealthy commoners and elites. By the Terminal Classic period, there were changes in the organization and in the control over the lowland trade system itself.

As the traditional lowland states declined, there was a corresponding decrease in trade via the overland and river routes across the lowlands. At the same time, there was an increase in the use of coastal routes that moved goods around the Yucatan Peninsula. These changes reflect a shift in the structure of economic power, from that held by kings to that exercised by the newer merchant class. These changes were promoted by increased demand for commodities, technological changes that allowed mass production of goods, and larger seagoing craft capable of carrying larger cargos over longer distances. As a result, more efficient seacoast trade distributed mass-produced commodities, including salt from Yucatan, pottery made on the Gulf coast or the Pacific plain of Guatemala, and green obsidian from Central Mexico, throughout the Maya area and beyond.

EXPANSION OF NORTHERN LOWLAND STATES

Archaeology has documented a long sequence of occupation in the northern lowlands, beginning in the Preclassic era. Other than subsistence crops, livelihoods in Yucatan were based on commerce in local resources, especially sea salt and agricultural products such as cotton. Populations in Yucatan were affected by the demise of southern lowland cities, but, while some northern cities also declined, changed political and economic conditions allowed many inhabitants to enjoy greater prosperity in the Terminal Classic period.

An important northern polity capital, Ek Balam, is located midway between Coba and Chichen Itza. Archaeological evidence reveals that it reached its maximum size between ca. 700 and 900. During this era, Ek Balam was the capital of a traditional Classic Maya state ruled by a dynasty of some five kings. The founding ruler, Ukit K'an Lek Tok', reigned at the end of the Late Classic period and was apparently buried in a tomb inside an elaborately decorated Ek Balam temple. The city's succeeding rulers reigned during the Terminal Classic era. The end of dynastic kingship at Ek Balam came by about 900, probably due to conquest by Chichen Itza.

Located among several lakes in northeastern Yucatan, the large city of Coba was one of several Classic states in the northern lowlands that survived the problems in the southern lowlands and continued to prosper, at least for a time. Coba was ruled by a long dynasty of kings portrayed on 23 carved stelae, like those seen in the capitals to the south. Unfortunately, most of its history cannot be read because the inscriptions have eroded. Coba's power peaked in the Late and Terminal Classic periods (ca. 730–1000). Thereafter, the city declined as it was surrounded by a greater northern power, Chichen Itza (discussed later). Cut off from its economic and political allies in Yucatan and bypassed by the new coastal trade routes, Coba was eventually abandoned.

The site of Yaxuna, in central Yucatan, reveals clues to the confrontation between Coba and Chichen Itza. Archaeological evidence indicates that Coba controlled Yaxuna in the Late Classic (ca. 600–750); the two cities were connected by the longest of all Maya causeways. This allowed Coba to consolidate its realm and to block further expansion by Chichen Itza. But not for long, for Coba's outpost at Yaxuna was soon overrun by Chichen Itza. Excavations reveal a defensive tower and palisades comparable to the fortifications at Dos Pilas and Aguateca, indicating that Yaxuna was besieged during the Terminal Classic. Evidence of building destruction and the appearance of pottery associated with Chichen Itza marks the conquest of Yaxuna around 950. Thereafter, Yaxuna was depopulated, although it may have been used as a support base for Chichen Itza's campaigns against Coba.

To the west, a number of Classic cities also prospered, some even reached their maximum growth during this Terminal Classic era. Two of the best known are Dzibilchaltun and Chunchucmil. Both were undoubtedly very reliant on the salt trade, and the resultant economic benefits may have shielded them for a time from the problems to the south. Chunchucmil is situated in one of the driest areas of Yucatan, so its prosperity depended on its proximity to diverse coastal resources. The city covered about 16 square kilometers and had an estimated population of more than 30,000 people. Chunchucmil does not have the usual monumental temples, palaces, plazas, and monuments of a Maya city. It is composed entirely of elite and nonelite residential compounds that reflect its specialized commercial function. A mercantile family specializing in salt and other coastal trade interests likely occupied each elite compound, while the commoner households provided the labor for these commercial enterprises.

Dzibilchaltun also depended on the production and export of salt for its prosperity, but, unlike Chunchucmil, it was a traditional Classic Maya capital. In fact, Dzibilchaltun was one of Yucatan's largest polity capitals in the Late and Terminal Classic periods. The city grew to its maximum size by about 800–900, with an estimated 25,000 inhabitants. Its carved but eroded stelae record its rule by a little-known royal dynasty. One date survives on Stela 9 (equivalent to 849). Stela 19 depicts a ruler named K'aloom Uk'uw Chan Chak holding a K'awiil scepter. A royal tomb excavated beneath one of its temples could be that of this ruler.

The Puuc States

Centered within the only hilly region in the northwest lowlands, the Puuc area is best known for its distinctive architecture. Some of the most beautiful and appealing of all Maya buildings are found in this region, with their distinctive upper zones decorated by intricate mosaic designs that define the Puuc architectural style. During the Classic period, the city of Oxkintok was a major polity capital in northwestern Yucatan. But, like its counterparts to the south, Oxkintok declined in the Terminal Classic; its latest monument dates to 859.

Oxkintok lost out to competition from a host of newer Puuc cities, including Uxmal, Kabah, Sayil, and Labna. These cities adapted to the changing conditions of the Terminal Classic period, which allowed them to grow and prosper for about 200 years. Their populations swelled due to local expansion and movements of peoples from the south. This was not a single mass migration but a gradual shift in population spread out over a century or more. Earlier settlements in the Puuc area had been limited by a long dry season and a lack of surface water sources. But the soils of this hilly region are among the best in Yucatan, so the construction of underground cisterns to collect and store rainwater allowed the Puuc to became more densely settled during the Terminal Classic.

There is evidence that the Puuc kings continued elements of traditional centralized political authority, reinforced by warfare. Carved monuments depict rulers dressed like other Classic Maya kings, often as warriors. High settlement densities and unusually close spacing between Puuc cities suggest a competitive environment. Remnants of walls surround several of these cities, and there are some carved depictions of captive taking. At least some Puuc rulers continued to dedicate carved monuments. Yet the Terminal Classic northern states were not replicas of the older southern Classic polities, for the northern kings apparently had learned from the traumatic downfall of the southern dynasties. Both the political and economic systems of these northern states were more decentralized than formerly. The greater number of palaces and the reduced number of funerary temples suggest that less emphasis was placed on the authority of individual kings. Many buildings now called "palaces" were probably administrative structures, indicating that these northern rulers relied more on power sharing with their royal courts and governing councils.

The largest Puuc capital was Uxmal, which at its peak controlled a polity of some 500 square kilometers. It also likely held the port of Uaymil, on the west coast of Yucatan. One of its rulers, Chan Chak K'ak'nal Ajaw, has

Figure 6.2 Uxmal, Mexico: Known as the House of the Governor, this is the largest palace at the site and one of the best examples of Puuc architectural style (Terminal Classic).

been identified from several monuments dating between 895–907. During this time, Uxmal took over neighboring Kabah and much of the eastern Puuc region, presumably under the leadership of Chan Chak K'ak'nal Ajaw. One of Uxmal's so-called palaces, popularly known as the "Nunnery Quadrangle," was likely a governmental complex where Uxmal's king, royal court, and governing council met to receive tribute, pass judgments, and make decisions.

Another powerful Puuc capital lies to the south. Investigated by archaeological research, the site of Sayil was first settled around 800. Thereafter, the city grew rapidly until it covered some 5 square kilometers, with a peak population of about 10,000 people (ca. 900). Another 5,000 to 7,000 people lived in the surrounding hinterland. Fragments of badly eroded monuments indicate that Sayil was ruled by a local royal dynasty. Crops grown in gardens and fields set among its residential compounds supported the city, each supplied by cisterns that stored water from seasonal rainfall. By about 950, Sayil began to decline, and within 50 years or so it was abandoned. This pattern of rapid growth and decline seems typical for most of the Terminal Classic Puuc cities.

The reasons for the decline and abandonment of the Puuc cities are not well understood. It is possible that they fell prey to the same problems that caused the Classic states in the southern lowlands to fail—a fatal combination of overpopulation, environmental damage, and warfare. However, lake core evidence seems to rule out drought as factor in the Puuc decline. Another possibility is that Uxmal and the other Puuc cities were victims of conquest by the rising military power of Chichen Itza to the east. It may be that the decline and abandonment of the Puuc cities resulted from the combination of internal problems and military conquest.

The Expansion of Seacoast Trade

Chontal Maya traders from the Gulf coast of the eastern Yucatan Peninsula began to expand their territory and trade routes during the Terminal Classic period. These formerly peripheral Maya peoples became successful merchants, warriors, and opportunists. As they expanded seacoast commerce, they stimulated economic and political changes throughout the Maya area. The Chontal comprised many independent groups that shared language and navigation skills but that had different social, political and religious traditions from most other lowland Maya societies. From their trading contacts, the Chontal adopted and combined non-Maya traditions from the Gulf coast and from areas inland as far as central Mexico.

The Chontal seized and controlled important resources, ports, and trade routes. Their most important coastal resource was salt evaporated from seawater. They founded new coastal trading centers and expanded salt production on the northern coast of Yucatan, which produced more salt than any other area in Mesoamerica. Their sea-trade network connected the east and west coasts of the Yucatan Peninsula and controlled commerce between the Gulf coast of Mexico and Central America. They also established or controlled a number of key ports along this coastal network.

One of these expanding Chontal Maya groups was known as the Itza in the Yucatecan chronicles. Because they spoke a language related to but distinct from Yucatec Mayan, they are described in the northern documents as people "who speak our language brokenly." The Itza established their first foothold in Yucatan at Isla Cerritos, an island port just off the northern coast. Remains of a sea wall and stone piers define the ancient harbor used by these coastal traders. From here the Itza expanded inland, first settling in the boundary region between the powerful polity of Coba to the east and the more numerous Puuc states to the west. But the base from which they were to dominate the political, economic, and religious life of Yucatan was Chichen Itza. The later Yucatecan chronicles record that the Itza established a new capital at this city, probably about 850. From their new inland base, the Itza expanded their power by trade, alliances, and conquest until they controlled most of the northern lowlands.

The Rise of Chichen Itza

Chichen Itza began its rise to power in the Late Classic period. But, in the Terminal Classic, it became the dominant capital in Yucatan, lasting longer than any other Classic city, until ca. 1050–1100. At its peak, Chichen Itza was the largest and most powerful Maya capital. It was also the most cosmopolitan of all Maya cities, for its heyday came at a time of increasingly widespread communication, political alliances, and migrations in Mesoamerica. Chichen Itza's commercial and religious institutions were connected to ports and cities throughout the Maya area and beyond. As a result, Chichen Itza's society and culture reflected many different Mesoamerican traditions and were the precursors of the cosmopolitan polities of Late Maya civilization.

At its height, Chichen Itza was probably the largest city in Mesoamerica. Its cosmopolitan architecture and art were inspired by a combination of its Maya heritage and traditions from throughout Mesoamerica, especially those of the Gulf coast and Central Mexico. Its success in maintaining control over its vast domain lay in its economic prosperity from trade, an effective political system, and a new religious ideology. But the rapid expansion of the Itza state was also promoted by military coercion and conquest.

An important factor in Chichen Itza's rise to power was its reliance on the Chontal trade network, but it soon controlled many of the critical coastal ports and trade routes itself. Earlier Maya polity capitals relied on alliances between cities to secure access to trade networks. But Chichen Itza maintained its own coastal ports and was able to exert direct control over its trade network, commanding the central position of this trading system on Yucatan's north coast. Chichen Itza gained wealth and power from its control of trade in prestige items made from gold imported from Panama and Mexico or turquoise that came from the American Southwest. But the foundation of its economic power came from controlling everyday products needed by every household. Chief among these was salt, and at least one of its ports was also a major salt production center. Judging from the extent of its solar-evaporation pans, it appears that it produced up to 5,000 metric tons of salt per year for export.

Wealth from trade is usually secured by military power. Murals depicting trade, ports, military conquests, and captives decorated Chichen Itza's buildings. One of its early texts refers to its ruler K'ak'upakal as a *yajaw* (vassal) of an unidentified king. But, by about 900, Chichen Itza began a campaign to dominate its rivals until it superseded the established order represented by Coba, the Puuc states, Dzibilchaltun, and the other older polities of Yucatan. At its peak, Chichen Itza probably controlled the largest and most populous state in Maya history. Its conquest of Yaxuna was a crucial step toward its dominance. Other polities in the northern lowlands declined during the period of Chichen Itza's expansion. Either by threat or by actual conquest, it achieved a level of military power that was successful in subduing its neighbors, including its largest competitor, Coba. It is likely that Coba was conquered by Chichen Itza, but Coba was also cut off from its economic and political allies and bypassed by the new coastal trade routes until it was abandoned.

Figure 6.3 Chichen Itza, Mexico: The Temple of the Warriors, with its great colonnade covered by a beam-and-mortar roof (Terminal Classic).

Figure 6.4 The summit building of the Temple of the Warriors, its central doorway columns in the form of K'uk'ulkan, the great feathered serpent deity.

The name Chichen Itza means "the wells of the Itza," referring to the two large limestone sinkholes or cenotes at the site. The cosmopolitan character of the city is reflected in its architecture, a blend of the Puuc style and Mexican characteristics, including the use of colonnades to provide extensive roofed areas. The most famous of Chichen Itza's colonnaded buildings is the so-called Temple of the Warriors. Although colonnaded buildings provided much more light and open space than traditional Maya buildings, they were often roofed with Maya-style corbel vaults. The Puuc-style buildings at Chichen Itza have typical fine Maya workmanship in their mosaic-decorated upper façades. Mexican styles can be seen in a temple known as the "High Priest's Grave," built over a natural cave, suggesting that it marks an original sacred entrance to the underworld. The Caracol is a distinctive round temple like those from Mexico, where they are associated with the wind-deity. The most famous of Chichen Itza's buildings is the Castillo. Like many Classic Maya examples, the Castillo has nine terraces, and its four stairways recall Classic period platforms at Tikal and other sites. But it also has plumed serpent columns and a flat roof similar to those on Toltec temples in central Mexico.

The Great Ball Court is the largest in Mesoamerica, and Chichen Itza has more ball courts (13) than any other Maya city. The famous carved frieze from the Great Ball Court depicts a victory by an Itza war leader with the decapitation of a vanquished foe, undoubtedly celebrated by a ritual ball game in time-honored Maya tradition. A causeway leads north from El Castillo to the edge of the sacred Cenote of Sacrifice. During the city's ascendancy, pilgrimages were made to this sacred cenote from all parts of the Maya area to cast offerings into its depths. The Great Ball

Figure 6.5 Chichen Itza, Mexico: The Castillo, the largest temple in the city (Terminal Classic).

Figure 6.6 Chichen Itza, Mexico: The Great Ball Court, the largest in Mesoamerica (Terminal Classic).

Court and its position as a famous pilgrimage center certainly contributed to the prestige and economic success of Chichen Itza. Overall, the new masters at Chichen Itza constructed a large and splendid capital from which they were able to rule one of the largest kingdoms ever seen in the Maya world. In fact, from their capital, the Itza Maya dominated Yucatan for some 200 years.

The Chichen Itza State

A core element of Classic society that disappeared during the Terminal Classic era was the dynasties of kings that had governed Maya states since the Late Preclassic. With the changing conditions of the Terminal Classic, the political systems of the north represent a transition from dynastic rule to a new political order that would come to characterize Late Maya civilization in the Postclassic period. This transition began with the less centralized political organization of the Puuc states. It culminated at Chichen Itza, the most powerful and successful Terminal Classic Maya state.

Although conquest helped create the Chichen Itza state, its success was a result of its governance by a flexible and stable political system. Chichen Itza's monumental buildings were intended to impress both its subjects and visitors from afar. Other northern capitals, including Coba, Dzibilchaltun, and Uxmal, continued the tradition of dynastic monuments with portraits of kings. But Chichen Itza's art and architecture do not proclaim the achievements of individual kings. Its buildings reflect a broad range of styles that, through carved and painted images of warriors, priests, merchants, and ball players, communicate the economic, military, and religious power of the Itza state. There are buildings for public spectacles, such as ball games, dances, and sacrifices. Instead of enclosed palaces like those associated with the kings of traditional Maya states, Chichen Itza features innovative buildings composed of extensive open galleries with roofs supported by colonnades.

Chichen Itza's colonnaded buildings were likely meeting halls for commercial and political activities, such as the *popol nah* (council house). The presence of these types of buildings and the lack of traditional royal texts and image suggest a changed political organization. Political authority at Chichen Itza was more decentralized, based on a power-sharing arrangement that included a supreme council composed of elite lords, including heads of the military, mercantile, and religious hierarchies within the state. Other councilors probably administered the polity's territorial divisions. Several Yucatan polities had this system, called *multepal* ("shared rule"), at the time of the Conquest, when the colonnaded structures were used for civic and ritual assemblies.

Yet, at least one ruler has been identified in Chichen Itza's texts, and Spanish sources refer to individual rulers at Chichen Itza. It is likely that both an individual ruler and a council of elite lords governed the Chichen Itza state. Even so, the authority of Chichen Itza's rulers was not based in the same ideological and symbolic foundations as traditional Maya kings. The lack of public displays of royal portraits and texts reflects a shift away from the concentration of power in the hands of a single ruler.

Of course, this form of power sharing had its beginnings in the Late Classic and was developed further in the Puuc states, so the *multepal* system probably derived from these prototypes. A shared power system was probably advantageous in the highly competitive Terminal Classic era, for it disassociated Chichen Itza from the failed rulers of the Classic Maya kingdoms. It also insulated Chichen Itza from political paralysis caused by the sudden loss of a king. The sharing of power between ruler and council also removed decision making from its dependency on the abilities of a single individual; instead, the experience and abilities of many leaders could be mobilized to govern. Finally, the later *multepal* system included an effective means of maintaining control over conquered areas by holding members of subordinate ruling families in the capital as insurance against revolts.

State Religion at Chichen Itza

Chichen Itza's success also depended on a religious cult that was as cosmopolitan as its architecture and commerce. Like its political system, the new cult represented a clear departure from the ideology that had supported the Maya kings of the past. The new Itza state religion was based on K'uk'ulkan, the feathered serpent, an appropriately cosmopolitan god that was also worshipped as Quetzalcoatl in Mexico. Images of K'uk'ulkan are prominent at Chichen Itza, including the feathered serpent columns that support the doorways of its greatest temples.

The cult of K'uk'ulkan played a major role in commercial success and communication throughout Mesoamerica. Chichen Itza was the setting for major religious celebrations and also benefited from its position as a major pilgrimage destination. In fact, it was such an important religious center that it continued to be a focus for pilgrimages long after its power had waned. It is likely that Chontal Maya merchants originally spread the feathered serpent cult throughout Mesoamerica. From these connections, K'uk'ulkan was adopted as the dominant deity at Chichen Itza, incorporated along with a pantheon of other gods with both Maya and non-Maya origins into a new cult sponsored by the Itza state to advance its major agendas, warfare and commerce.

The cult of K'uk'ulkan/Quetzalcoatl was the first religion that transcended the ethnic and linguistic divisions of Mesoamerica. As such, it promoted a new cosmopolitan culture and the interchange of ideas. At a more practical level, the sharing of a common religion fostered communication and the peaceful interchange of goods among merchants and traders from many different cultural and social backgrounds.

Figure 6.7 Chichen Itza, Mexico: The Cenote of Sacrifice, which continued to be the destination of religious pilgrimages long after the city declined.

CHANGES IN THE SOUTHERN MAYA AREA

Chichen Itza's power was felt far to the south over much of the Maya highlands and the Pacific plain. Trade ties with the north increased the distribution of highland products like obsidian, along with cacao and mass-produced pottery from the Pacific plain. From this time on, ruling houses in much of the Maya area claimed ties to Chichen Itza to reinforce their authority. This is seen in art and architecture, especially in feathered serpent motifs reflecting the K'uk'ulkan cult.

The southern Maya area was also impacted by the first of several waves of peoples from Central Mexico in the Terminal Classic period. The Pipil settled parts of the southern area from Guatemala to El Salvador and into Central America. Linguistic evidence suggests that the Pipil language diverged from that of the group's Nahua-speaking ancestors in Central Mexico during the Late Classic.

These new groups contributed to the rise of the Cotzumalguapa state on the central Pacific coast of Guatemala. Its innovative monumental sculptural tradition combined Maya and Mexican elements and revived an ancient southern Maya tradition that had all but died out at the end of the Preclassic era. The Cotzumalguapa state rose to power after ca. 700 and reached its zenith during the Terminal Classic period. The Cotzumalguapa sculptural style has ties to the Gulf coast Chontal Maya and to Chichen Itza, where a jade plaque carved in this southern style has been recovered.

An expansion of peoples southward from the Gulf coast was probably responsible for changes in site planning, architecture, and artifacts seen in the northern Maya highlands by the Terminal Classic period. Some of these migrants into the highlands were people fleeing the turmoil at the end of the Classic lowland states. It is also likely that Chontal colonists and traders also began moving into the highlands by way of the upper Usumacinta tributaries by this time.

In any case, the Terminal Classic changes in Maya highland society begin by about 800. Some earlier sites were abruptly abandoned; others were rebuilt and expanded. There were also population increases, since entirely new sites were founded. Both the rebuilt centers and the newly founded Terminal Classic highland centers were often larger than older Classic sites within the same region. Some new hilltop settlements from this time have been identified, especially in the western highlands. Yet, most highland and Pacific plain sites continued to be unfortified and situated in open settings, indicating that conflict levels remained low for much of the Terminal Classic.

OVERVIEW OF TRANSFORMATIONS
IN MAYA CIVILIZATION

The Terminal Classic era saw important economic, political, and religious changes. The traditional institution of dynastic kingship concentrated political, economic, and religious power of each Maya state into the hands of a single ruler whose power was reinforced by the religious beliefs of the common people. The problems and disruptions at the end of the Classic period were complex and multifaceted, but in the end they exposed the all-too-human failures of individual kings. Most lowland areas were over-populated by the end of the Late Classic, and food production from a depleted environment was in decline. Increased competition, along with warfare undertaken to augment the threatened resources and power of kings, only accelerated the problems. Combinations of famine, disease, violence, and even periodic droughts probably triggered the collapse of most lowland states as their surviving inhabitants abandoned their houses and fields seeking a better life elsewhere.

Some polities declined about the same time in Yucatan, but in many areas there was an expansion of population and prosperity. As most of the polities in the southern lowlands lost population and were eventu-ally abandoned, increasing numbers of people migrated to resettle new areas—on the coasts, in the highlands to the south, and into Yucatan to the north.

The changes wrought by the events of the Terminal Classic period can be seen in the Maya highlands and on the Pacific plain. The latter region was impacted by the first in series of migrations of new peoples, many of whom came from central Mexico. These newcomers spawned new developments, such as the Cotzumalguapa state, which revived the art of carved monuments rendered in a new cosmopolitan style.

Some of the refugees who moved north may have been elites intent on founding new polities and continuing their privileged lives outside the devastated Classic heartland. But most people were simply looking for undevastated areas to settle, like the Puuc region in northwest Yucatan. These migrations helped trigger the rapid rise of new cities and polity capitals in the north, while some older Yucatecan polities such as Coba were not only able to survive the changes of this era but also expanded and prospered for a time.

The last Classic Maya capital, Chichen Itza, ruled the largest and most powerful of all Maya states. It was a dominant military power and a major religious center ruled by a more flexible system in which rulers and an advisory council shared power. But a key to Chichen Itza's success also lay in its promotion of a new economy based on utilitarian commodi-ties such as salt, cotton, and cacao, rather than traditional prestige goods. Chichen Itza joined with Chontal Maya traders to control the efficient sea-coast trade route around the Yucatan Peninsula, which made most inland routes controlled by Classic-period kings obsolete. These changes, in turn, promoted further growth in the mercantile elites and in the middle class that managed the operation of this new economy.

The Terminal Classic was a time of political transition. With its author-ity undermined, the institution of dynastic kingship declined and was ultimately replaced by institutions with more dispersed political, economic and religious power, such as *multepal* or "shared power" systems. The trend toward a more decentralized political system can be seen first in the Terminal Classic resurgence of the Puuc states. But the decentralized government of Chichen Itza is a culmination of the political changes made in response to the failures of the more centralized power of earlier Maya kings.

Yet, Chichen Itza maintained the traditional foundations of power within Classic Maya states—control over critical commodities, labor, warfare, and religion. Chichen Itza accumulated vast wealth by controlling its trade network and used its resources and labor to construct a monumental capital of imposing civic and religious buildings. It also used warfare and captive taking to dominate its neighbors and sponsored huge public religious spectacles, including ritual dances, ball games, and human sacrifices. Chichen Itza was also innovative; its commercial success supported a capital city that was far more international in its outlook than any of its predecessors. Its cosmopolitan art, architecture, and religion combined the Maya past with the present. In this sense, Chichen Itza profoundly shaped the direction of Maya civilization during its final development before the Spanish Conquest. Chichen Itza dominated the Maya lowlands for more than two centuries and had a greater impact throughout Mesoamerica than any other Maya city. Its cosmopolitan economic, political, and religious institutions promoted a new pan-Mesoamerican culture that set the stage for the final era in pre-Columbian America.

In the end, however, like most of its Classic-period predecessors, Chichen Itza declined and was abandoned. While the causes of its downfall are unknown, it may have succumbed to the same combined effects of overpopulation, a depleted environment, warfare, and failures of leadership seen in earlier times.

FURTHER READING

Andrews 1983; Andrews et al. 2003; Chase and Rice 1985; Culbert 1973; Dahlin 2000, 2003; Demarest 2004; Demarest, Rice, and Rice 2004; Fash 2001; Gill 2000; Grube 2001; Haug et al. 2003; Kowalski 1987; Lowe 1985; Marcus 1992b; Martin and Grube 2008; Sabloff 1994; Sabloff and Andrews 1986; Sharer and Traxler 2006.

7

LATE MAYA CIVILIZATION

The final episode of Maya civilization, corresponding to the Postclassic era, ca. 900–1500, is characterized by increasing population and more prevalent warfare. In some cases, the Postclassic has been described as a period of cultural decline or decadence because of shifts in artistic expression or other aspects of life. But such judgments reflect an application of our modern standards to ancient Maya society. It would be more accurate to view Late Maya civilization as a time of political and economic reformulation, when more widespread Mesoamerican traditions were adopted into Maya culture.

The institution of dynastic kingship did not survive the changing conditions of the Terminal Classic period. The rise of Chichen Itza marked the emergence of a cosmopolitan culture based on expanded commerce, communication, and the interchange of ideas throughout Mesoamerica. The arrivals of new peoples created many of these changes. These include Chontal Maya groups from the Gulf coast and Nahua-speaking Pipil populations from Central Mexico. At the same time, Mesoamerican societies expanded further into both North and Central America by migrations and trade routes. These increased contacts brought new products, political ideas, military tactics, and religious practices to the Maya people.

The Postclassic was a period of change, and many cultural traditions that began in the Preclassic and developed throughout the Classic era were permanently altered. These changes affected political institutions and the economic and ideological foundations of society. The Yucatecan Maya saw their past as a time when people "adhered to their reason....At that time the course of humanity was orderly." But, like most peoples, the Maya resisted change and saw the arrival of new peoples and ideas as bringing about misfortune and instability marked by "the origin of the two-day throne, the two-day reign.... There were no more lucky days for us; we had no sound judgment."

These words, from a translation of a chronicle recorded by the Maya in the *Books of Chilam Balam* (Edmonson 1982, 1986), reflect a traditional Maya view of history. We have records of Postclassic history from accounts written by both the Maya and the first Europeans to arrive in the Americas. The Maya used the past to reconcile actual events with prophecy, which was an important element in their religious beliefs. In fact, Maya writings often modify sequences of events to fit their prophecies. Thus, the histories of events recorded by the Maya do not always agree with the results of archaeological research. By compensating for these differences, however, we can outline the major sequence of events as revealed by both archaeology and Maya history.

The most significant developments of Middle Maya civilization were in the southern lowlands. The most significant developments of Late Maya civilization were in the northern lowlands of Yucatan, in the lake region of the southern lowlands, and in the southern area, especially the Maya highlands. We will look each of these areas in turn.

LATE MAYA CIVILIZATION IN THE NORTHERN LOWLANDS

The power and prestige of Chichen Itza were in decline by ca. 1050. Later historical sources say Chichen Itza was destroyed by conquest, probably around 1100. Some buildings show evidence of sudden abandonment and destruction that might support these accounts. Yet, like the end of some Classic Maya cities to the south, it is not clear if Chichen Itza's fall was caused by violence or if this destruction happened after its power had already disappeared.

Chichen Itza was succeeded by a new capital, Mayapan, as the dominant power in Yucatan. Yet, the reasons behind this shift of power remain unclear. The Maya chronicles describe political intrigue, including the dramatic kidnapping of the queen of the ruler of Chichen Itza by the ruler of another kingdom, Izamal. This started a war that ended with the ruler of Mayapan, Hunak Keel, leading the conquest of Chichen Itza.

Rule by Mayapan

Mayapan became the new capital of the Itza state with a *multepal* government modeled after its larger and more splendid predecessor. The chronicles indicate that Mayapan controlled a fairly unified state in central Yucatan for nearly 250 years. This was done through a strategy of alliances and the simple but effective means of keeping the heads of each local ruling family at Mayapan—and therefore under direct control of the Itza ruling elite.

Mayapan is located about 100 kilometers west of Chichen Itza. Described by Bishop Landa in the sixteenth century and the subject of several archaeological investigations, it was a smaller city than its predecessor but better prepared to survive in an age of increasing conflict. An encircling wall with four gateways that were carefully planned against attack protected the new capital. The wall encloses an area of about 2 square kilometers, covered by about 4,000 buildings, and these probably housed as many as 20,000 people. Most of Mayapan's buildings were irregularly spaced commoner houses, many of which were partially of masonry construction. Low, dry-stone property walls surround these houses, enclosing irregularly shaped yards that average about a quarter of an acre. Meandering among the houses are lanes, their irregular limits defined by property walls. However, even in this unusually dense settlement, each household had enough open space for a small kitchen garden and other activities, such as beekeeping.

The densely packed settlement pattern inside the wall contrasts with the layout of earlier Maya cities, where houses were more dispersed to allow for larger intervening garden plots. Mayapan's major buildings are near the center of the city, gathered around a public plaza that was the focus of the capital's civic and ceremonial activity. Many of its buildings were patterned after those at Chichen Itza but were not as large or well constructed. The Temple of K'uk'ulkan and the Round Temple were clearly modeled after Chichen Itza's El Castillo and Caracol, respectively. A cenote and an adjacent shrine are located within the central area, just south of the Central Plaza. Near the center of the plaza are the remains of a round platform that once supported several carved stelae dedicated to K'atun ending ceremonies held during the first part of the site's history. Surrounding the Central Plaza is a series of small temples and shrines. A carved altar in the form of a miniature jaguar was excavated from a shrine on the east side of the plaza. Its beautifully carved form demonstrates that the art of fine sculpture continued in Postclassic Mayapan.

On the north side of the plaza is the Temple of the Niches, with murals dating to Mayapan's final period of occupation. More than 20 examples of colonnaded buildings are in the center of the site, grouped around the Central Plaza and its temples. All are rectangular buildings, set on platforms, with frontal colonnades and solid rear walls that supported flat beam-and-mortar roofs. Solid masonry benches line the rear wall, with an altar in the center. They likely served both residential and administrative functions for the city's elite.

Unlike the earlier finely shaped blocks of Chichen Itza and the Puuc sites, Mayapan's buildings were made of roughly shaped stones, set in

Figure 7.1 Mayapan, Mexico: Colonnaded buildings like this excavated example were the elite palaces and centers for the administration of the Mayapan state (Postclassic).

mortar. This poorer quality masonry was covered by plaster, often painted and modeled into decorative forms. Excavations have found remnants of these stuccoed decorations, along with and painted murals within its buildings. The styles of these stuccoed architectural motifs and murals are very different from those found at Classic Maya sites. Mayapan's architecture and murals were rendered in the prevailing styles of Postclassic Mesoamerica and reflect its wide-ranging commercial contacts.

Excavations indicate that Mayapan's earliest constructions date from its founding era (1185–1204) described by ethnohistoric accounts. These include the round platform that supported several monuments, including Stela 1, which marks a K'atun ending in 1185. The first buildings around Mayapan's Central Plaza cenote and several colonnaded buildings also date to this time.

According to the *Books of Chilam Balam*, Itza groups from the Gulf coast and from Chichen Itza joined forces with Mayapan during it first century of rule. One of these was the Cocom, a noble Itza family descended from the ruling houses of Chichen Itza. After their arrival, the Cocom took over the rulership of Mayapan. To enforce their power, the Cocom brought in foreign ("Mexican") mercenaries. Mayapan's major buildings, including large colonnaded palaces and other structures that emulated earlier buildings at Chichen Itza, were rebuilt under Cocom leadership.

If this reconstruction effort was intended to transform the new capital into a reborn successor of Chichen Itza, it was successful, since Mayapan became the dominant power in Yucatan. Under Cocom rule, Mayapan also led a revived K'uk'ulkan cult associated with the past glories of Chichen Itza. This is seen in representations of the feathered serpent throughout the city and the introduction of distinctive incense burners adorned with modeled deity figures. These Mayapan-style incensarios are found over a wide area, from the Gulf coast to the Maya lowlands. They continued to be used after Mayapan's fall, for the Spaniards reported destroying large numbers of such "idols" found in Maya temples.

Mayapan also grew into a major commercial center. It controlled a portion of coastal salt production. It also controlled the source of rare clay that was combined with indigo to make a highly prized pigment known as "Maya blue." Mayapan's merchants traded these and other products such as cotton textiles, honey, pottery, and slaves for goods like copper bells from western Mexico and obsidian and jade from the Maya highlands. These products were distributed by a series of ports along the sea routes along the coast of Yucatan. They have also been found along revived trade routes that ran through the central Petén lake region. The Mexica ("Aztecs") in Central Mexico imported Maya blue pigment from Yucatan to decorate buildings in their capital of Tenochtitlan.

The Mayapan State

The houses of the lords and priests of Mayapan can be identified from the ruins of its colonnaded buildings in the central area of the site. The Maya chronicles suggest Mayapan was governed by a *multepal* system of shared rule among several elite houses known as the Xiu, the Chel, and the Canul, in addition to the Cocom. Both the Cocom and the Chel came from Chichen Itza. The Canul were descended from the foreign mercenaries imported by the Cocom to support their rule. The Xiu were from Uxmal. It appears that members of each elite house held a share of the civil and priestly offices.

Mayapan ruled over a large territory divided into provinces administered as a confederacy under Mayapan's control. Each province was ruled from a prominent town. The leaders of these subordinate towns lived in Mayapan, supported by their subjects. By living in the capital, Mayapan's rulers could keep a close watch over their subordinate lords. Since they had to be supported by their own subjects, the rulers of Mayapan also avoided providing for their upkeep.

Mayapan used warfare and captive taking to expand and maintain the power of the state, just as in earlier times. Archaeology provides evidence for ritual sacrifices of captives at Mayapan. Excavations have found the bones of human sacrifices, including some that had been decapitated. Bound captives were probably tied to stone rings found still set into floors or the rear walls of several of Mayapan's buildings.

The organization of the Mayapan state changed over time as the balance of power between the ruling elite houses shifted. Although later accounts say the Cocom were the founders and the rulers of Mayapan, the Xiu may have been in power for the first century of its history (ca. 1180–1280). The evidence suggests at this time there was an Uxmal-inspired revival of stelae dedications marking traditional K'atun ending ceremonies. The chronicles also record that Mayapan, Uxmal, and Chichen Itza cooperated under an alliance after the fall of Chichen Itza. But, in time, the Xiu apparently lost their leading role at Mayapan. By about 1300, the Cocom gained complete control, supported by their Canul mercenaries. Sometime around 1400, a major contingent of the Xiu was expelled from the city. But, after their ouster, the Xiu plotted their revenge.

The Fall of Mayapan and the Rise of Petty States

Mayapan's dominance in Yucatan ended in violence shortly before the Spanish Conquest when, in 1441, the expelled Xiu took their revenge. Aj Xupan Xiu led a successful revolt against the Cocom, and all members of the Cocom house in Mayapan were killed, except one who was away on a trading mission. Mayapan was sacked and abandoned, an event verified by archaeology. Excavations at the site have revealed evidence of burned buildings, looted ceremonial deposits, and the bones of individuals who may have been killed during the revolt.

After the destruction of Mayapan, most of the larger northern cities declined, and many were abandoned. The prominent elite houses of Mayapan dispersed to found new cities. The Chels established their principal settlement at Tecoh. The only surviving son of the slain Cocom ruler gathered the remnants of his people and established his rule at Tibolon. The victors, the Xiu, founded a new capital, called Mani. With these events, Yucatan fragmented into at least 18 petty kingdoms.

Yet the Cocom waited for an opportunity for revenge, which came a century later during the wars of the Spanish Conquest (discussed later in this chapter). In 1536, the Xiu ruler and his court planned to make a pilgrimage to offer sacrifices at Chichen Itza's Cenote of Sacrifice. By this time, the newly arrived Spaniards had withdrawn from Yucatan to prepare for a renewed invasion. Aj Tzun Xiu, ruler of the Xiu at Mani, saw this as an auspicious time for a pilgrimage to make offerings for success to the Maya gods. He asked and received assurance of safe conduct from Nachi Cocom, the ruler of Sotuta, to pass through their province to reach Chichen Itza. Permission was needed since the Xiu ruler feared reprisals by Nachi Cocom because his great-grandfather, Aj Xupan Xiu, had slain Nachi Cocom's great-grandfather during the sacking of Mayapan.

Indeed, Nachi Cocom had not forgotten the murder of his great-grandfather, so he welcomed the Xiu request as a long-awaited chance for revenge. Unaware of this and reassured by the promise of safe passage, Aj Tzun Xiu, his son Aj Ziyah Xiu, and 40 other Xiu leaders set out for Chichen Itza. Nachi Cocom and a large delegation met them near the Cocom capital. The Xiu pilgrims were royally entertained for four days, but, at a banquet on the evening of the fourth day, the Cocom suddenly turned on their guests and slaughtered them all. This act of treachery pitted the two most powerful kingdoms in Yucatan against each other and prevented a united stand against the Spaniards, who resumed their conquest of Yucatan a few years later.

The East coast of Yucatan was the setting for a series of small independent states that prospered up to the time of the Conquest. Shrines built during this period have been identified at Coba and several other Classic era sites, indicating that these earlier centers were reoccupied during the final centuries of the Postclassic era. The southernmost was Chetumal. Its capital was recorded by the Spanish in the sixteenth century as being a large and prosperous city. The best-preserved Postclassic architectural remains in the northern lowlands are at the walled city of Tulum, overlooking the sea on the east coast of Yucatan. Other ports of trade are off the east coast on the Isla de Mujeres and Isla de Cozumel.

Cozumel

Cozumel was a major port of trade for the sea routes passing around the Yucatan Peninsula. Archaeological research documents the growth of its Postclassic populations and commerce. The island was administered from its capital, San Gervasio, well connected to several ports and storage areas by a road network. Cozumel's elite rulers were far less concerned with using their subjects to construct great temples and palaces like those from the Maya past. Instead, their labor was used to build port facilities, roads, and large platforms to support warehouses. Prosperity from the new mercantile economy had diminished the distinctions between elite and nonelite classes, and the standard of living for Cozumel's population had increased as a result. Goods once largely reserved for elite use were now widely distributed throughout Postclassic society. Status was still marked in familiar ways, such as in elaborate residences. But, to save labor and material costs, Postclassic houses on Cozumel (and on the mainland) were built with front walls of well-plastered stone that looked like an imposing masonry house. But behind this false front, the remainder of the house was constructed of low-cost pole and thatch.

Tulum

The small port city of Tulum is situated just south of Cozumel along Yucatan's eastern coast. Although the city is much smaller than Mayapan, its location gave it direct access to the Caribbean and seacoast trade. Dramatically situated on sea cliffs, its small Postclassic buildings retain much of their original plastered and painted surfaces. Investigations reveal that Tulum was occupied in the Late Postclassic, beginning about 1200. Its principal structures show parallels with Chichen Itza and the later buildings of Mayapan, except that Tulum's architecture was executed on a much smaller scale. One motivation for its founding was likely a wish to establish a trading center on Yucatan's east coast, probably by a Chontal Maya group in alliance with the rulers of Mayapan.

The city's eastern or seaward side is protected by sea cliffs averaging some 12 meters high. It is defended on its landward sides by a masonry wall once equipped with a walkway, parapet, and corner watch towers, averaging some 6 meters thick and 3–5 meters high. The wall is broken by five narrow gateways, one on the west side and two each on the north and south. The city covers a rectangular area of about 0.6 square kilometers enclosed by the wall. Its most conspicuous feature is a series of masonry platforms and buildings, including colonnaded palaces and elevated temples. Water was provided by a small cenote near the northern wall.

Tulum's masonry is roughly fashioned and covered with thick plaster, like that of Mayapan and other Postclassic sites. A low masonry inner wall defines the central precinct. Its principal building, the Castillo, supports a small vaulted two-room temple with two feathered-serpent columns, similar to those at Chichen Itza. The largest palace-type buildings have colonnades in the style of Chichen Itza and Mayapan. As its name implies, the Temple of the Frescoes contains murals. These are rendered in a non-Maya

Figure 7.2 Tulum, Mexico: Buildings and defensive wall in the distance; this small city was still occupied at the time the first Spaniards arrived in the sixteenth century (Postclassic).

style dated to about 1450 or later. The temple's façade is decorated with stucco reliefs, including niched figures of the "diving god," identified as *Xux Ek'*, the Maya "wasp star," or Venus deity.

North of the Castillo, there is a gap in the sea cliff that forms a cove and landing beach suitable for Maya trading canoes. A break in the barrier reef lies offshore from the site, and canoes seeking to make port at Tulum could have used this for safe passage to the landing beach. Tulum remains a landmark to mariners along the east coast. Occupied until Conquest times, it was probably the Maya city sighted by Juan de Grijalva during his reconnaissance of the coast in 1518 and compared to Seville in an account from an earlier Spanish voyage.

Chaktemal

To the south on the border between Mexico and Belize lay the Postclassic realm of Chaktemal, now known as Chetumal. Spanish accounts in the sixteenth century describe its large and prosperous capital city. Chaktemal was one of the most important ports on the Caribbean coast, well situated where the New River flows into Chetumal Bay. Over time, this large bay was the location of a succession of ports, beginning with Cerros in the Late Preclassic (chapter 4). In the Classic period, the port of Lamanai became a major transshipment center for trade up and down the New River. Lamanai has one of the longest spans of occupation of any Maya city. It escaped the decline and abandonment of most of its lowland neighbors at the end of the Classic period, for its prime location supported commercial activity continuously from the Preclassic through the Postclassic era. Archaeological excavations at Lamanai have revealed Postclassic pottery, incense burners, and objects of both gold and copper from its trade connections with Yucatan, Central Mexico, and Central America.

In the final centuries of the Postclassic period, the port of Chaktemal became a major transshipment center for inland and sea-borne commerce. Salt, textiles, and other products from Yucatan arrived by large seagoing canoes and were unloaded for transport inland by smaller river canoes and then by porters overland to the Gulf coast and the Maya highlands. Feathers, copper, and other products from inland sources were loaded on seagoing canoes at Chaktemal for shipment north to Yucatan or south to Central America. It was also a major port for exporting cacao, since the Chaktemal polity was an important cacao-growing area. A channel was cut through the peninsula that separates Chetumal Bay from the Caribbean to shorten the passage to and from Chaktemal land other sites around the bay.

Santa Rita Corozal was another important site within the Chaktemal (Chetumal) polity. Heavily disturbed by present-day occupation, most of its archaeological remains are poorly preserved. But investigations have documented a long occupation span. Santa Rita grew rapidly during the last few centuries before to the Spanish Conquest. Commercial ties with Yucatan are indicated by effigy incensarios and pottery related to that of Mayapan found at Santa Rita and other east coast sites. In the early twentieth century, a Postclassic mural was excavated at Santa Rita that is closely related to the murals at Tulum. Postclassic murals at ports along the Caribbean coast reflect their economic prosperity. Most were the work of skilled foreign artists commissioned by wealthy local elites.

Ambergris Caye, the largest of the Belize cayes, bounds Chetumal Bay to the east. Investigations on Ambergris have revealed a sequence of occupation associated with trading activity beginning in the Late Preclassic era. In the Late Classic, a series of ports was situated along the protected western shore of Ambergris Caye. Each port was adjacent to a natural or constructed harbor and controlled a share of the commerce to and from Lamanai and other mainland centers. Obsidian was a major commodity, transported from the Maya highlands down the Motagua Valley and up the Belize coast by seagoing canoes.

The Classic period pattern of many competing coastal trade centers like those documented on Ambergris Caye changed in the Terminal Classic, when the Chontal and other Maya merchant elites consolidated seaborne commerce. A more efficient system took over, based on having fewer and larger ports, spaced about 40 kilometers apart, corresponding to a day's journey by large oceangoing canoe. On Ambergris Caye, the earlier series of ports was replaced by a single transshipment center, which maintained commercial links with Lamanai and the New River trade during the Postclassic period.

REVIVAL OF STATES IN THE PETÉN LAKES REGION

The expanded Postclassic economy documented at ports along the east coast of Yucatan fostered a revival of prosperity in the southern Maya lowlands and east into Belize. Some settlements, like Lamanai, located on the rivers and lakes of this region, remained occupied even after the abandonment of the Classic cities. This continued occupation was sustained by strategic locations on overland and river trade routes and by enduring markets for local forest products like cacao, copal, feathers, and pelts. Spanish records indicate the populations in the Petén lakes region spoke Yucatec Mayan in the sixteenth and seventeenth centuries.

This region was subdivided into at least three Maya polities. The best known was the Kan Ek' polity south and west of Lake Peten Itza. Its capital, Tayasal, was on *Noj Peten* ("large island") in the south arm of the lake, now occupied by the town of Flores, capital of the Guatemalan Department of the Petén. The rulers at Noj Peten held the title Aj Kan Ek' and claimed to be descendants of Itza Maya who migrated into the Petén after the fall of Chichen Itza. Archaeology at Flores and along the lakeshore has revealed evidence of substantial Postclassic occupation linked to Yucatan and the

Caribbean coast. The use of Postclassic effigy incense burners reflects connections between the people of the Kan Ek' kingdom and Mayapan's religious cults and trade network.

The Kan Ek' polity competed with at least two other petty states in the Petén. The Kowoj polity was north of Lake Peten Itza and had twin capitals. The Kowoj reportedly arrived from Mayapan after its fall. The Yalain polity ruled the eastern lake region—an area probably controlled by Tikal in Late Classic times. Archaeology indicates that Yalain retained an identity distinctive from that of the rest of the lakes region up to the Spanish Conquest. Further east, the ruins of Topoxte, apparently unknown to the Spaniards, may represent another Postclassic polity capital.

Topoxte is on an island in Lake Yaxha, opposite the large Classic period city of Yaxha, on its shores. Archaeology shows that it was an important Postclassic city with close ties to Mayapan and an important link in the north-south trade routes into Yucatan. Postclassic occupation at Topoxte began around 1100 with the construction of temples and colonnaded buildings similar to structures at Mayapan. Plain stelae—probably once covered by plaster and painted—reflect a revival of K'atun ending celebrations like those at Mayapan. Topoxte's pottery is also linked to Mayapan, and both cities were abandoned about the same time (ca. 1450).

The kingdoms of the central Petén remained independent for nearly 200 years after Spain had subjugated both Yucatan and the Maya highlands. Although the Spaniards knew about Tayasal, the Petén region was surrounded by dense rain forest, which put it beyond the reach of Spanish colonial authorities until the end of the seventeenth century. Finally the Spaniards raised an army to invade the Petén, and, in 1607, after a dramatic naval battle on Lake Peten Itza, Tayasal was captured and destroyed. Following this defeat, the surviving Maya populations were forced to abandon the Lake Peten region and were resettled closer to the coast in areas controlled by the Spanish crown.

NEW MASTERS IN THE SOUTHERN MAYA AREA

Among the Maya chronicles recording the history of the Postclassic highlands, the most famous is a book written in K'iche Mayan, the *Popol Vuh* (with English translations by Christenson 2003; Tedlock 1985). From sources such as this we can trace a history of Postclassic peoples in the southern Maya area that was similar to that of Yucatan. Outsiders invaded several southern areas, including Pipil migrants from central Mexico who resettled on the Pacific coast (chapter 6), and Chontal Maya groups from the Gulf Coast lowlands who brought non-Maya cultural elements into the highlands. Recorded names of some Postclassic highland ruling families reflect "Mexicanized-Maya" origins, such as *K'umatz* ("serpent") and *Xiuj Toltecat* ("Toltec Xiu"). These names suggest Chontal Maya connections or even links to the Itza kingdoms in Yucatan.

Increasing competition and warfare in the Postclassic era caused a dramatic shift in settlement location throughout the highlands. The highland chronicles tell of conquests led by invading warrior elites. Indeed, earlier open-valley sites were abandoned in favor of settlements in well-defended locations, such as hilltops or promontories surrounded by steep-sided ravines, often reinforced by ditch-and-wall fortifications. These Postclassic highland sites often provide evidence of connections to lowland Chontal or Itza Maya areas, including references to the K'uk'ulkan religious cult, including sculptures of open-mouthed, feathered-serpent heads. There are also specific examples of architecture, murals, and sculpture comparable to examples at both Chichen Itza and Mayapan.

Postclassic sites have been identified along the natural routes into the highlands via both the Motagua and upper Usumacinta drainages. The Usumacinta River was a direct route from the Chontal homeland in the Gulf coast lowlands, and the Motagua Valley provided a route from the Caribbean coast to the east, where coastal trading outposts had been established during the Terminal Classic. It was during this era that invading warrior groups began moving into the highlands. The *Popol Vuh* describes how one of these groups, the ancestors of the K'iche Maya, first occupied mountain strongholds from which they conducted raids and subjugated the local populace. As time passed, these initial bases became capitals of new kingdoms forged by warfare and alliances. Although they maintained their elite status as the new masters of the land, later generations of the Chontal Mayan-speaking warrior elites gradually adopted the local Mayan languages of the original inhabitants, including the Mayan languages now known as K'iche and Kaqchikel.

The K'iche and Kaqchikel Highland States

By the Postclassic period, these invading Maya groups had established a series of kingdoms in the Maya highlands, many of which were described by the Spaniards during their conquest in the early sixteenth century. These highland kingdoms included the Pokomam Maya, with their capital at Jilotepeque Viejo; the Tz'utujil Maya, with their capital at Atitlan on the famous lake of the same name; the K'iche Maya, with their capital at Utatlan; and the Kaqchikel Maya, with their capital at Iximche. From their bastions, the capitals of each of these kingdoms competed for control over the people, products, and commerce within the highlands. Warfare was used to settle disputes, and two of the most successful of these highland kingdoms, the K'iche and the Kaqchikel, expanded as far as the Pacific coastal plain to control trade routes, cacao production, and other resources.

The *Popol Vuh* gives the most complete history of the development of the K'iche Maya kingdom. According to this account the ancestral K'iche warriors, led by Balam Quitze, came into the highland region shortly about 1200. There they began to forge their kingdom from a stronghold known as Jakawitz. A century later, three K'iche elite leaders traveled to the east to gain the proper symbols of authority to rule over their expanded domain. This direction may have taken them to Copan, which by then was abandoned but still a sacred and powerful place that represented the past glories of the Maya ancestors. It is more likely that they journeyed to the pilgrimage site of Chichen Itza or to Mayapan, both of which were reached by traveling east via the Motagua Valley, then north following the Caribbean coastal canoe route. In any case, the proper symbols of authority were secured, and the three princes returned to their highland kingdom. After this journey, one of the leaders, C'ocaib, assumed the title of Ajpop ("he of the mat"), the highest political office in the K'iche kingdom.

About 1350, the K'iche consolidated their kingdom and, led by Ajpop Conache, founded a new capital, Ismachi. During the reign of his successor, Ajpop Cotuja, an unsuccessful revolt led to a further expansion of the kingdom. Early in the fifteenth century, during the reign of Ajpop K'u'k'umatz ("feathered serpent"), a new and well-defended capital was founded at Q'umarkaj ("place of the rotten reeds") or Utatlan, as it is now known. Utatlan was situated on a defensible plateau surrounded by ravines. K'u'k'umatz extended the power of the K'iche to the north and west and was glorified in the *Popol Vuh:* "All the other lords were fearful before him...when Lord Plumed Serpent [K'u'k'umatz] made the signs of

Figure 7.3 Utatlan, Guatemala: View of one of the temples at the highland K'iche Maya capital of Utatlan, a target of the invading Spaniards in the sixteenth century (Postclassic).

greatness. His face was not forgotten by his grandsons and sons" (Tedlock 1985: 213).

The K'iche kingdom was further expanded by K'iq'ab, his successor. But, around 1470, during the reign of Vahxaqui-Caam, the Kaqchikel Maya—who had been subjects and allies of the K'iche—revolted and established an independent kingdom southeast of Utatlan. The Kaqchikel founded a new fortified capital, Iximche, from which they began a new cycle of conquests. The K'iche made several attempts to subdue the Kaqchikel but were unsuccessful. One highland document, *Annals of the Kaqchikels*, records how the Kaqchikel forces annihilated an attacking army from Utatlan. Thousands of K'iche warriors were killed, while their leaders were captured and sacrificed. The Kaqchikel were still expanding their kingdom in the early sixteenth century, when the Spaniards arrived.

THE SPANISH CONQUEST

The first reported contact between Europeans and the Maya occurred during Columbus's final voyage of 1502, when he discovered a Maya oceangoing trading canoe in the Gulf of Honduras. After Spanish colonies were established in the Caribbean, several voyages of exploration sent from Cuba discovered Maya settlements along the Yucatan coast. Some contacts were peaceful; most produced attacks. They also transmitted European diseases: "11 Ajaw was when the mighty men arrived from the east. They were the ones who first brought disease here to our land, the land of us who are Maya, in the year 1513" (*Book of Chilam Balam of Chumayel* [Roys 1967: 138]).

In 1511, the Maya on the east coast of Yucatan captured several shipwrecked Spaniards. One of these men, Gonzalo de Guerrero, was adopted by Nachan Kan, ruler of Chaktemal, and married his daughter. Eight years later, when offered rescue by the Spaniards, Guerrero declined, and he spent the rest of his life with his Maya family.

In 1518, an expedition returned to Cuba from the Gulf coast with gold and reports of the Mexica (Aztec) empire in central Mexico. A new expedition, commanded by Hernán Cortés, was fitted out to explore this new land of Mexico. Its official goals were to convert the natives to Christianity and to establish Spanish sovereignty, but the expedition's members joined for a share of the gold and other booty that armed conquest would provide. Two captains who went with Cortés, Pedro de Alvarado and Francisco de Montejo, would later lead conquests in the Maya area.

After stops on the Isla de Cozumel and in Tabasco, Cortés landed in Veracruz on the Gulf coast and, after a brutal struggle that lasted several years, ultimately conquered the Mexica. After the fall of Tenochtitlan, the Mexica capital, Cortés sent one of his captains, Cristóbal de Olid, to subdue Honduras. Once in Honduras, Olid rebelled. When news of this defection reached Cortés, he set out on a six-month march overland to

Honduras to punish Olid. As a result, Cortés and his army were the first Europeans to pass through the southern Maya lowlands.

Cortés took an army of about 140 Spanish soldiers and more than 3,000 native warriors from Mexico, with horses, artillery, munitions, and supplies. They entered the Maya area in what is now central Tabasco and crossed the Río Usumacinta. After this, they came to Lake Peten Itza, where Kan Ek', the Itza ruler of Tayasal, met Cortés on the north shore of the lake. Cortés had his Catholic priests celebrate mass, after which Kan Ek' promised to destroy his idols and replace them with the Cross. At his invitation, Cortés visited Tayasal with 20 Spanish soldiers. Leaving Tayasal, the army entered the rugged Maya Mountains. After many more days of struggling through the forest, the army became lost the hills north of Lago de Izabal. The Indian guides deserted the Spaniards, but a Maya boy who led them to safety saved them from starvation. On his march across the Maya lowlands, Cortés visited one important Maya capital, Tayasal, and passed within a few miles of several ruined Classic cities.

Firearms and cavalry facilitated the Spanish conquest of the Maya. But the Spaniards could not have succeeded without the assistance of far larger Mexican and Maya armies who joined their cause. In both the Maya highlands and Yucatan, native forces joined the Spaniards to settle long-standing rivalries among the independent states in both regions. Yet the most overwhelming factor for Spanish success was biological. European diseases against which the Maya had no immunity produced epidemics that decimated Maya armies and their entire population long before the battle lines were drawn.

Conquest of the Southern Maya, 1524–1527

In 1522, Cortés sent some of his Mexican allies to reconnoiter the borders of the southern Maya area. On the Pacific coast of what is now Chiapas, the patrol met delegations from the Kaqchikel capital of Iximche and from the K'iche capital of Utatlan. Cortés later reported that both delegations declared their vassalage to the King of Spain. But, according to his account, he heard later that the Kaqchikel and K'iche had broken their pledges. So he sent Pedro de Alvarado to investigate the matter, accompanied by 120 cavalry (with 50 spare horses), 300 infantry, a large number of Mexican warriors, and four artillery pieces.

Alvarado was infamous for his cruelty and his inhuman treatment of his foes. While temporarily commanding the Spanish army in Tenochtitlan, he led a brutal massacre of unarmed Mexica dancers. His later conquest of Guatemala was punctuated by many reports of similar events. According to Bartolomé de Las Casas, Alvarado's Maya conquests were accomplished by killing, ravaging, burning, robbing, and destroying everything in his path. Alvarado's own letters report the terror tactics he employed against defenseless Maya populations.

In late 1523, Alvarado's left Mexico, following the ancient trade route along the Pacific coast. No opposition appeared until the Spanish reached a K'iche coastal province in what is now western Guatemala. A native force tried and failed to block the Spaniard's progress. The invaders then rampaged through the nearby settlements, hoping to strike terror into the K'iche who still resisted.

The Spaniards then turned north to attack the heartland of the highland K'iche state. In a mountain pass, Alvarado's contingent of Mexican warriors was driven back by the K'iche, but a charge by the Spanish cavalry brought about a victory, since the K'iche warriors had never seen horses before. Alvarado's force then entered the deserted city of Xelahu, called Quezaltenango by Alvarado's Mexican allies (many place names in Guatemala now bear Nahuatl names, because the Mexicans, Nahuatl speakers, served as interpreters for the Spaniards).

Six days later, a climactic battle was fought in the valley of Quezaltenango, as the K'iche made a desperate attempt to stop the invaders. One of the K'iche commanders was Tecun Uman, a hero of his people. But Tecun Uman and many other Maya leaders were killed in the battle, and the K'iche resistance was spent. The K'iche asked for peace, offering tribute, and invited Alvarado to enter their capital, Q'umarkaj, known as Tecpan Utatlan in Nahuatl. The ever-suspicious Alvarado sensed a trap. So, when the Spanish came to Utatlan, he arranged for gifts of friendship to be given to his hosts. While the K'iche were distracted by the gift-giving ceremony, Alvarado ordered the capture of the ruler of Utatlan, the Ajpop Oxib-Queh, and his heir, the *Ajpop c'amha*, Beleheb-Tzy. As reported in his account to the king of Spain, Alvarado then had both men burned at the stake to ensure goodness and peace.

With Utatlan destroyed and its rulers dead, Alvarado sent a delegation to the Kaqchikel at their capital, Iximche (or *Tecpan Quauhtemalan*, "City of Guatemala"), asking them to join him in the final defeat of the K'iche. At the time, the Kaqchikel were the paramount power in the highlands and the traditional enemy of the K'iche, so they sent a force of warriors and joined the Spanish against the K'iche.

His new Maya allies welcomed Alvarado into Iximche. The Kaqchikel thought that they could use their new alliance to vanquish not only the K'iche but other enemies, as well. Indeed, the Spaniards and their Kaqchikel Maya allies attacked the neighboring Tz'utujil, who then offered tribute and allegiance to the King of Spain.

From the highlands, Alvarado launched an expedition to the Pacific coast and east to conquer the Pipil province of Cuscatlan, in what is now El Salvador. Upon his return to the Maya highlands at Iximche, on July 25, 1524, he founded the first Spanish capital of the province of Guatemala. But the new capital was short-lived, for the Spanish provoked revolt from their Maya allies. After demanding gold and not receiving enough to satisfy his demands, Alvarado threatened to burn the Kaqchikel leaders as he had done with the K'iche.

Figure 7.4 Iximche, Guatemala: Temple and palace platforms at the Kaqchikel Maya capital; during the Spanish Conquest, this Maya city became the first colonial capital of Guatemala (Postclassic).

In response, the Kaqchikel attacked and drove the Spaniards from their new capital. For the next several years, the highland Maya, led by the Kaqchikel, fought a desperate campaign to drive the Spanish out of their lands. But, in the end, the Maya were defeated. On November 22, 1527, a new Spanish capital, known today as Ciudad Vieja, was founded at the foot of Agua volcano. Fourteen years later, it was devastated by a mudslide from the volcano, and the colonial capital was reestablished nearby in the city known as Antigua Guatemala. With the highlands more or less subdued, the Spaniards could turn their attention to the Maya of the north.

Conquest of Yucatan, 1527–1546

A royal decree of December 8, 1526, authorized Francisco de Montejo to raise an army for the conquest and colonization of Yucatan. Montejo outfitted an armada of three ships and 400 men and landed on the Isla de Cozumel in late September 1527. Aj Naum Pat, ruler of Cozumel, received them peaceably. Montejo then sailed for the mainland, where he took possession of the land in the name of God and the King of Spain.

The first Spanish settlement was established at Xelha, near Tulum. After leaving 40 men at this base under the command of Alonso d'Avila and another 20 in a nearby town, Montejo set out with 125 men to subdue the towns and villages of northeastern Yucatan. During the march, the chiefs of the towns were called together to swear allegiance to the Spanish crown. However, in the spring of 1528, the Maya attacked the Spaniards. Another battle was fought at Ake, 16 kilometers north of the modern town of Tizimin, in which more than 1,200 Maya were killed. Following this battle, all the neighboring Maya chiefs surrendered. From Ake, Montejo returned to Xelha, where he found only 12 survivors of the 40 Spaniards left there; all 20 of those stationed nearby had been wiped out. By this time the entire Spanish force numbered fewer than a hundred men. So Montejo retreated to New Spain (Mexico), ending the first attempt to conquer Yucatan.

In 1531, Montejo returned to his campaign in Yucatan, taking with him his son, also named Francisco de Montejo. This time, they made their base in Campeche, on the west coast. Soon thereafter, they were attacked, and the elder Montejo was nearly killed. However, the Spaniards prevailed, and their Maya attackers surrendered. Montejo's son marched a force to the province of the Cupules and, at the former Itza capital of Chichen Itza, founded a new Ciudad Real ("royal city").

The Cupules soon became dissatisfied with Spanish rule, and, after six months, their ruler, Naabon Cupul, tried to kill Montejo. Although he failed and was killed, this only increased the hatred for the Spaniards by the Cupul Maya. By mid-1533, they lay siege to the Spanish garrison at Chichen Itza, and the younger Montejo was forced to abandon his Ciudad Real and retreat to his father's base in Campeche.

At this point the Spaniards had been fighting in northern Yucatan for seven years, and had only found enough gold to fill a few helmets. They now realized that there would be no riches like those found by the soldiers of Cortés in Mexico, or by Pizarro in Peru. So, the Montejo's abandoned the conquest of Yucatan for a second time.

In 1540, Montejo the elder turned the task of conquering the northern Maya over to his son. Early in 1541, Montejo the younger established a new headquarters in Campeche, which became the first permanent Spanish *cabildo*, or town government, established in Yucatan. His army again numbered between 300 and 400 soldier-colonists. By this time, resistance to the Spaniards was at low ebb. Not only were the Maya deeply divided following the Cocom's revenge-motivated slaughter of the Xiu in 1536, described previously; they were also decimated by disease.

Montejo summoned the Maya lords to Campeche to submit to the Spanish crown. The Xiu ruler and a number of neighboring leaders obeyed the summons, but the Canul polity refused. In response, Montejo dispatched his cousin to subdue the Canules. His cousin succeeded, and, near the ruins of the Maya city of T'ho, on January 6, 1542, "The Very Noble and Very Loyal City of Mérida" was founded as the second Spanish *cabildo* in Yucatan.

Seventeen days after the founding of Mérida, Montejo's sentries sighted a throng of warriors escorting a young Maya lord seated in a palanquin. The Spaniards feared an immediate attack, but the lord had come in peace, bringing with him food for a feast. He was the lord Tutul Xiu, supreme ruler of Mani, who expressed his admiration for the bravery of the Spaniards. He also wanted to see their religious ceremonies, so Montejo ordered the army chaplain to celebrate a solemn Adoration of the Holy Cross, in which all the Spanish soldiers took part. The Xiu ruler was deeply impressed and said that he wished to become a Christian. He stayed at the Spanish camp for two months, during which time he was instructed in the Catholic faith and baptized Melchor.

The results of this visit were far-reaching. Since the fall of Mayapan a century earlier, the Xiu polity of Mani had been the most powerful state in northern Yucatan, and the other western polities followed its peaceful submission to the Spaniards. Don Melchor Xiu sent ambassadors to the other Maya lords, urging them to submit to Montejo, and western Yucatan was conquered and pacified without further fighting.

However, eastern Yucatan remained unconquered. After a brief but bitter campaign the Spaniards defeated one Maya force. But, soon afterward, most of the eastern polities rebelled after massacring 18 Spaniards and more than 400 Maya allies. Both Montejos were called to action, and, after raising a new army, in 1546 they defeated the coalition of eastern Maya lords in a single battle. With this victory, the conquest of Yucatan was completed.

More than 150 years would pass before the Spaniards conquered Tayasal, the last independent stronghold of the Maya. Overall, the subjugation of the Maya was a long and brutal process, accomplished by campaigns that ultimately succeeded in destroying the last remnants of Maya independence and Postclassic Maya civilization. In succeeding, of course, the conquest of the Maya also marked the beginning of a long period of suppression by Europeans that has shaped much of the world of the Maya people today.

OVERVIEW OF LATE MAYA CIVILIZATION

Late Maya civilization emerged in the Postclassic era from the failures and decline of Middle Maya civilization. New polities succeeded by reformulating the socioeconomic, political, and ideological foundations of Maya states, while looking to the past for inspiration and ways to reinforce their authority. Their immediate inspiration was the Terminal Classic city of Chichen Itza. The most cosmopolitan of all Maya cities, Chichen Itza reached beyond the Maya area to secure resources and ideas from throughout Mesoamerica. These foreign connections increased during the Postclassic era and continued to bring the Maya new products and ideas that produced further changes.

After Chichen Itza fell, a new northern lowland capital was founded at Mayapan, which revived Chichen Itza's economic, political, military, and religious institutions. Mayapan dominated Yucatan during the Postclassic era until just before the Spanish Conquest. With its downfall, the northern lowlands fragmented into a series of independent rival states that failed to unite against the European invaders.

Postclassic Maya states were sustained by an economy based on seaborne commerce that provided more efficient and widespread distribution of everyday products. These new trade routes tied together the diverse regions of the Maya area and Mesoamerica, promoting widespread growth and prosperity that transformed Maya society. The "middle class" expanded along with the mercantile economy. The prosperity of the new economy also decreased the distinctions separating the elite class from the rest of Maya society.

The Postclassic political system consolidated its control over economic, military, and religious institutions. The heart of the governing system at Mayapan and other Postclassic capitals was a collective sharing of power among elite ruling lords. Decision making and responsibility were shared, rather than concentrated in a single individual, although one lord was usually identified as paramount among the ruling council.

A new state-sponsored transcendental religious cult based on the cult of K'uk'ulkan reinforced the new mercantile economy. By its widespread adoption throughout Mesoamerica, this cult encouraged commercial interaction and communication. Yet, the new religion was less centralized and more focused on family-based ritual and pilgrimages than its predecessors. It required fewer and smaller temples, thereby lessening the huge expenditures for temple constructions found in earlier times.

Postclassic populations increased along the coasts of the Maya lowlands and in many areas of the highlands. Revived inland trade routes restored the fortunes of the Petén lakes region of the old Classic heartland. This supported the rise of several small states that claimed to have their origins in Chichen Itza or its successor, Mayapan. By their isolation, these revived Postclassic realms remained independent from Spanish control far longer than Maya states in Yucatan or in the southern area.

Maya states in the southern highlands followed a similar course and often traced real or fictive origins back to the Gulf coast Chontal Maya or to the Itza of Yucatan. The aggressive K'iche Maya state grew rapidly by conquest and political consolidation. In the fifteenth century, the K'iche and their chief competitors, the rapidly rising Kaqchikel state, fought for supremacy in the highlands. But the Spanish Conquest cut short their independent careers, as it did those of the petty states of Postclassic Yucatan.

FURTHER READING

Alvarado 1924; Andrews, Andrews, and Robles 2003; Chamberlain 1948; Chase and Rice 1985; Demarest 2004; Christenson 2003; Edmunson 1982, 1986; Fox 1978; Freidel and Sabloff 1984; Grube 2001; Innes 1969; Jones 1998; Las Casas 1957; Milbrath and Peraza 2003; Recinos and Goetz 1953; Roys 1967; Sabloff 1994; Sabloff and Andrews 1986; Sharer and Traxler 2006; Tedlock 1985; Tozzer 1941.

8

MAYA ECONOMY

The daily lives of ancient Maya people were taken up with economic activities that provided the resources for the development of Maya civilization, including food, raw materials, labor, and manufactured goods. Our information about this ancient economy comes from archaeology and ethnohistory, plus a few references to market and tribute goods recorded on pottery and murals.

The elite class controlled some aspects of the ancient Maya economy, while others were fully in the hands of the silent majority—Maya commoners. For thousands of years, the basis of the Maya economy rested on the productive capabilities of individual Maya households and communities. The daily round of activities by each member of the Maya household provided most of the family's needs—labor for the construction of houses and food from hunting, gathering, and agriculture. Yet, all households were dependent to some degree on goods from outside producers. The labor needs of local communities were met by pooling the efforts of each household. Maya communities included specialists that made a variety of necessities, such as pottery, basketry, textiles, grinding stones (manos and metates), hunting and fishing equipment, and other tools. What could not be produced locally was usually available from traveling peddlers or local markets, exchanged for locally available raw materials or produce.

Local economies changed over time and varied from one area to another. One of the most important changes was the gradual emergence of a "middle class," composed of people who left the traditional household economy to specialize in the production or distribution of commodities. Some people made mass-produced goods, such as mold-made ceramics and copper axes and bells. Others were merchants who managed trade routes or middlemen who bought and sold goods in markets. Although barter was the oldest means for exchanging goods, in time the economy depended on several monetary systems that facilitated buying and selling throughout the Maya world and beyond. At various times, greenstone beads, cacao beans, and copper bells were used as Maya money, all of which had standardized value and could be exchanged for other goods and services.

The ability to manage critical resources contributed to the growth of social and economic differences, which led to the rise of a ruling elite within Maya society. Ultimately, the power of kings depended on their ability to control resources. Maya rulers managed the production and distribution of status goods used to enhance their prestige and power. They also controlled some critical exotic (nonlocal) commodities that included critical everyday resources each family needed, like salt. Some rulers managed critical water resources, especially in cities, like Tikal, that required reservoirs for rainwater storage. But all Maya kings controlled one of the most important resources in their kingdoms—the labor of their subjects.

Over time, Maya rulers managed larger portions of the economy. By the Classic period, major states such Calakmul and Tikal competed to control the important river and overland trade routes through the lowlands. These states sponsored colonies and established alliances with other polities to extend their control over goods and trade routes. In the Terminal Classic and Postclassic periods, new states such as Chichen Itza and Mayapan controlled the production and distribution of cacao, cotton, salt, and other goods. These states exercised more direct authority over production facilities and ports, as their long-distance seacoast trade routes dominated commerce throughout Mesoamerica. Yet, throughout the history of Maya civilization, large segments of the economy remained in the hands of household producers and a rising "middle class" of merchants who operated outside state control.

LABOR

Control of human labor provided one of the cornerstones of the power exercised by Maya kings. This included labor invested in producing tribute that provided the elite with everyday needs, such as food and clothing, and the manufacture of high-quality status goods. It also included corvée (labor tax) quotas each subject fulfilled to construct palaces, temples, and other public works. Rulers who were successful in war enjoyed increased labor and wealth through the extraction of tribute from defeated enemies. The famous Late Classic murals at Bonampak depict sacks of cacao (chocolate) beans given as tribute to the local ruler by a defeated enemy. The cacao beans are bagged and neatly labeled with the numbers of beans each contains.

Archaeologists can estimate the amount of labor mobilized in the past by excavating the remains of irrigation canals, temples, palaces, and everyday houses. Some building projects were accomplished by volunteer labor—communal efforts undertaken without coercion or direction from a political authority. Like today, commoner houses were built and maintained by the families that used them. Most likely the men of each community working together constructed other buildings in residential communities, such as meeting halls, shrines, or small temples. Such family and communal labor efforts were always a part of Maya society and do not reflect centralized political power. On the other hand, ancient Maya constructions that directly benefited the elite ruling class, such as palaces, major temples, or royal tombs, and those that required effective management because of their size and complexity (like reservoirs and irrigation canals) were usually built and maintained by corvée labor. As such, these efforts reflect centralized management and are indications of the authority of the ruling class in Maya society.

A full range of Classic period household buildings has been excavated at several Maya sites and has been studied to determine the amount of labor each required for construction. These calculations are based on observing the number of workers and days required for modern Maya people to carry out specific construction tasks. In the case of a typical Maya house today, these activities include quarrying and shaping stone for foundations, gathering timber and thatch for walls and roof, transporting all materials to the house site, preparing cement for the floor, and assembling the house. These studies show that ancient commoner residences could have been built relatively rapidly by small numbers of people and were well within the capabilities of family and community groups.

However, the labor requirements rise dramatically for the monumental buildings in ancient Maya cities, implying the use of large amounts of corvée labor. At the site of Copan, excavation data from the Acropolis have been used to make construction labor estimates based on observations of modern workers conducting similar construction tasks, such as acquiring, preparing, and transporting masonry, sand, plaster, and water. These labor calculations have been applied to a succession of buildings constructed during the first century of growth of the Copan Acropolis after the dynastic founding in 426. The results show that more than 175,000 person-days of labor were required to construct the platform and buildings of the new royal complex during its first decade of use (ca. 426–437).

On the basis of population estimates for this period, every adult male in the Copan Valley would have had to devote about one month every year for 10 years to construct this complex. Since this was only one of several construction projects undertaken during this era, the actual requirements for corvée labor must have been even greater, probably two to three months each year. The corvée labor requirements increased during later periods of Acropolis construction. These studies show that one of the basic consequences of Copan's dynastic founding was the institution of centrally controlled monumental construction projects that placed a heavy burden of corvée labor on the shoulders of the subjects of Copan's new rulers.

DAILY LIFE AT CERÉN

An unknown number of ancient Maya communities lived beyond the control of the major capitals of the Classic period. One of these, ruled by a small elite capital now known as San Andrés, was situated in the southeastern borderlands of the Maya area, within a minor polity in the Zapotitan Valley in western El Salvador. Although the ancient name of the community is lost to history, its ruins form the World Heritage site of Cerén. Its excavation by an archaeological project directed by Payson Sheets from the University of Colorado has revealed its amazingly well-preserved remains. As at Pompeii, ash from a sudden volcanic eruption preserved Cerén's buildings, household items, even nearby gardens and fields. But, unlike Pompeii, Cerén was a small rural community, and its 100 or so inhabitants apparently escaped before being buried by the ash fall.

The eruption occurred about 1,400 years ago, in the middle of the Classic period. By carefully excavating the ash layers archaeologists have revealed a wealth of evidence about everyday life in a small Maya community. They have uncovered the remains of houses, fields, and a nearly complete inventory of items made and used by its inhabitants, including agave fiber, manos and metates, painted gourd containers, pottery cooking and serving vessels, and incense burners for household rituals. There were also imported obsidian cutting tools, pigments, and polychrome-painted pottery—all likely acquired from nearby markets.

Who were the ancient inhabitants of Cerén? At the time of the Spanish Conquest, El Salvador was inhabited by several different ethnic groups that spoke different languages, such as Lenca, Pipil, and two Mayan languages, Ch'orti and Pokomam. While there is no direct way to know the identity of the people of Cerén, all the evidence indicates that they were Maya, most likely Ch'orti Mayan speakers. The best indication of this comes from their houses. Lenca families built rectangular houses, which were subdivided inside for various household activities. Like most Maya groups, the Ch'orti Maya constructed separate buildings for these household activities, which is the pattern seen at Cerén. In addition, the religious buildings at Cerén also reflect prevailing Maya customs and beliefs. Thus, the evidence indicates that the people who lived at Cerén 1,400 years ago were culturally Maya and probably spoke Ch'orti Mayan.

Examples drawn from the Cerén evidence will be used in this chapter, along with several that follow, to provide a unique view of daily life in a rural Maya community.

FOOD

The development and growth of all civilizations requires efficient means for producing food. The most important is usually agriculture—the harvesting of domesticated plants and, to a greater or lesser extent, the use of domesticated animals for food (animal husbandry). Food remains recovered by archaeologists at Maya sites typically include maize and other crops, animal and fish bones, shells, and similar traces of both domesticated and wild species. The combination of agriculture, animal husbandry, and hunting and gathering ensured a nutritious diet and was well adapted to the variety of environments found throughout the Maya area.

As populations increase, there is pressure for food production to expand; this process is known as intensification. Agricultural systems, for example, can be intensified by increasing the amount of land being cultivated or by increasing the yield in each unit of land under cultivation. Yields can be increased by developing more productive crops, irrigating, and fertilizing. Although it is likely that the Maya used more means to produce food than can be documented by either archaeology or history, they clearly adopted various methods to intensify food production through time. As their populations grew, they opened new lands to cultivation, built terraces, drained swamps, and irrigated fields. The evidence also suggests that some lowland areas were used for large-scale food production, so the harvests must have been transported to major cities for distribution.

The Ancient Diet

Foods consumed by the Maya in the past were similar to the traditional diet of Maya peoples of today. The major differences come from new domesticated plants and animals introduced after the Spanish Conquest (such as rice, wheat, chickens, and pigs). The core of the Maya diet—past and present—consists of maize, beans, and squashes. Maize is usually dried, removed from the cob, and soaked in water and lime to remove the casing around each kernel. This process also releases amino acids that would otherwise not be utilized when consumed, which boosts the food's nutritional value. The maize is then ground on a metate and mixed with water to form a dough that can be formed into flat tortillas and cooked on a pottery griddle (*comal*) or wrapped in leaves and steamed in a clay pot to make tamales. These vessels are supported over the fire by three stones; traces of three-stone hearths are sometimes found inside the remains of ancient Maya kitchens, which are often separate structures next to a sleeping house. On the basis of present practices, we can assume that food was prepared and cooked by women.

A variety of different kinds of beans are still grown, but among the most favored are the black beans of the Maya highlands. A major source of protein, beans are cooked and served whole or mashed and refried.

In fact, the combination of either tortillas or tamales and beans provides most of the protein essential to human nutrition. A variety of squashes also form part of the traditional diet. Both the flesh of the squash and the seeds (often dried and roasted and used in sauces) are consumed. Several kinds of chiles were used fresh, roasted, or dried as a condiment. A variety of root crops, such as cassava (manioc), were also grown. The diet was further supplemented by fruits that were either domesticated or collected wild from the forest, including avocados, papayas, guavas, and ramón (breadnut).

The major source of animal protein was the domesticated turkey, supplemented by other birds and animals. A rich and spicy turkey soup remains an especially important festive dish among the Maya today. Because the Maya kept only a few domesticated animals besides the dog, most animal protein came from wild animals and birds. A great variety of wild forest animals were hunted or trapped. The most important food animals included deer, rabbits, peccaries, tapirs, agoutis, armadillos, and monkeys (see Table 8.1). These could be roasted or stewed with chiles and other condiments. Rivers, lakes, and the sea were harvested for snails, shellfish, and fish that could be roasted or cooked in soups.

Table 8.1:
Common Wild Animals Used by the Maya

Agouti (*Dasprocta ssp.*)

Armadillo (*Dasypus novemcinctus*)

Brocket deer (*Mazama americana*)

Coatimundi (*Nasua narica*)

Cougar (*Felis concolor*)

Howler monkey (*Alouatta villosa*)

Jaguar (*Felis onca*)

Jaguarundi (*Felis jaguarondi*)

Macaw (*Ara macao*)

Manatee (*Trichechus manatus*)

Ocelot (*Felis pardalis*)

Opossum (*Didelphis marsupialus*)

Paca (*Agouti paca*)

Peccary (*Tayassu tajacu*)

Rabbit (*Sylvilagus brasiliensis*)

Spider monkey (*Ateles geofroyi*)

Tapir (*Tapirus bairdii*)

White-tailed deer (*Odocoileus virginianus*)

The Maya stingless bee was kept in hives, especially in Yucatan, and the honey they produced provided sugar. Cacao (chocolate) was used as a beverage, mixed with water, honey, chiles, or other spices. *Atole* is a beverage made from maize and water; another ceremonial drink is made of ground beans and squash seeds. A potent intoxicating beverage can be made from the bark of the balche tree, along with a variety of fermented drinks made from maize, honey, and fruits.

Honey, cacao, and salt were the most commonly traded dietary items, but almost any food product could be dried and transported. Salt was produced by evaporating sea water or water from salt springs. In Yucatan, extensive saltpans were constructed along the northern coast to harness the sun to evaporate seawater. In the highlands there are several areas with salt springs; there and along the Pacific and Caribbean coasts, the Maya boiled saltwater in large pots to produce salt.

Hunting and Gathering

All pre-Columbian peoples relied in part on wild-food resources. After all, there were far fewer species adaptable for domestication in the Americas than in the Old World. Thus, fishing and hunting provided vital sources of animal protein for Maya families. Hunting was done by bow and arrow, spear, and blowgun, along with traps and snares. The use of snares to trap deer is depicted in an ancient Maya codex. The blowgun was used to hunt birds, monkeys, and other arboreal animals. The most common forest animals used by the Maya are listed in Table 8.1. Not all hunted or trapped animals were eaten; some, especially the carnivores, were used for their pelts, teeth, claws, and other products.

Aquatic species were very important parts of the ancient Maya diet. Fired-clay net weights and carved bone fishhooks are often found at Maya sites. The Maya used dugout canoes, which are depicted on murals and artifacts. Fish and shellfish were a major source of food for people living along the coasts, and dried fish were traded far inland, just as is done today in parts of the Maya area. Freshwater lakes and rivers throughout

Figure 8.1 Canoes were used by the Maya for fishing and transport; this scene, engraved on bone from a Tikal royal tomb, shows Maya deities fishing from a canoe (Late Classic). Courtesy of Tikal Project, University of Pennsylvania Museum.

the highlands and southern lowlands provided a variety of fish and fresh-water mollusks. The importance of both fish and shellfish is indicated by their frequent representations in Maya art.

A variety of useful wild plants are found throughout the Maya area. Today many of these are still collected for food, fibers, medicines, and other uses. Doubtless the same was true in the past, as well. A number of forest trees and plants used by the Maya were also tended and cultivated in household gardens.

Animal Husbandry

Although the Maya did not rely on domesticated animals for food, they did raise several species. The most important was the turkey, although doves and the Muscovy duck may have been raised for food. The Muscovy duck was domesticated in South America but was known to the Maya before the Spanish Conquest. As in many societies, dogs were the most important domestic animal. They were used as household guardians and as hunting companions. Special species of dog may have been fattened and eaten, as was the custom elsewhere in Mesoamerica. The Maya also raised captured wild animals, such as deer, in pens for food. In addition, the drainage canals in raised field systems (discussed later) could have been used to raise fish and mollusks.

Today the Maya keep many different wild animals as pets. The most favored are parrots, monkeys, coatis, and kinkajous. In the sixteenth century, Bishop Diego de Landa wrote that the Maya of Yucatan did likewise: "there is an animal which they call *chic* [coati]; the women raise them and...other domestic animals, and let the deer suck their breasts...and make them so tame that they never will go into the woods" (Tozzer 1941: 204; trans. of Landa's original manuscript of ca. 1566).

Agriculture

The most important means of producing food for the Maya was agriculture. Their most common food plants are listed in Table 8.2. Over time, farmers perfected a variety of cultivation methods: nonintensive systems, in which fields are allowed to lie fallow between periods of cultivation, and intensive systems, in which fields are cultivated continuously.

The most common form of nonintensive agriculture is slash and burn or swiddening. This involves clearing new fields from overgrowth or virgin forest, burning the debris, and planting for several years until the soil is depleted. In areas with better soils, the fallow periods may be from one to three years for each year of cultivation. In areas with poorer soils, the fallow periods may increase to three to six years for each year of cultivation. Large trees and species that provided wild foods or other useful products were probably left to grow with the stands of maize, beans, squashes,

Table 8.2:
Common Domesticated Food Plants Grown by the Maya

Amaranth (*Amaranthus ssp.*)

Avocado (*Persea americana*)

Cacao (*Theobroma cacao*)

Chili (*Capiscum annuum*)

Common bean (*Phaseolus vulgaris*)

Guava (*Psidium guajava*)

Maize (*Zea mays*)

Malanga (*Xanthosoma sp.*)

Manioc (*Manihot esculenta*)

Papaya (*Carica papaya*)

Pineapple (*Ananas comosus*)

Squash (*Cucurbita pepo*)

Sweet potato (*Ipomoea batatas*)

Yucca (*Yucca elephantipes*)

manioc, and other planted species. In most areas, the fields could be planted and harvested for several successive seasons, depending on rainfall and soil fertility. When a field was depleted, it was abandoned to lie fallow and recover its fertility while other areas were cleared for fields.

Swiddening was probably the oldest form of agriculture used by the Maya, for it was undoubtedly used in the first colonization of forested areas. But this method produces low yields while requiring large areas of land and therefore can support only relatively small and scattered populations. As populations increased, fallow periods were shortened and more efficient methods were developed. Fallow periods can be shortened by weeding and intercropping (growing several complementary species together, such as maize and beans). These techniques decrease competition for the food plants, reduce soil depletion, and even replenish nutrients in the soil.

Although Maya farmers today still raise traditional crops, they rely on steel tools, such as machetes and axes. Machetes are used to clear overgrown (fallow) fields with relative ease, and the ax is used to clear new lands of large trees. Because the ancient Maya did not have steel tools, they used sharp blades of flint or obsidian and flint axes. Without steel cutting tools, clearing new forest or second growth in fallow areas requires more energy and time. Thus, once the time and effort had been invested in clearing a new field, Maya farmers probably maintained it by constant weeding to prevent new growth from taking over.

Indirect evidence for the use of swiddening by the Maya comes from the analyses of pollen samples in sediment cores from the beds of several southern lowland lakes. These show that the earliest settlers of that region grew maize. Remnants of ash fallout, possibly from field burning, indicate swiddening.

Archaeologists have found relics of past agricultural use. Remnants of stone terraces have been identified in several areas of the lowlands. These were used to retain soil and water to increase productivity in hilly landscapes. Archaeological excavations in these areas show that these terraces were constructed during Middle Maya civilization. Such agricultural features require a heavy investment of labor, which implies that they may have been used for more intensive forms of agriculture.

The Maya used several other intensive agricultural methods, including continuous field cultivation, household gardens, arboriculture, and hydraulic modifications. Continuous field cultivation involves growing crops with little or no fallow periods so that fields never become overgrown. This requires constant weeding and maintenance. Continuous cultivation could have been used in areas with fertile soils and plentiful rainfall, such as alluvial valleys in parts of the southern and coastal lowlands. Alluvial valleys provide especially fertile soils on natural river levees and bottom lands where periodic flooding replenished fertility by depositing new soils.

There is indirect evidence to indicate that the Maya used continuous cultivation. It is likely that some constructed agricultural features, such as terraces, were used for continuous cultivation. Estimates of peak sizes and densities of Maya populations in the southern lowlands suggest that continuous cultivation was a necessary part of the ancient system. The high potential yields from alluvial soils suggests that continuous cultivation could have transformed these areas into "breadbaskets" supplying large amounts of maize, beans, and other staples to feed the great Maya cities.

Household gardens are a common form of intensive agriculture in Maya communities today. Gardens are cultivated in the open spaces adjacent to each house. These gardens usually provide a great variety of foods from annual root crops, maize, beans, and other field species, as well as perennial shrubs, vines, and trees. Because weeding and other maintenance are minimal and the rate of soil depletion is low, household gardens continuously supply large quantities of foods per unit of land. Intercropping minimizes soil depletion; fertilization comes from plant residues and human and animal wastes from the household.

Gardens and Fields at Cerén

Excavations at Cerén, El Salvador, reveal the remains of both household gardens and maize fields. The cultivated crops were identified from dental plaster casts made from the voids in the volcanic ash left by the original

Figure 8.2 A contemporary Maya household; many families continue to raise maize and other crops in gardens next to their houses.

plants after they decayed. The food crops under cultivation at the time of the eruption at Cerén include maize, cacao, and two root crops, manioc and malanga, along with agave (used for fiber). The products found in household storage provide an additional inventory with achiote (a condiment), common beans, lima beans, cotton, and squash. There is no evidence for irrigation at Cerén, but the length of the rainy season allowed two annual plantings of maize. The eruption appears to have occurred midway through the rainy season (probably in August), shortly after the second planting had sprouted.

One garden was excavated next to a household storage building. It consisted of six rows about a meter apart, with plants spaced about every 75 centimeters. The row closest to the storage building was planted in root crops, manioc and malanga (*Xanthosoma*). The other five rows alternated malanga and cebadilla (*Schoenocaulon officialanis*), a medicinal plant reputed to relieve stomach upsets. Another household garden that was excavated contained more than 70 agave plants and a cacao tree.

A maize field cultivated with a series of ridges and furrows was also excavated. The ridges run roughly north-south, are about 60 centimeters apart, and were used to grow clusters of maize from two to five plants each, spaced about 50 centimeters apart. The recently sprouted maize plants were about 20 to 40 centimeters high at the time of the eruption.

Figure 8.3 Cerén, El Salvador: A sudden volcanic eruption buried and preserved a farming village; including casts of a cane corncrib and the maize ears stored inside (ca. 600). Courtesy of Payson Sheets, El Cerén Archaeological Project.

Nearby was a fallow maize field. Another excavated field contained a matured first planting crop of maize, and the plaster casts reveal that the corn stalks had been bent over to allow the ears to dry, just as is done by Maya farmers today.

The excavated exposures represent only the edges of far more extensive gardens and fields at Cerén. But it is virtually certain from the available evidence that the community produced enough food to be self-sufficient.

There is also indirect evidence for household gardens within ancient Maya cities. Settlement studies show a near-uniform spacing of residences throughout most sites. The spaces between these house remains, not large enough for agricultural fields, are just the right size for household gardens. Tikal and other Maya capitals could be aptly described as green cities, for their buildings and plazas were set amidst an array of productive gardens. Some food trees, such as ramón, cacao, and avocado, may have been also cultivated in extensive groves in low-population areas. Studies of the yields from ramón trees show that they produce 10 times more food per unit of land than maize. Ramón is a starchy food that can be processed and used like maize to make tortillas. Tree crops require little labor, and the fruit or nuts of some species may be collected from the ground as they fall. By mingling different food tree species, the Maya would have discouraged pests or diseases that thrive on a single species.

Both archaeological evidence and ethnohistorical accounts indicate that tree crops were once important to the Maya. Cacao was a highly valued tree crop in lowland environments. In addition to their use as a beverage, cacao beans were used as money in economic exchanges (even counterfeit cacao beans made of clay have been found). Pottery effigies of cacao pods have been found on incense burners at Copan, Quirigua, and other Maya sites, indicating the importance of chocolate productions for these cities.

The Maya used hydraulic modifications to intensify food production. They dug extensive networks of ditches to irrigate crops and to drain excess water from saturated soils, thus allowing better growth. Huge irrigation ditches have been found at Kaminaljuyu in the Valley of Guatemala. Edzna in the northern lowlands has an impressive canal and

Figure 8.4 Pulltrouser Swamp, Belize: One of many swamps and shallow lakes the Maya converted into productive agricultural land by digging drainage canals to form raised fields visible in this aerial photograph. From B. L. Turner and P. D. Harrison, "Prehistoric Ridged-Field Agriculture in the Maya Lowlands." *Science* 213 (4506): 399–405. Copyright 1981, American Association for the Advancement of Science. Reprinted with permission from AAAS.

reservoir system capable of irrigating at least 450 hectares of cultivated land. Both hydraulic systems were constructed during Early Maya civilization (ca. 300–50 B.C.E.) and were probably used for several centuries thereafter.

Even more extensive are the remains of raised fields that were constructed in low-lying areas. These provided fertile and well-drained growing conditions for a variety of crops, including maize, cotton, and cacao. Raised fields are built by digging narrow drainage canals in water-saturated soils and heaping the earth to both sides, forming raised plots for growing crops. By periodically dredging the muck from the drainage channels, the Maya gathered fresh soil and organic debris to replenish the raised plots, allowing continuous cultivation. As already mentioned, these canals also may have been used to raise fish, mollusks, and other aquatic life.

The traces of raised fields have been detected by aerial photography in several areas of the Maya lowlands, and several of these field systems have been excavated. Although additional research is needed to recover more evidence of the kinds of crops grown on raised fields, it is obvious that hydraulic agriculture was a major source of food in the lowlands beginning in Early Maya civilization and became increasingly important during Middle Maya civilization.

PRODUCTION OF GOODS

Archaeology provides evidence for the production of a variety of goods by the ancient Maya, organized on three different scales. We have already described household production, the earliest and most persistent pattern, where each household produced the food and goods to sustain its needs. A second pattern was household specialized production, where the household manufactured a surplus beyond its requirements that was exchanged for other goods to supplement its needs. This kind of production involved part-time specialization usually aimed at manufacturing particular types of tools, pottery, or other goods. But this production activity remained secondary to the central activities of the household, such as subsistence farming, cooking, and childbearing. The third pattern, workshop production, was associated with full-time occupational specialists. As the name implies, this involved distinct manufacturing facilities that were often adjacent to domestic residences. Kin or service personnel provided food and other needs for the full-time specialists engaged in producing goods.

Over time, the Maya increasingly relied on workshop production. Most pottery came from household specialized production, but by the Terminal Classic ceramics were being mass-produced in specialized workshops using pottery molds. At Colha, in Belize, stone tools were made from local chert in two stages, each within its own specialized workshop facility. In a variation of this pattern, by the Late Classic many fine polychrome vessels were formed and fired by nonelite household specialists, then painted by

Figure 8.5 Palace scene on a painted polychrome pottery vessel made in a royal workshop at Tikal, Guatemala; it shows Tikal's twenty-sixth king, Jasaw Chan K'awiil, seated on his throne (Late Classic). Courtesy of Tikal Project, University of Pennsylvania Museum.

highly skilled artisans in specialized workshops adjacent to elite or royal palaces.

Production efficiency was increased by the introduction of new technologies, a reduction in the variety of goods produced, and the use of mass-production techniques. A good example of new production technology is the already mentioned use of molds to form pottery and figurines, introduced during at the end of the Classic period. Mass-production techniques involved separating each manufacturing step to create an assembly line. The production of standardized pottery vessel shapes also facilitated shipment of stacks of vessels, loaded either in canoes or on back racks for overland transport. Another innovation in the Maya highlands was the making of tortilla griddles with a talc slip, imparting a nonstick surface long before modern Teflon was invented.

The Maya produced and traded both utilitarian and nonutilitarian goods (Table 8.3). These can be defined by their use—utilitarian items were used for common household tasks like cooking, while nonutilitarian goods were used for displaying status or prestige. Utilitarian and non-utilitarian goods are also defined by their relative value based on their relative costs for production and distribution and the laws of supply and demand. But, for the ancient Maya, social and ideological factors were also crucial to value. Commodities we would consider utilitarian, such as pottery vessels, were also imbued with ideological meanings. In fact, food storage and serving vessels are often found in Maya ritual contexts such as in tombs and cave burial sites.

The Maya also associated unusual and exotic materials with prestige goods. Jade, for example, had a high value because it was relatively rare, difficult to obtain, and very hard, making it costly to shape and carve. Thus, low supply and high production costs gave it high value. Jade also had social value from its association with the ruling elite class. Most important of all, jade was imbued with ideological meanings, including the belief that its blue-green hue represented the sea upon which the world floated and the sky of the celestial world. Together, all these factors made jade the most highly valued substance known to the ancient Maya.

There were other highly valued prestige goods produced by the Maya, including carved Spondylus shells, feathered headdresses, fine polychrome pottery, mirrors, and, in later times, copper and gold objects. Most prestige goods were manufactured by specialized artisans, who usually worked in palace workshops as clients of Maya kings and other elites. In some cases, these artisans were members of the elite class, as documented by their names and titles found inscribed on individual objects. Excavations at the conquered Classic lowland capital of Aguateca, Guatemala, have revealed the remains of high-status goods preserved inside the remains of burned elite residences. This evidence shows that members of the Maya ruling elite were managing and even creating fine stone, bone, and shell objects, in addition to performing their administrative and ritual duties as part of Aguateca's royal court.

In contrast, utilitarian goods were available in great quantities, had low production and distribution costs, and carried little social or ideological value. There is evidence that some mass-produced utilitarian goods made by full-time specialists may have been controlled to a degree by elite managers. But most everyday items—the containers, tools, and utensils with relatively low value—were produced by commoners in local households and workshops. Nonetheless, studies show that the production of utilitarian goods was well organized and efficiently supplied the needs of the population at large.

Stone Artifacts

A variety of utilitarian and prestige items were made from stone. Chipping was used to shape lowland flint and highland obsidian (volcanic glass) to make sharp cutting and scraping tools for many uses, from

Figure 8.6 An "eccentric flint" scepter from San Andrés, El Salvador, depicting the profile figure of a ruler seated on a throne, probably made in a household specializing in making chipped-stone items (Late Classic). Photograph by Stanley Boggs.

food preparation to ritual bloodletting. The finest examples of chipped stonework were created by expert artisans. These include beautiful ritual objects, sacrificial knives, scepters, and eccentrics—elaborately shaped sacred objects shaped into profile human or deity figures, used as emblems of office, and carried by Maya kings. Highland basalts and other igneous stones were shaped by grinding to make manos and metates, chisels, axes, and bark beaters for softening fibers to make paper used in Maya books.

Jade was the most precious substance for the Maya. It was obtained from outcrops and water worn stones in the streams of the highland Motagua Valley. Because of the stone's hardness, jade working was a specialized skill. Some jade objects are fashioned from unmodified cobbles. Most jade was cut into pieces and used for beads, pendants, plaques, and similar objects. Jade was cut by sawing with tough cords embedded with fine stone abrasives and water and perforated with drills of bone or hardwood and abrasives. After the jade was shaped and drilled by an apprentice, master artisans carved the delicate portraits and other scenes found on the finest examples.

Highly skilled artisans fashioned masks, mirrors, and mosaics from jade, obsidian, pyrite, turquoise, and shell for kings and their elite kin.

Mirrors were sacred symbols of high status worn by rulers and made of fitted pyrite or obsidian mosaics attached to wood or stone backs. Maya kings were often buried with jade mosaic masks fitted over their faces; a spectacular mask of jade, shell, and pyrite was excavated from a royal tomb at Tikal. The finest examples of Maya jade mosaics are two cylindrical vessels from Late Classic royal tombs, each adorned with mosaic portraits of the king.

Stone Carving

The Maya carved in both stone and wood. Obviously, only a few wooden examples have survived, so most of the sculpture we have today is of stone. Most surviving Maya sculpture is of limestone, the most available resource. Maya sculptors were specialists and artists, most likely sponsored by Maya rulers and elite supervisors. They used tools of harder

Figure 8.7 Life-sized mosaic mask of jade and other materials from a royal tomb at Tikal, Guatemala, made in a royal workshop and commissioned for the funeral and burial of the king (Early Classic). Courtesy of Tikal Project, University of Pennsylvania Museum.

stone, along with wooden mallets and wedges, to work the stone. Large chisels and hammer stones were used to quarry and roughly dress the stone. Celts or chisels did the final shaping; the actual detailed carving by small chisels usually two to six centimeters in length, then finished by abrasion and painted.

Wood Carving

A few examples of carved wood survive, created by skilled artisans using chipped-stone chisels and sharp finishing tools, probably of obsidian. These include beautifully carved small wooden boxes. Wooden architectural elements include the well-preserved carved lintels over the doorways in the Late Classic temples at Tikal. These and most other examples were carved from the sapodilla tree, one of the hardest woods known. The Tikal lintels were formed of from 4 to 10 beams, with texts and royal scenes carved in low relief. Carved wooden lintels have also survived at Chichen Itza, Uxmal, and a few other sites.

Ceramics

A variety of objects were made of fired clay—pottery vessels, figurines, beads, and other items. Household specialists made the bulk of everyday pottery—most likely women in countless farming communities. Workshop production used molds to mass-produce vessels and figurines. Maya rulers also managed workshops for artists who painted the intricate scenes that mark the finest Maya vases. Finished ceramics were fired in open fires or enclosed kilns. Maya potters produced lustrous polished monochrome wares in many colors—cream, orange, red, brown, and black. They also made unusual resist-decorated wares, elaborate modeled vessels, beautiful polychromes, including the famous portrait vases of the Late Classic period, and the only glazed wares in the Americas. Modeled and mold-made figurines often give us information about clothing, adornments, and hairstyles of both commoners and elites in ancient Maya times.

Metalwork

The Maya used several metals, more for their sacred qualities than practical applications (such as tool making). Mercury had powerful symbolic meanings. Archaeologists have found mercuric sulfide (cinnabar) and mercury in burned ritual deposits. Cinnabar is brilliant red, symbolizing blood. During fire rituals, Maya priests burned cinnabar, transforming it into metallic mercury with its mysterious qualities.

Beginning in the Late Classic era, the Maya used copper, silver, and gold for adornments and for ritual objects. These metals came largely from trade with societies in lower Central America and central Mexico.

Copper bells are the most common metal objects. A large assemblage of gold disks, necklaces, bracelets, mask elements, pendants, rings, earplugs, bells, and beads has been recovered from the Cenote of Sacrifice at Chichen Itza, where these objects had been offered to the rain god. Maya craftsmen reworked some of these imported objects, including cast-gold disks depicting battle scenes.

Textiles

The Maya cultivated cotton and wove an array of beautifully decorated textiles for clothing, but only small fragments of ancient Maya weaving have survived in a few tombs. The best examples of this well-developed craft come from representations in Maya art. Clothing depicted on sculptures indicates that cotton fabrics were made by several complicated weaves and elaborately embroidered. The Bonampak murals portray a variety of beautiful fabrics used for capes and clothing. Woven cotton textiles (*patis*) of fixed size were articles of trade and after the Conquest became the principal form of tribute exacted by the Spanish. In the Maya highlands, this ancient household craft still flourishes, and Maya women weave a variety of textiles on the traditional back strap loom.

Baskets and Mats

Woven baskets and mats made from natural fibers were important for both practical and symbolic uses. Although some specimens have survived, these ancient crafts are best known from depictions in carved or painted art. Elaborately woven baskets appear on painted vases and in sculpture. Fragments of woven textiles, baskets, and mats were recovered from an Early Classic royal tomb at Copan. A burial of a sacrificed warrior wrapped in a mat was found at the same site. Woven mats are still used for sleeping in Maya households, and they played an important symbolic role in ancient times. Sitting on a mat was a mark of authority, as indicated by the royal title *ajpop*, "lord of the mat," used by Maya rulers.

Feather Work

Impressions found in tombs and representations from Maya art show that feather working was a highly developed craft, closely associated with royal status. The best examples can be found in the Bonampak murals, and almost every sculptured portrait of a Maya king includes a feathered headdress. These show that feathers were used in making headdresses, crests, capes, and shields and in decorating canopies, fans, personal ornaments, and pendants for spears and scepters. Feather work was also used in embroideries on cotton fabrics and baskets. The feathers came from birds trapped in the highlands and lowlands, such as the scarlet macaw.

Long tail feathers from the sacred quetzal of the northern highlands of Guatemala were reserved for the use of Maya kings.

DISTRIBUTION OF FOOD AND GOODS

Environmental diversity allowed the Maya people to develop many local economic specializations. The rich resources of the Maya area provided many different food and nonfood products. The forests produced firewood, the essential fuel for cooking, firing pottery, and making lime plaster. By preserving forested areas, the Maya could maintain supplies of wood, thatch, and fibers for buildings, baskets, rope, nets, and bark cloth. The most important cultivated fiber, cotton, was spun into thread, colored with a rich variety of vegetable and mineral dyes, and woven into clothing and textiles. Animal bone, teeth, and pelts were used for adornments and ritual objects. Aquatic species, especially coral and seashells, were used in similar ways. The diversity of products and varied local economic specializations of the Maya area created the need for transportation and exchange networks to distribute resources, goods, and services.

Archaeology reveals the distribution of goods by the locations of excavated artifacts. Durable utilitarian goods such as chipped-stone tools and domestic pottery are recovered from household settings. Prestige goods are usually found in royal tombs and ritual deposits (caches). Various prestige items were used for tribute, funerary offerings, and gifts exchanged between rulers to celebrate alliances or other events. Bishop Landa mentions that the elite of the northern lowlands controlled trade in copal, honey, and salt at the time of the Spanish Conquest. Copal was resin incense vital to religious rituals conducted by commoner and elite alike. By controlling a critical ingredient for ritual (copal), the only available source of pure sugar (honey), and a dietary necessity (salt), Maya elites had a lucrative monopoly and a powerful hold on the rest of society.

Production and Exchange at Cerén

Archaeology at Cerén reveals that household production at this Classic period community met their own needs for food and some implements, such as ritual incense burners. There was also household specialized production of clothing by weaving, metates for processing food, and pottery vessels, especially the plain wares made for storage and cooking. Yet there were a number of items found at Cerén that came from elsewhere, including obsidian blades, knives, and scrapers, jade beads, seashells, celts (small chisels or axes), cinnabar and hematite pigments, and polychrome-painted pottery serving vessels. These exotics were probably acquired in exchange for products made at Cerén.

Each household produced one or more items beyond its own needs, and these surplus items could be exchanged for products with neighbors or in nearby centralized markets. The men of one household made manos and metates used to grind maize and other food products, as well as donut-shaped stones, used as mortars to grind nuts and other hard seeds and as digging stick weights for planting maize. The women of the same household were weavers who likely produced surplus textiles for exchange. Another household manufactured painted gourds, used as containers, especially for food serving bowls. A third household produced cotton-seed oil and cordage from agave fibers. These items were undoubtedly exchanged to acquire the imported obsidian tools, artifacts of jade and shell, pigments, and polychrome pottery found in each household.

In addition, two Cerén households provided community services for which they probably received payments in local goods. One household operated the large steam bath located immediately south of its compound. Another household apparently maintained the community ceremonial building and provided the ground maize for the communal feasts held there. Furthermore, a woman member of this household was probably a shaman who conducted divination rituals in her own specialized building adjacent to her household compound.

Markets

Sponsoring markets was a source of power for Maya rulers, a way of attracting large numbers of people to polity capitals on a regular basis. This provided mutual benefits beyond the opportunity to buy and sell goods, since markets are arenas for social interaction and the exchange of ideas. These conditions still hold true today in the Maya highlands and Yucatan, where markets allow the exchange of foods and other goods between producer and consumer. This gives everyone a central place to gather and to acquire products from different areas that otherwise would be unavailable. Both men and women sell the products of their labor—everything from fruits and vegetables to pottery, textiles, and charcoal. At the same time, these markets also allow people to exchange news and ideas.

Today Maya markets are usually held on one or two days each week (often on Sundays in conjunction with religious services in many rural communities) or daily in larger cities. In the past, markets were probably scheduled by the ritual calendar to coincide with major ceremonies or pilgrimages to local religious shrines, as at Chichen Itza. During Late Maya civilization, there were important shrines on Cozumel Island, off the Yucatan coast, that attracted many visitors. These pilgrims were also consumers, and it is no accident that Cozumel was also a major port for the seacoast trade around the Yucatan peninsula.

Thus, it is likely that in the past Maya families obtained at least some of their food, and a variety of products from markets like those described by the Spanish in the sixteenth century. Studies suggest that the production and distribution networks for products such as pottery vessels were well integrated within Maya polities, which indicates that centralized markets served the populace in each ancient kingdom. In addition, the presence of imported goods with a high degree of uniformity recovered from household contexts indicates they came from centralized markets, in contrast to more variable locally produced goods. This pattern has been found among artifacts excavated from household remains at Cerén, El Salvador.

The largest market described by the Spaniards was in the Mexica capital in central Mexico (present-day Mexico City). An arcade surrounded the market, and the stalls were arranged in a grid pattern around a central elevated platform used for public announcements and the executions of thieves. A court where disputes were settled stood at one corner. Goods from all over Mesoamerica were sold, including a variety of foods and beverages, baskets, mats, pottery, obsidian blades and other tools, clothing, jewelry, medicines, rubber, paper, and building materials.

The Aztec example suggests that larger Maya markets were permanent facilities and were under government control to enforce rules, settle disputes, and collect taxes. Well-organized markets with designated areas for various commodities would attract more buyers and sellers, thus contributing to the prosperity of the entire community. In fact, at some Maya archaeological sites, markets can be identified at central locations in large plazas, often near causeways and reservoirs or other water sources. They usually contain distinctive architecture, such as standardized rows of small rooms or stalls. While some larger markets have masonry architecture, most are difficult to detect because of their use of perishable pole-and-thatch stalls. But, even in such cases, markets often leave distinctive residues, such as clustered remains of different artifacts or chemical "signatures" (high phosphorus levels).

A central market was identified at Tikal in the East Plaza, located at the intersection of several causeways that provided easy connections throughout the city. The market was housed in a large rectangular masonry complex unlike any other building at Tikal. Each of the four sides was composed of standardized rooms that opened outward onto the plaza and that were probably occupied by market stalls. The East Plaza was next to Tikal's royal palace, which allowed the ruling elite to monitor market activities.

At the much smaller site of Quirigua, Guatemala, a market was identified in the southern portion of the site's Great Plaza, adjacent to its royal Acropolis, ball court, and river landing area. Archaeologically, it was recognized by a concentration of artifacts on the plaza floor, in contrast to most of the plaza, which was without artifacts or other traces of human activity.

Another market constructed of masonry architecture has been identified in Calakmul's Late Classic Chiik Nahb group by its location in a large central plaza and by the arrangement of buildings in long parallel rows. Although only one structure has been excavated, it is decorated with unprecedented pictorial and textual evidence for a market. There are murals depicting commodities and individuals engaged in market activities, identified by hieroglyphic captions. Several of these apparently identify vendors of specific products, including "Maize Person," "Salt Person," "Tobacco Person," Tamale Person," and "Atole Person."

Scholars have long assumed that Classic Maya art did not depict commoners or everyday activities. The Chiik Nahb murals at Calakmul show otherwise. It has also been assumed that Maya commoners were illiterate and that texts were intended for only the elite. The hieroglyphic captions on the Calakmul murals appear to have been intended for all to see and read.

Trade Networks

Beyond the local level, the Maya have always traded a variety of products to more distant destinations. Individual traders who buy products in one area and then sell in another area maintain the traditional trade networks in the Maya highlands today. Before the advent of motorized transportation, these traders carried their goods on their backs, secured by tumplines (cords running from the backpack around the forehead). Similar individual traders undoubtedly operated in the past. The Spaniards also found wealthy elite merchants who managed the transportation and distribution of goods overland and via waterways. On land, teams of porters transported cargoes on their backs (the Maya did not utilize beasts of burden or wheeled vehicles). On the rivers and lakes and along the seacoasts, fleets of canoes carried goods.

The Maya and other societies in Mesoamerica were never united by a single political system, but they were integrated by commerce. Both archaeological evidence and documents (such as surviving native tribute lists and Spanish accounts) indicate the existence of a complex system of trade routes throughout Mesoamerica. This trade network kept the ancient Maya in contact with neighboring societies throughout Mesoamerica. Trade routes were a conduit not only for goods but also for the movement of people and ideas. Indeed, the management of people to acquire, transport, and distribute goods required efficient organization. Individuals who controlled these organizations were able to secure both wealth and power.

The Maya were an important part of Mesoamerican long-distance trade networks. The trade that supplied the populous Mexican states with goods from Central America and beyond had to pass through the Maya area. This enabled Maya merchants to control much of this commerce. The Maya area was also blessed with many critical resources that not only could be used by the local inhabitants but were traded throughout Mesoamerica (Table 8.3). Some goods were traded to even more distant areas; pyrite mirrors and macaw feathers from the Maya area have been found as far north as the Southwest United States.

Table 8.3:
Important Trade Goods from the Maya Area

Utilitarian Goods		
Pacific Plain	*Highlands*	*Lowlands*
Agricultural products	Agricultural products	Agricultural products
Balsam	Basalt (manos and metates)	Cotton
Cotton	Hematite	Flint
Dyes and pigments	Obsidian	Lime (plaster)
Fish & sea products	Pottery	Pottery
Pottery	Salt	Salt
Salt	Talc	Shell
Shell	Textiles	Sugar (honey and wax)
Tobacco	Volcanic ash	Textiles
Nonutilitarian Goods		
Pacific Plain	*Highlands*	*Lowlands*
Bark paper	Amber	Bark paper
Cacao	Cinnabar (mercury)	Cacao
Feathers	Feathers (esp. quetzal)	Copal
Shark teeth	Jadeite	Coral
Spondylus shell	Pyrite (mirrors)	Feathers
Stingray spines	Serpentine	Jaguar pelts and teeth

The Maya area was also economically tied together by many overland north-south trade routes that connected the southern Maya area and its resources with the lowland areas to the north. At the same time, the longest routes ran generally east-west, linking the cities in Mexico, in the Maya area, and those in Central America. Many of the earliest routes appear to have been land-based, including those that connected the Gulf coast with the Mexican highlands and those than ran eastward along the Pacific coastal plain to the resources in the Maya highlands and Central America. Other routes extended more directly east to west through the Maya lowlands, using both land and river-canoe transport. These could reach the resources in the Maya highlands via the Usumacinta River and extended into Central America via the Caribbean.

Consequences of Trade

During past eras, some areas dominated trade networks by controlling supplies of critical materials and forming trading alliances to manage distribution. In the Preclassic period, growing powers in the Maya high-lands and along the Pacific coast gained wealth and power by control-ling trade between Mexico and Central America. One of the reasons for the growth of several centers of Early Maya civilization, especially Kaminaljuyu and El Mirador, was undoubtedly their control over trade goods and routes. During the era of Middle Maya civilization, a series of states dominated segments of the Mesoamerican economy, including the great city of Teotihuacan in central Mexico, which controlled several major sources of obsidian. At the same time, the highland power of Kaminaljuyu controlled much of the Maya trade in obsidian and was probably allied with Teotihuacan. Concurrently, Tikal and Calakmul inherited the posi-tion of El Mirador in controlling east-west trade across the lowlands.

Eventually, the rise of sea trade based on larger and more efficient canoes expanded the water routes around the Yucatan Peninsula at the expense of many of the trans-lowland routes. Water transport was an ancient tra-dition among the Maya. Canoes followed riverine routes across the low-lands and exploited the islands off the east coast of Belize and the coastal margins of Yucatan. But, from their homeland along the Gulf coast of Tabasco, the Chontal Maya rose to power largely because of their control over seacoast commerce. The key to prosperity and power for Chichen Itza and its successor, Mayapan, came from their control of seaborne com-merce around the Yucatan Peninsula. A single large seagoing canoe could carry more goods and required less manpower than land-based porters or even river craft, which required large crews for portages.

We know far more about Maya trade at the time of the Spanish Conquest because of the accounts written by Europeans. On his fourth voyage to the New World, Columbus recorded a famous encounter with a Maya trad-ing canoe off the north coast of Honduras. The canoe was described as being as long as a European galley and two-and-a-half meters wide, with a cabin amidships and a crew of some two dozen men, plus its captain and assorted women and children. It carried a cargo of cacao, copper bells and axes, pottery, cotton clothing, and *macanas* (wooden swords set with obsidian blades).

The rise of sea trade resulted in profound changes for Maya society. It contributed to the decline of the southern lowland cities, especially those (like Tikal and Calakmul) that were located far inland and depended on the older trans-Petén trade routes. But cause and effect in past societies are not always clear. It is also possible that the breakdown of Middle Maya civilization disrupted the older riverine and land-based trade routes, thus encouraging the rise of seacoast commerce. Regardless, it appears that, during Late Maya civilization, sea trade created a shift in settlement toward the seacoasts of the Yucatan Peninsula.

Even though sea trade was important to the economy of Late Maya civilization in Yucatan, porter-borne overland trade continued in the highlands and elsewhere. With the Conquest, Maya coastal trade soon disappeared. During the sixteenth and seventeenth centuries, unconquered Maya groups such as the Tayasal Itza maintained a vestigial riverine and overland trade network through the southern lowlands. Because of the rugged terrain, overland trade has always been primary in the Maya highlands. Today, the last vestiges of traditional Maya commerce are being replaced by modern transport using bus and trucks, and supermarkets are replacing traditional Maya markets.

FURTHER READING

Abrams 1994; Ardren 2002; Bell, Canuto, and Sharer 2004; Fedick 1996; Flannery 1982; Freidel and Sabloff 1984; Harrison and Turner 1978; Helms 1993; Hirth 1984; Lohse and Valdez 2004; Masson and Freidel 2002; McAnany 2004; Osborne 1965; Sabloff 1994; Sharer and Traxler 2006; Sheets 2006; Turner and Harrison 1983.

9

MAYA SOCIETY

Although their ancient civilization is gone, the Maya people and their cultural traditions continue in today's world. In this chapter, we will look at the organization and lifeways of ancient Maya society. Our information about past Maya society comes mostly from indirect sources, for the Maya's own writings say little about this subject. And what is recorded deals almost exclusively with the kings and the elite class; nothing is said about the great majority of ancient Maya society, the common people. Fortunately, there is excellent archaeological evidence for everyday life in small communities. This, combined with ethnohistorical sources—records made after the Spanish Conquest—allows us to reconstruct all levels of ancient Maya society.

The following discussion will consider archaeological studies of Maya households and settlement patterns, family organization, kinship, descent, and the development of social stratification and other changes in Maya society over time.

SIZE AND ORGANIZATION OF SOCIETY

The location and size of human settlements are conditioned by the availability of critical resources, such as water and good agricultural soils. Patterns of settlement allow us to reconstruct ancient social organizations. As we shall see, information about the size and organization of Maya families can be obtained by studying the patterns of household remains—cooking vessels, tools, storage and disposal areas, and the size and shape of the houses themselves. Moreover, the patterning of all household remains within a village or city reflects the social ties that once defined ancient communities.

Population Reconstructions

To understand how past Maya society was organized, we need to determine the size of the population—how many people made up a typical family or how many people lived in Maya villages, towns, and cities. Archaeologists estimate past population sizes by counting houses or other features that reflect population numbers. Ancient Maya households are identified from low but distinctive mounds that are the remains of domestic structures. At some sites, population can be estimated from the number and size of water storage facilities (wells, cisterns, or reservoirs). Regardless of what is counted, there is always an unknown proportion of features that have been completely destroyed or remain undetected. At Maya sites, it is estimated that the actual number of ancient houses ranges anywhere from 10 to 100 percent greater than the total identified by archaeological study.

Thus, reconstructions of ancient population size from archaeological remains yield only approximations. Nonetheless, settlement studies provide a basis for comparing the numbers and densities of structures at different Maya sites. Such studies reveal that lowland sites usually contain between 200 and 450 houses per square kilometer. Central Copan is outside this range, with the greatest constructional density of any Maya site (1,450 structures per square kilometer), because of the close confinement of the Copan Valley. Mayapan shows the second highest density (996 structures per square kilometer), due to crowding within its defensive wall. At the low end of settlement density are both Quirigua (129 structures per square kilometer) and Uaxactun (124 structures per square kilometer).

Populations can be estimated by applying figures for the average number of people in a Maya family to these house counts. Census figures from shortly after the Conquest show that in several Maya communities the size of Maya families ranged from 5 to 10 people per household. Ethnographic studies show that traditional Maya families today average between 4.9 and 6.1 people.

To arrive at population estimates for Maya cities, a reasonable average of 5.5 people per family can be used. Multiplying this figure by the number of identified houses within the site defined by the 120 square kilometer area bounded on the north and south by earthworks shows that an estimated 65,000 people inhabited Tikal in the Late Classic period. By including the estimated 30,000 additional people within a 10-kilometer radius of the site center provides a "greater Tikal" population of between 90,000 and 100,000 people. For comparison, "greater Copan" was about one quarter this size, with an estimated peak population of 20,000 to

25,000 people in this period. These are estimated populations for cities, not total polities.

Studies of lowland Maya settlement in areas between cities show that rural areas also supported large numbers of people. For example, the hinterland in the central lakes region of the Petén supported about 190 people per square kilometer during the Late Classic. This means that, at its peak, occupation density in parts of the southern lowlands was comparable to that of China and Java, with some of the most densely settled areas of the world. Such high population densities illuminate the pressure exerted on the lowland environment and the critical role of overexploitation in leading to the drastic decline of Middle Maya civilization.

These reconstructions also show the patterns of growth and decline of population through time. Two peaks of highest population are apparent: one at the end of Early Maya civilization (ca. 200) and another at the end of Middle Maya civilization (ca. 800). The later peak was the higher. Both peaks were followed by population decreases, but the decline at the end of Middle Maya civilization was the most severe in the southern lowlands. Research has also shown that substantial occupation continued after 800 in some southern lowland areas, notably the central lake region of the Petén and parts of Belize.

Maya Household Activities

The daily activities of Maya families today are little different from those of ancient times. The center of everyday life for each Maya nuclear family is the household compound—a cluster of several separate buildings. This typically consists of a main house or domicile where the family members work, eat their meals, and sleep, a kitchen for preparing food, one or more storerooms, and, in some cases, a workshop and a steam bath. Over time, additional domiciles may be built within the compound—perhaps for sons of the original family who marry and begin new nuclear families.

Traditional Maya houses are also little changed from those of the past. They are built with walls woven together and framed with poles and with thatched roofs. This provides shelter but is open enough to remain fairly cool in tropical climates. In the colder regions of the highlands, the walls are often plastered with dried mud (*bajareque*) or made of adobe (sun-dried mud mixed with straw binder). Of course, today many Maya families live in houses built with modern materials, such as concrete blocks.

The daily activities of Maya families today show a clear division of labor between women and men. Both ethnohistory and archaeology confirm the same practices in the past. Young children are given more responsibilities as they grow older—girls help their mother, while boys assist their father. The daily round of activities in Maya families begins before dawn when women wake to build a fire in the hearth and prepare tortillas and beans for the first meal of the day. After eating, men may take wrapped tortillas with them to their fields or wherever they work. In addition to cultivating fields of maize, beans, and other crops, men may hunt, fish, and tend hives of honeybees. Some are part-time craftsmen who may do leatherwork or carve wood or stone, making objects to sell to tourists. Men are also responsible for constructing and maintaining their household buildings. They clear new land for their fields and cut down trees for firewood, although women and children often gather and carry the firewood to the house. Men are in overall charge of representing the family to the world, in everything from paying taxes to conducting agricultural and household rituals. Fathers also train their sons to carry out these activities against the day when they have their own families. The day usually ends at dusk, when men return to their homes for the evening meal.

Most activities within the household are a family affair. Mothers with small children usually spend their days doing household tasks while keeping an eye on their youngsters, except when an older daughter can assume this duty. Daily tasks include carrying water for household use, washing dishes, and tending kitchen gardens near the family household. When help is needed in the fields, older women and young girls may assist the men with weeding, harvesting, transporting, and processing

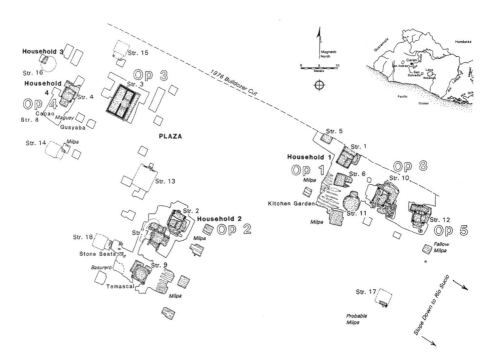

Figure 9.1 Cerén, El Salvador: Map of excavated remains of several households, each consisting of several buildings occupied by a family, with adjacent fields (milpas) and gardens (ca. 600). Courtesy of Payson Sheets, El Cerén Archaeological Project.

maize and other crops. Women are also responsible for meal preparation and cooking, marketing, sewing, childrearing, and keeping the house and yard swept clean. One or more times each week, women wash the family's clothes in a nearby river or stream or at a *pila* (community laundry fountain). Many Maya women also make pottery or weave textiles. Of course, women train their daughters in these household activities so that they will be prepared to raise their own families. Women also often collect some wild foods and tend domestic animals—today these usually include species with Old World origins like chickens and pigs. Before the arrival of Europeans, Maya household animals included dogs, ducks, and turkeys. The day ends with the family gathered for the evening meal.

HOUSEHOLDS AT CERÉN

Cerén's household buildings were constructed on low square or rectangular earthen platforms, finished with fine clay, and fired to make them durable and waterproof. Most had *bajareque* walls linked to adobe corner columns that supported a pole-and-thatch roof. The wall poles were tied to the pole framework of the roof to make a strong yet flexible earthquake-resistant structure that prevented serious injuries even if damaged by a powerful quake. A few nonresidential special-purpose structures were constructed of much heavier solid adobe walls.

Cerén had about a dozen households built around a small central plaza that was flanked by public buildings. In keeping with the typical Maya pattern, each household consisted of a cluster of several buildings, a domicile where the family worked, ate its meals, and slept, a kitchen for preparing food, a storeroom, and, in some cases, a workshop and a steam bath. Each household tended adjacent kitchen gardens and surrounding agricultural fields, where its crops were preserved by volcanic ash after the eruption 1,400 years ago that buried the town (see chapter 8).

The evidence indicates that the people of Cerén led good and prosperous lives before the eruption. They had a wide variety of tools, goods, and pottery, including "fancy" polychrome bowls probably imported from the Maya capital of Copan. Cerén's inhabitants produced a diverse and plentiful supply of food, judging from the amount of food storage within each household compound. They did not live under crowded conditions but had plenty of room to conduct their daily activities, including protected interior and exterior roofed areas and areas for their household gardens.

Excavation exposed the remains of four household compounds at Cerén. Two are located southeast of the plaza and are excavated enough to document their composition. Household 1 contains four buildings: a two-roomed domicile, a round one-roomed kitchen, a small one-roomed storage shed, and a smaller one-roomed auxiliary structure used for craft manufacture. Household 2 has three buildings: a two-room domicile, a one-room storage building, and a steam bath. An unexcavated building identified by remote sensing nearby is probably Household 2's kitchen.

Figure 9.2 Cerén, El Salvador: Reconstruction of Household 1 included (left to right) a kitchen, storeroom, domicile (main house), and workshop (ca. 600). Courtesy of Payson Sheets, El Cerén Archaeological Project.

The information from the excavation of these household buildings provides details of everyday family life in an ancient Maya community.

Domiciles

The main house or domicile is where adults work during the day, children learn and play, meals are taken, and the entire family sleeps at night. But daytime activities often take place outside, as well. Maya domestic buildings usually have overhanging roofs and sometimes a veranda that protect against sun and rain and allow room for craft making and other activities around building exteriors. Household compounds have a yard, often bounded by fences, which can be used for a variety of activities—sun drying, firing pottery, children's games, and so on. Yards are also used for household gardens to grow foods, condiments, flowers, and other products.

The excavated domiciles at Cerén follow this pattern. The Household 1 domicile was constructed of *bajareque* on a low platform with about 16 square meters of floor area divided between two rooms. The north-facing front room was actually a veranda, open to the front, with a thatched roof that covered a lower northward extension of the building platform. A pottery-smoothing tool and a clay nodule found on this surface indicate that it was used to make pottery. The clay's composition matches that of the household's domestic pottery. The family's painted pottery bowls used for serving food were made elsewhere and probably came from a local market.

Several pottery vessels were found where they had been abandoned in the domicile and other household buildings. These include incense burners used in family rituals and serving vessels used for meals. The dinnerware found in Household 2's domicile included remains of painted gourd vessels and three polychrome pottery bowls. One of these bowls preserved the finger swipe marks from the person who had just finished the evening meal, indicating that the eruption occurred before there was time to wash the dishes.

Both excavated domiciles had a larger southern room entered by a doorway from the front room. This interior space was divided between an open floor area and an adobe bed platform that filled half the room. Woven mats were spread on the bed for family members to sleep on. During the day, these were rolled and placed in the rafters so that the bed could be used for other purposes. Obsidian cutting tools, sharper than a razor, were stored in the roof thatch to keep them from small children. These were made by craftsmen and likely also came from the local market. The floor of Household 1's southern room held seven pottery vessels. One of these contained items that probably belonged to a woman—pieces of imported seashell, lumps of hematite (red pigment), a small metate used to grind hematite, and a clay spindle whorl used to spin cotton thread.

Excavation outside the west wall of Household 2's domicile found a whetstone used to sharpen celts. There were also sun-dried adobe bricks stored under the overhanging roof. The east side of Household 1's domicile was used for weaving, indicated by a clay spindle whorl still on its wooden spindle. This space was also used for food preparation, for a metate was found still positioned on its *horquetas*, forked sticks used to elevate it to permit grinding at waist level. The east side was also a walkway leading to the kitchen and storage shed.

Kitchens

Household 1's kitchen is located about 6 meters south of the domicile; its doorway and narrow veranda also face north. The kitchen is on a low earthen platform. It was circular and of open construction, with upright poles and a porous thatch roof to allow cooking fire smoke to easily escape. Instead of fired adobe, the kitchen floor was paved with volcanic ash that absorbed food spills and could be periodically replaced.

The kitchen interior was spacious (about 30 square meters) and organized into three activity areas: food storage, food preparation and cooking, and food grinding and vessel storage. The southern end of the building was used for food storage. It held remains of common beans, lima beans, achiote seeds, cacao, chiles, and squash. The chiles were hung from the roof, but other foodstuffs were stored on a wooden shelf and in pottery vessels and baskets on the floor. The beans were on a layer of leaves that acted as a moisture barrier.

The eastern side of the kitchen was for preparing and cooking food. The traditional Maya three-stone hearth was in the center of this area. The fire had burned out, so the evening meal had been cooked and served before the eruption. A metate on the floor had a mano ready for use. Nearby were a bowl and a pottery scoop to hold the *masa* (dough of ground maize and water) as it was prepared on the metate. There was also a pot full of maize that had been soaked in water, ready for making *masa* the next morning. The Cerén households used *masa* to make tamales and atole (a maize-based drink) rather than tortillas, since no *comales* (tortilla griddles) were found.

The kitchen also held another *horqueta*-supported metate. Cooking pots, empty storage jars, and serving vessels were stored in the kitchen's western area. Food was served in pottery and gourd bowls, both often decorated with colorful patterns. The painted gourd bowls were fashioned from half of a dried and scraped gourd, painted red, yellow, green, and other colors. Serving vessels were found in domiciles and several other buildings, indicating that meals were prepared in the kitchen, placed in large serving bowls, along with smaller individual bowls and drinking cups, then carried to the domicile for consumption by the family.

Steam Baths

The *temascal* or steam bath has been an essential part of Maya life for thousands of years. To this day, many Maya household compounds include a steam bath, little changed from those of ancient times. Enclosed structures were equipped with fireboxes to heat rocks that, when doused with water, produce steam to cleanse body and spirit. Classic period elite palaces were furnished with elaborate masonry steam baths. Judging from their size, ancient steam baths held several people and thus housed social events for both practical and ritual purposes.

Cerén's communal *temascal* was built on a half-meter-high earthen platform surfaced with flat stones. Its solid adobe walls, about a meter high, supported an adobe dome, 10 to 15 centimeters thick (reinforced by embedded sticks), that rises another .75 meter at its center; this was damaged by lava bombs from the volcanic eruption. A circular vent in the dome, fitted with a removable adobe plug, allowed smoke to escape and provided ventilation. A pole-and-thatch roof protected the adobe dome from rainfall. The adobe dome's interior steam chamber was covered with soot from many fires contained within a central firebox of stones set in adobe. A small doorway on the north side provided access, and a stone-paved bench around the chamber's perimeter could seat up to about 10 bathers at a time. A waiting area of exterior benches along the north and west side could hold 10 or 12 people.

The *temascal* was located adjacent to Household 2, so it is likely that this family operated and maintained the facility. Because it held more than an average family, the steam bath was probably a communal gathering place where Cerén's inhabitants could relax, converse, and enjoy the bath's cleansing and therapeutic benefits.

Storage Buildings

Three storage buildings have been excavated at Cerén. The Household 1 storage building was adjacent to its kitchen and was placed on a low, 3.2-meter square platform. It had a single doorway in its adobe-plastered eastern wall. Its other three walls were vertical poles that were open to allow air circulation. The Household 2 storage building had *bajareque* walls. A third example from Household 4 (its other buildings are unexcavated) was also built of *bajareque* but had two rooms. All three were used to store seeds, beans, cacao beans, and similar items in pottery vessels, baskets, and net bags. While the pottery vessels in the Household 1 storage building were on the floor, most of those from Household 2 were suspended from the rafters by cords. The Household 4 storage building was the only one with cottonseeds, stored in pottery vessels. Nearby was a metate used to grind the seeds to extract cottonseed oil, identified from the residue on its surface. The same building contained dried chiles, likely suspended from the rafters in bunches.

The two-room storage building also held a circular crib, a meter in diameter, constructed of wooden poles. It was used to store husked maize, revealed by plaster casts of the voids in the volcanic ash that covered the crib. Nearby a cylindrical vessel held residue of a maize-based liquid, likely atole or *chicha* (fermented maize beer). The Household 2 storeroom contained five small jars containing different hues of red pigment made from cinnabar (mercuric sulfide), a rare and symbolically important mineral. There were also seven jade beads, two beads of shell and stone, and a star-shaped pendant that together likely formed a necklace, indicating that this family had accumulated some wealth.

Workshops

The Household 4 storage structure was also used for processing agave fiber. Next to it were several pairs of sticks used to de-pulp agave (or maguey) leaves. Processed agave fibers were used to make string and rope for a variety of purposes. Excavations south of this storage building discovered a garden of some 70 agave plants. Some had missing leaves, suggesting that they had already been harvested for processing.

Household 1 was involved in food production beyond its family needs. The *horqueta*-mounted metate in its storage shed identifies an area devoted to grain grinding. Household 1 contained five metates; more than needed for everyday family use, indicating that the household was preparing food for a community feast planned for the ceremonial building located just east of its compound. A duck tied to the west wall of the storage building was probably intended for a feast that never happened. The storage shed also contained five hammer stones used to make ground stone manos and metates. Household members also made pottery vessels and woven textiles. Finally, Household 1 had a small workshop in a *ramada* (roofed platform without walls) west of its domicile. Obsidian wastage found just to the south indicates that it was used to resharpen obsidian scrapers and similar tools.

THE ORGANIZATION OF MAYA SETTLEMENT

The small mounds found at most lowland Maya sites are the remnants of low earthen or rubble platforms that once supported oblong or rectangular houses of one or more rooms. These were the dwellings of commoners who formed the bulk of ancient Maya populations. In the past, there was clear variation in house materials and size according to the status of the occupant. A Maya elite house (*nah*) was much larger than those of the common people, was built of masonry blocks, had a vaulted roof, and was supported by a higher masonry platform. The houses of Maya kings were so large and elaborate that they are usually referred to as palaces.

As we have seen, Maya houses often form clusters of several related structures (*nahlil*), each serving different purposes (e.g., domiciles, kitchens, storage). Over time, the *nahlil* often expanded to shelter new families. The largest or most elaborate house in the group often indicates the family head's domicile. A repeated pattern found in the *nahlil* clusters at Tikal consists of a central patio bordered on three sides by houses. A smaller but higher eastern building is identified as the family shrine where the senior member or founder of the group was buried and became the focus of ancestral veneration rituals.

Clusters of *nahlil* often form wards or barrios (*chinah*). These may have been occupied by larger kin groups or, in some cases, families sharing a common profession (such as pottery makers or stone masons). Retainers, servants, and other people who were clients of other residents may have occupied some houses within a *chinah*. Thus, common interests or professions, as well as kinship, often united residential groups.

Although they could be organized in various ways, the sum total of people living together in one place defined the *cah* or Maya community. The *cah* could be of any size, from the smallest agricultural village (*chan cah*), like Cerén, to the largest political capital (*noh cah*), like Tikal. Yet even the largest of Maya cities included the same residential components— some much larger and more complex than others, of course. At the heart of a capital such as Tikal was the *noh nahlil* (palace complex) of the royal family, along with those of the other elite extended families. Larger Maya cities also included many more public buildings and facilities than the smaller communities. But, regardless of its size, the *cah* was the setting for the organizations that gave society its basic structure.

THE INDIVIDUAL LIFE CYCLE

The day-to-day activities and the entire life cycle of each person were set by custom and governed by religious beliefs, much as they are among the Maya of today. The Maya kept their lives in harmony with their world—their family, their community, and their gods. The key to this harmony was the calendar that tracked the cycles of time, beginning with the 260-day sacred almanac (discussed in chapter 12). Every person's destiny, from birth to death, was tied to this almanac.

Childhood

The date of each person's birth in the 260-day almanac had different attributes, some good, some neutral, some bad. In this way, a person's birth date controlled his or her temperament and destiny. To this day, the Kaqchikel Maya name their children after their date of birth in the 260-day almanac. In Yucatan, at the time of the Spanish Conquest, each child's *paal kaba,* or given name, was determined by a divining ceremony conducted by a shaman. The Maya are given multiple names. In Yucatan, these are the *paal kaba,* the father's family name, the mother's family name, and an informal nickname.

Children are greatly desired and treated to a great deal of love and affection. At the time of the Conquest, women would ask the gods for children by giving offerings, reciting special prayers, and placing an image of Ix Chel, goddess of childbirth, under their beds. Today, having many children is seen as beneficial for the family. Sons assist their father in the fields, and older daughters assist their mother at home. Children take care of their parents in their old age. These roles were probably little different in the past.

The Maya performed ceremonies marking a child's acceptance into society. In Yucatan, this ceremony is called *hetzmek,* performed when the baby is carried astride the mother's hip for the first time. For girls the *hetzmek* is held at three months, and for boys, at four months. Three months symbolizes the three stones of the Maya hearth, an important focus of a woman's life. Similarly, four months symbolizes the four sides of the maize field, the focus of a man's life. Participants in the ceremony, besides the infant, are the parents and another husband and wife who act as sponsors. The child is given nine objects symbolic of his or her life and carried on the hip nine times by both sponsoring parents. The ceremony closes with burning copal incense, offerings, and a ritual feast.

Mothers raised their children until the age of three or four. At about age four, girls were given a red shell, which was tied to a string around their waists. At the same age, boys received a small white bead, which was fastened to their hair. Both of these symbols of childhood were worn until puberty, when another ceremony marked the transition to adulthood.

There is no evidence that the ancient Maya had formal schools. They received their education at home. Some children were selected by their social status or aptitude for specialized training in an apprentice system. Scribes, priests, artists, masons, and other occupational groups recruited novices and trained them. Today, among some highland Maya peoples, shamans continue to recruit and train the next generation of these religious specialists.

Adolescence

In colonial Yucatan, the 260-day almanac was consulted to select an auspicious day for the community puberty ceremony marking the end of childhood. It was held every few years for all the children deemed ready to take this step. A shaman conducted the ceremony with four assistant shamans called *chaaks* (after the Maya rain god), and a respected community elder. The parents, the children, and their sponsors assembled in the patio of the community elder's house, which was purified by a ritual conducted by the shaman. The patio was swept and covered by fresh leaves and mats.

After the *chaaks* placed pieces of white cloth on the children's heads, the shaman said a prayer for the children and gave a bone to the elder, who used it to tap each child nine times on the forehead. The shaman used a scepter decorated with rattlesnake rattles to anoint the children with sacred water, after which he removed the white cloths. The children then presented offerings of feathers and cacao beans to the *chaaks*. The shaman cut the white beads from the boy's heads, while the mothers removed the red shells from their daughters. Pipes of tobacco were smoked, and a ritual feast of food and drink closed the ceremony. After this, both the girls and boys were considered adults and eligible to marry.

Until they married, young women continued to live with their parents and were expected to follow the customs of modesty. When unmarried women met a man, they turned their backs and stepped aside to allow him to pass. When giving a man food or drink, they lowered their eyes. In colonial times, young unmarried men of the community lived in a house set apart for them; this was probably an ancient custom. They painted themselves black until they were married but did not tattoo themselves until after marriage.

Adulthood and Marriage

In colonial times, marriages were often arranged between families while the couple were still very young. The wedding then took place when they came of age, usually when the couple was around 20 years old. Today, in most Maya communities the average age of men at marriage is about the same, and the average age of women at marriage is 16 or 17 years.

In colonial Yucatan, it was customary for fathers to approve of the prospective spouse for their sons, ensuring that the young woman was of the same social class and of the same village. In accordance with marriage taboos, it was incestuous to marry a girl who had the same surname or for a widower to marry the sister of his deceased wife or the widow of his brother. On the other hand, because the couple would always have different surnames, cross-cousin marriages were fairly common (marriage between the children of a brother and sister). A professional matchmaker (*aj atanzahob*) was often used to make the arrangements, plan the ceremony, and negotiate the dowry.

For the dowry, the groom's father usually provided dresses and household articles for the bride, while the groom's mother made clothing for both her son and her prospective daughter-in-law. Today, in Yucatan, the groom or his family usually covers the expenses of the wedding, including the bride's trousseau.

The wedding ceremony was traditionally held at the house of the bride's father. A shaman, who began by explaining the details of the marriage agreement, performed the ceremony. After this, he burned incense and blessed the new couple. Everyone then enjoyed a special feast that concluded the ceremony.

Monogamy is the most common form of marriage. But in pre-Columbian times, polygyny was permitted. Because polygyny imposed greater economic demands, multiple wives were probably more widespread among the elite than the nonelite. Divorce was uncomplicated, consisting of a simple repudiation by either party. Widowers and widows remained single for at least a year after the death of their spouses. They could then remarry without ceremony; the man simply went to the house of the woman of his choice; if she accepted him and gave him something to eat, they were considered married.

After the marriage, the groom lived and worked in the house of his wife's parents (uxorilocal residence). His mother-in-law ensured that her daughter gave her husband food and drink as a token of the parental recognition of the marriage, but, if the young man failed to work, he could be put out of the house. After a period of no more than six or seven years, the husband could build a new house adjacent to that of his father and move his new family there (patrilocal residence). The family slept in one room, using mats on low bed platforms. Today, in the highlands, mats are still used, although hammocks are now often favored in the hotter lowland regions.

Roles and Occupations

As already discussed, the traditional roles for men and women are probably essentially the same today as in the past. Beyond the home, it can be assumed that nonelite women undertook several community-level specializations in ancient times, such as midwives and matchmakers, as they do today. Also like today, they may have shared the responsibilities of their husbands when they held community offices. We can only assume that many nonelite women also served as cooks and servants for the noble and royal families within each kingdom. Some probably became successful and even famous for the pottery and textiles they produced. Other women may have prospered as merchants, as suggested by the portrait of a woman in the Chiik Nahb murals at Calakmul (chapter 8). But beyond such speculations we do not know how many occupations were open to women in the past.

At the elite level of society, we know from Classic period texts and portraits that the wives and mothers of royalty played essential roles in the civil and religious duties of Maya kings. Some royal women assembled considerable wealth and power, as suggested by the elaborateness of the tomb of the presumed queen of Copan's dynastic founder. Mothers of kings were vital to the ceremonies held for the designation of the heir to the throne and at the inauguration of the new ruler. The royal histories of Tikal and Palenque record that in each kingdom a royal daughter assumed the throne in the absence of a male successor and held the position of ruler until the male heir took the throne. The royal dynasty at Naranjo was restored by the arrival of a royal woman from Dos Pilas who also ruled her new kingdom until a male ruler came of age.

It can be assumed that nonelite men took on a variety of roles in the past. Most men had to provide a portion of their time and labor to their community and king. Like women, many nonelite men must have been servants to noble or royal families. During the dry season, when their agricultural duties were minimal, men were obligated to help construct and maintain buildings, causeways, reservoirs, and other essential facilities. Some undoubtedly became skilled masons, carpenters, and other craftsmen. Of course, in time of war, these men were also called upon to serve in the lower ranks as soldiers. Some men probably became peddlers and merchants, engaged in manufacturing specializations, or became shamans or priests within their communities. The various low-level political offices were filled by the men of each community selected by their seniority or abilities for such roles.

Elite men held the majority of political and religious offices in each Maya kingdom, advancing according to their age and abilities within the governmental or priestly hierarchy. Other elite occupations were probably concerned with economic affairs; these included court officials charged with collecting and recording tribute, managers of plantations for growing valuable crops such as cacao, or wealthy merchants directing major trading expeditions over land or water. Warfare also created roles for elite men in positions of military command. In addition, there were elite men who became artists, artisans, and scribes, sometimes even signing their names to their works.

Figure 9.3 The costumes and adornments worn by elite Maya men are often depicted in Maya art; this scene depicts the presentation of tribute to the king on a painted pottery vessel from a royal tomb at Tikal, Guatemala (Late Classic). Courtesy of Tikal Project, University of Pennsylvania Museum.

Personal Appearance

The Maya marked social status by their personal appearance, clothing, and adornments. There were several means to alter physical appearances. For example, crossed eyes were considered a mark of beauty among the Maya in the past. In colonial times, mothers induced crossed eyes by tying a lump of resin to their children's hair so that it would hang between their eyes. In another mark of beauty, the Maya pierced the ears, lips, and septum of the nose to hold a variety of ornaments that indicated the individual's status. Incisors were notched or inlaid with jade and other materials. Flattened foreheads were also considered a mark of beauty and status. Such foreheads were achieved by binding the heads of babies with boards, one at the back of the head, another against the forehead. Once the cranial bones had set, the desired flattened appearance remained for life. Carved and painted representations of profile heads show that this practice was often used in the past to indicate elite status.

Clothing marked gender and status differences. Men wore loincloths (*ex*), a band of cotton cloth that went between the legs and wrapped around the waist. The *ex* is represented in Maya art, from elaborately decorated examples worn by kings and other elite men to simple, undecorated versions worn by commoners. Elite men often wore a large square cotton cloth (*pati*), elaborately decorated with different patterns, colors, and feather work according to the wearer's status, around their shoulders. Simple versions of the *pati* were worn by commoners and also served as a bed covering at night.

Men wore sandals made of untanned deer hide bound to the feet by two thongs. Kings and elite men, depicted on carved monuments, wore very elaborate versions of these sandals. Although the *ex* and the *pati* are no longer worn—today most Maya men wear Western-style clothing—some still wear sandals similar to the ancient examples.

In ancient times, Maya men wore their hair long, usually braided and wound around the head, except for a queue in back. Body paint was often used to mark special groups. Priests were painted blue, the color associated with sacrifice, and warriors painted themselves black and red. War captives are shown painted black and white. Paint was also used in tattooing, the painted designs being cut into the skin with an obsidian knife.

The principal woman's garment was a woven cotton skirt (*manta*). According to Bishop Landa's colonial-era account, "The women of the coast and of the Provinces of Bacalar and of Campeche are more modest

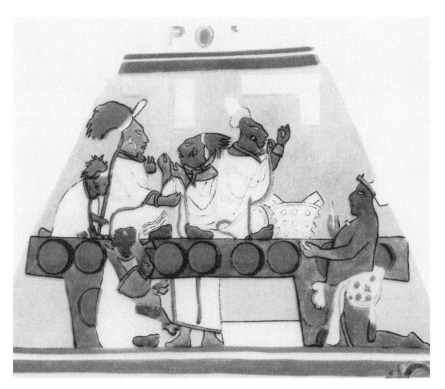

Figure 9.4 The costumes and adornments worn by elite Maya women are also depicted in Maya art; here a group of royal women are shown in the murals from Bonampak, Mexico (Late Classic). From Ruppert, Thompson, and Proskouriakoff 1955. Reprinted by permission of the President and Fellows of Harvard College.

in their dress, for, besides the [skirt] which they wore from the waist down, they covered their breasts, tying a folded manta underneath their armpits" (Tozzer 1941: 126; trans. of Landa's original manuscript of ca. 1566). Women also covered their head and shoulders with a cotton shawl (*booch*).

Today, the traditional Maya women's garment is the *huipil*, a Nahuatl word from central Mexico. In the Guatemalan highlands, the *huipil* is a hand-woven blouse, beautifully embroidered in cross-stitch, worn over a wrap-around skirt. Traditionally, each highland community had its unique design, so a women's hometown could be recognized from her *huipil*. In Yucatan, the *huipil* is a white, loose-fitting cotton dress with arm-holes and a square opening at the neck. A long white petticoat (*pic*) is worn underneath. Today, some Maya women go barefoot or wear slippers of European style, but formerly they may have used sandals.

As in the past, most Maya women and girls wear their hair long, arranged in various ways. In the past, married and unmarried women each had distinctive hairstyles. Both women and men anointed themselves with a sweet-smelling red ointment, the odor of which lasted for many days. Like men, married women also tattooed themselves, except for their breasts, with delicate designs.

The costumes worn by the highest status men in society, Maya kings, were the most elaborate and were decorated with symbols of supernatural power. Portraits of Classic period kings show them arrayed in beautifully decorated loincloths, capes, sandals, and huge headdresses. The belt holding the *ex* was adorned with jade masks and suspended jade plaques. Earlier belts often included a chain dangling a small image of a royal patron god. A large jade god mask was often worn on the chest, along with necklaces of jade beads. Jade, shell, and other materials were formed into beads, pendants, and mosaics; these were worn in the ears, nose, lips, and around the neck, arms, wrists, and ankles. The king's *pati* was a magnificent cape of embroidered cotton, accompanied by jaguar pelts and feather work.

Completing the royal display was a huge headdress adorned with an array of iridescent tail feathers from the sacred quetzal bird. The head-dress framework was probably of wood, including a front piece carved to represent one or more heads of Maya gods. The headdress was also adorned with mosaics and carved jades. On early representations, the ruler wore a headband with a tri-lobed element, sometimes personified by three heads of the maize god. Royal inaugurations included the "taking of the white headband" as a symbol of kingship. Kings used specialized headdresses for special events, including one associated with warfare. At Copan, each ruler of the royal dynasty is often shown wearing a distinctive turban headdress.

Commoners also wore jewelry, usually simple nose plugs, lip plugs, and earrings of bone, wood, shell, or stone. Adornments worn by the elite were much more elaborate and were made of jade, stone, obsidian, coral, and shell. The most precious of these items were delicately made mosaics and inlays. The elite also wore collars, necklaces, wristlets, anklets, and knee bands made of feathers, jade beads, shells, jaguar teeth and claws, crocodile teeth, or, in later times, gold and copper.

Recreation

In ancient Maya society, each person's time and labor was critical to ensure that the daily needs of life were maintained. Besides meeting family needs, adults had labor and tribute obligations to fulfill for their king and kingdom. Thus, there was little leisure time for most of the Maya population, and recreation as we know it today was almost nonexistent. Even children, as soon as they were old enough to help their parents in their tasks, had to put work before play.

Nothing is known about the games children played in the past, but we believe that at least some used balls made from the elastic gum of the rubber tree, cultivated and widely traded by the Maya. We can also assume that people found time between their labors to relax and enjoy themselves. Certainly the great religious feasts and festivals held periodically throughout the year provided an important means to break the difficult routine of everyday life. It is also certain that when they could find free time, both children and men played various kinds of ball games.

Maya ball games are known from both archaeological evidence and carved representations, although these tell us mostly about a formal version that was played in the major capitals of Maya kingdoms. We can assume that nonelite people also played a more everyday version of this game in their communities.

The formal version of the ball game was played in a specially constructed ball court. One or more of these are found at most larger Maya cities, usually in a central area. These ball courts have a level paved surface between two masonry platforms and an open end zone at both ends of the playing alley. Sometimes there are provisions for large crowds, as at Copan and Quirigua, where the ball courts are near extensive stepped terraces that could have been used by several thousand spectators. The size of the playing alley varied from court to court but was generally smaller than a baseball infield (the playing alley of the Great Ball Court at Chichen Itza, the largest known, was about the size of a football field). Classic period ball courts have sloping sidewalls, whereas most later ball courts have vertical side walls with a single vertically set stone ring placed high up in the center of each wall.

The game was played between two teams with a hard rubber ball that could be struck with the body but not with the hands or feet. For protection, ball players wore special padded garb around the waist and on the head. There were at least two versions of the game.

The Classic era game was played with a large heavy ball, larger than a basketball. The rules are unknown, but the objective apparently was to keep the ball moving back and forth between the two teams, each defending one end zone. Points were probably scored if one team failed to properly strike the ball or if the ball landed in their end zone. The later version was played with a smaller rubber ball. The rules are also unknown, but the objective was probably similar. We do know from Bishop Landa's description that the team that managed to put the ball through one of the stone rings would instantly win the game. But this was a rare event, so much so that the winning team and their spectators could seize the clothing and possessions from the losing team and their spectators, provided they could catch them!

We also know that the Maya ball game was linked to religious belief and ritual. The Hero Twins of Maya myth (see chapter 11) were expert players who defeated the death gods in a ball game. Because of this religious association, a ritual version of the ball game was played to dramatize military victories. It is clear that this ritual had no recreational value for the losing side. In such rituals, defeated captives, on rare occasions including captured kings, were forced to play a ball game with the victors. The result of this ritual contest was preordained, and after the defeated captives lost the game they were sacrificed. Defeated kings might be decapitated, just as the Hero Twins decapitated the defeated death gods in the Maya myth. We actually know more about this ritualized version of the ball game than we know about the game itself. But the original ball game played in every Maya community was a far less fatal contest.

Health

Bishop Landa's colonial-era account describes Maya shamans "who cured with herbs and many superstitious rites...(and) by bleedings of the parts which gave pain to the sick...[the Maya] believed that death, sickness and afflictions came to them for their wrong doing and their sin" (Tozzer 1941: 106, 112; trans. of Landa's original manuscript of ca. 1566).

As in other matters, the Maya believe that their personal well-being depends on their harmony with the world about them. Illness is a sign of disharmony. When a person is ill, a shaman is summoned and uses a variety of divination techniques to reveal the cause of illness. The prescribed cure includes measures to correct the cause of the illness discovered by the shaman—usually some harm done to another person, animal, or spirit. Curing rituals include prayers and burning of incense, along with the taking of medicines made from local plants. There are many medicinal herbs and plants in the Maya area, and shamans to this day preserve an extensive knowledge of these cures. Several colonial-period Maya manuscripts list a series of illnesses and their cures, and many of these remedies are considered effective.

Death

In colonial times, the Maya believed the dead went to Xibalba, the underworld beneath the earth, just as the sun did when it "died" each night at sunset before being reborn each dawn. Xibalba was a place of rest but not a paradise. There is evidence that Maya kings promoted special rituals to grant divine status to their dead predecessors. Several examples of this ritual apotheosis are recorded in Classic period texts. Once deified, these dead kings, it was believed, escaped Xibalba to dwell in the sky as stars.

The common people did not have the luxury of deification. According to Bishop Landa, the Maya expressed deep and enduring grief over the death of a loved one: "During the day they wept for them in silence; and at night with loud and very sad cries...(a)nd they passed many days in deep sorrow. They made abstinences and fasts for the dead" (Tozzer 1941: 129; trans. of Landa's original manuscript of ca. 1566).

The body was wrapped in a shroud and the mouth filled with ground maize and a jade bead. Commoners were buried under the floors or behind their houses. Into the grave were placed figurines of clay, wood, or stone and objects indicating the profession or trade of the deceased. Archaeologically excavated Maya burials usually have offerings that vary according to the sex and status of the deceased but almost always include a jade bead in the mouth.

Burials of the elite were the most elaborate. Bishop Landa reports that, in colonial-era Yucatan, the bodies of high-status individuals were cremated and their ashes placed in urns beneath temples. The construction of funerary shrines over tombs is well documented by archaeology. But, while evidence of cremation is not often found, there is evidence of burial ritual involving fire. At Copan, for example, several royal tombs were re-entered for rituals that included fire and smoke and the painting of the bones with red cinnabar.

During the time of Late Maya civilization, the Cocom ruling house at Mayapan reduced their dead to bones by boiling. The front of the skull was used as the base for a face modeled from resin, and this effigy was kept in their household shrines. These effigies were held in great veneration, and on feast days offerings of food were made to them so that they would remain well fed. When the Cenote of Sacrifice at Chichen Itza was dredged, a skull was recovered that had the crown cut away. The eye sockets were filled with wooden plugs, and there were the remains of painted plaster on the face.

KIN AND DESCENT

In Maya communities today, the life and destiny of every person are bound to the person's family, kin, community, and the supernatural world.

Steps in the life cycle are marked by ritual, as they were in ancient times. This includes marriage, which allows the individual and his or her family to establish ties with another family group.

The nuclear family is the foundation of Maya society. But the Maya have long defined social groupings larger than the nuclear family. Membership in these groups is based on descent through the male or female line. Recognition of membership in a patrilineal descent group is by the father's family name, transmitted from generation to generation just as in our own society. People with the same last name, therefore, are at least potentially members of the same patrilineage and in Maya society are prohibited from marrying. More than a last name is inherited from the father; property, titles, status, and even offices may be transmitted from one generation to the next according to patrilineal descent. In the past, these Maya patrilineal kin groups also seem to have had their own patron deities and social obligations, as well.

There was also a matrilineal principle in Maya society. In colonial Yucatan, children inherited surnames from both their father and their mother. In Postclassic Petén, there is evidence for both patrilineal and matrilineal descent. Each person was a member of two groups, a *ch'ibal*, defined by patrilineal descent, and a *ts'akab*, defined by matrilineal descent. Individuals inherited a surname and property from their father's *ch'ibal* and a second surname and religious identifications from their mother's *ts'akab*.

In ancient times, social and political offices were probably transmitted within patrilineal descent groups, from father to son, brother to brother, or even uncle to nephew. During the Classic period, the succession of kings is sometimes specified as from father to son. There are also examples of younger brothers succeeding older brothers as king. But succession in even the highest offices did not occur according to a single inflexible rule. At some sites, historical texts stress descent through both the male and the female lines, as at Palenque, while other sites emphasized the male line, as at Tikal and Copan. There are prominent portraits of elite women associated with kings at Piedras Negras, Coba, Yaxchilan, and Palenque and paired male and female portraits at both Calakmul and El Peru.

SOCIAL STRATIFICATION

The Maya recognized a number of distinctions within their society, beginning with those based on age and gender. There were also distinctions based on differences in status, prestige, and wealth. The latter are usually defined as disparities between the elite and the nonelite (or commoners). In Yucatan, these two classes were known as the *almehenob* (elite) and the *aj chembal uinicob* (commoners). Among the K'iche Maya of the highlands, the elite class was called the *ajawab*, while the nonelite were called the *al k'ajol*. Social stratification refers to the different rights, roles, and obligations accorded to two or more groups according to their place in society.

While these two categories are based on ethnohistoric descriptions and are reflected in differences in the archaeological record, the elite-nonelite distinction defines a very complex reality. There clearly was an elite class within ancient Maya society. But this class was not uniform, and the same can be said of the far more numerous commoners in Maya society.

Although there were clear differences between the huge masonry residences of kings and the small thatched houses of rural farmers or between elaborate royal tombs and simple commoner graves, these represent two extremes of a continuum of material remains based on size, elaborateness, and preservation. It is often impossible to see the boundary between elite and nonelite in the middle of this continuum. This indicates that the social distinctions between elite and nonelite were not always marked by material differences—there were undoubtedly relatively impoverished elites and wealthy commoners. Some of these people formed a middle class, which emerged with the changing economic conditions at the end of the Classic period (see chapter 8). Therefore, although the terms *elite* and *nonelite* (or commoner) are used here to refer to a basic division within Maya society, these labels only approximate the true diversity and complexity of past Maya society.

The elite class was divided by higher and lower status positions. Obviously, kings occupied the highest positions within the elite class. Not all kings and their kingdoms were equal. At any one point in time, there were wealthy and powerful kings and polities, while there were also less wealthy and less powerful kings and polities.

Below the king and the royal house there was a variety of other elite positions. Some were probably determined by kinship; a member of the elite class might have inherited his or her status and position in society from his father. Bishop Landa distinguished a title for priests, *aj k'inob,* who were members of the elite class. The K'iche Maya distinguished several elite occupational groups, such as merchants (*aj beyom*), professional warriors (*achij*), and estate managers (*uytzam chinamital*).

The elite certainly controlled far more resources, labor, and power (as decision makers) than the nonelite. Skeletal remains indicate that the elite enjoyed better health and longer lives. But these differences were not absolute. Maya commoners also controlled significant resources and labor. As food producers, they controlled most of the basic necessities of life. They even possessed potential power as decision makers, although they were seldom able to exert it. For, in choosing where they lived and to whom they owed allegiance, they could sometimes make or break the reigns of kings.

Gradations in nonelite burials and houses suggest that there were internal divisions of wealth and status. Commoners lived outside the central areas of the towns and cities, the core areas being reserved for the elite.

Generally speaking, the greater the distance a family lived from the central plaza, the lower its position on the social scale. Some distinctions probably derived from occupations—for example, skilled craftsmen were probably held in higher regard than unskilled laborers. Farmers defined the largest occupational group, whose toil supported both themselves and the king. Most Maya farmers probably worked their own land (or that of their family). In some areas, there was also a group of landless peasants, (known as the *nimak achi* among the K'iche Maya) who worked estates owned by the elite and were inherited along with the land.

The lowest status was that of slaves or captives owned by the elite. These were known as *p'entacob* in Yucatan or *munib* among the K'iche Maya and included commoners captured in war, sentenced criminals, and impoverished individuals sold into slavery by their families. Elite captives were often ritually sacrificed. Nonelite captives were either enslaved for labor or adopted by families to replace members lost to war or disease. Thieves were sentenced to become slaves of their victims until they could repay what they had stolen. Children of slaves were not considered slaves but were free to make their way on the basis of their abilities. But unwanted orphans could be sacrificed, especially if they were the children of slave women. Slaves were usually sacrificed when their masters died so that they could continue serving them after death.

All commoners had obligations to pay tribute to their rulers, their local elite lords, and the gods by offerings made through the priests. Tribute consisted of agricultural produce, woven cotton cloth, domesticated fowl, salt, dried fish, and hunted game. The most valuable offerings were cacao, *pom* (copal) incense, honey, beeswax, jade, coral, and shells. The corvée labor obligations of commoners were used to build temples, palaces, and other buildings, as well as causeways (*sacbeob*) that connected the principal Maya cities. Bishop Landa wrote, "The common people at their own expense made the houses of the lords [and]...cared for his fields and harvested...for him and his household; and when there was hunting or fishing, or when it was time to get their salt, they always gave the lord his share" (Tozzer 1941: 87; trans. of Landa's original manuscript of ca. 1566).

Elite and Nonelite Architecture

Maya buildings had practical and religious meanings. Residences reflected the status of their occupants and defined the center of the world for the family. Most buildings were constructed on platforms that raised them above the surface of the world, ranging from low earthen platforms for the simplest houses to the terraced masonry-faced "pyramids" for the loftiest temples. The most humble of ancient dwellings represent skillful engineering and beautiful craftsmanship applied by nonelite families to produce practical and well-adapted houses. These were constructed in the same manner as contemporary Maya houses; a pole framework supported a thatched roof, with walls made from a lattice of sticks, sometimes plastered with a thick coating of adobe. Commoner houses represent the oldest known examples of Maya architecture and are the basis for all later elaborations built of stone and plaster.

Far grander masonry structures are the best-known examples of Maya architecture. Elite architects and other specialists designed and supervised the construction of public buildings and the palaces used by kings and elite families, built and maintained by commoners to fulfill their obligations to the king and state. Nonelite specialists, such as stonemasons, and the artisans and artists who decorated buildings, probably filled many of the more skilled jobs. But the majority were part-time laborers fulfilling their corvée obligations during the dry season, when most agricultural activities ceased.

The basic raw material for masonry construction was limestone, found throughout most of the Maya the lowlands and in parts of the highlands. Plaster produced by burning limestone was used to pave plazas and to give a smoothed finish to walls, floors, and roofs of Maya buildings. Most buildings were also painted, sometimes in red or other solid colors, sometimes with painted motifs on the exterior or murals on the interior.

Because of the need for thick walls to support their roofs, Maya palaces and other masonry buildings have less interior space in proportion to their mass than the pole-and-thatch houses of the nonelite class. In most cases,

Figure 9.5 Maya corbelled arch forms the entrance to a Puuc-style palace complex at Labna, Mexico (Terminal Classic).

Figure 9.6 Elaborate masonry mosaic deity masks often frame palace doorways, as in this example from Chicanna, Mexico (Terminal Classic).

Figure 9.7 Modeled and painted plaster depiction of the "diving god" on a palace at Tulum, Mexico (Postclassic).

walls were built of rubble cores faced with masonry blocks and roofed by corbelled vaults. These were shaped like an inverted "V," constructed of a series of overlapping blocks, each projecting farther inward until a row of capstones could bridge the gap between the walls. Two- and three-story masonry buildings were constructed with especially massive walls and narrow vaults.

Many palaces and temples were adorned with displays of mosaic or stuccowork. Temples often had high, decorated roof combs that rose above the building. Some masonry palaces and other buildings had less weighty roofs made of wooden beams and mortar. Exteriors of palaces, temples, and other buildings had three-dimensional motifs rendered in both plaster and stone. These included portraits of kings and elites on palaces and funerary temples and large deity masks and a variety of other sacred elements on temples. Decorations made from modeled plaster are found on buildings from the time of Early Maya civilization to the Conquest. Beginning in the Classic period, carved stone mosaics (covered with thin plaster) gradually replaced modeled plaster. As mentioned, building surfaces were also usually painted.

Today we give labels to Maya structures that suggest their ancient functions: temples, palaces, ball courts, causeways, steam baths, shrines, and the like. Yet, to the ancient Maya who built and used them, buildings had multiple meanings that it is not always possible to decipher. Buildings were a means of realizing the Maya social and cosmological order. The locations, elaborateness, and decorations of residential buildings reflected the status and activities of their occupants. Thus, at Copan, the palace of the king's elite scribe was adorned by carved stone busts of the scribe holding his writing brush. Building orientations represented the order of the Maya universe, where east meant birth and life, west death and the underworld, north the sky and the supernatural abode, and south the earth and the human realm. Thus, at Tikal, the palaces of living kings were located south of the North Acropolis, where the ancestral kings were buried. Temples were sacred places, "mountains" with summit doorways that represented entrances to the abode of the gods. The ball game was played in "courts of creation" that recalled the myth about very origins of Maya society (chapter 11).

THE DEVELOPMENT OF MAYA SOCIETY

Our knowledge of past Maya society comes from archaeology, documents, and studies of Maya peoples today. Through these sources of information, we can outline the size and organization of ancient Maya society, how individuals lived out their lives, and the ways groups were defined by status and occupational specialties.

The foundation of Maya society has always been the nuclear family. Today the father or eldest male family member is the authority figure;

the same can be assumed to be true for the past. But the domestic authority of the mother or eldest female in the family is also important in the social system. In fact, in traditional Maya communities, important offices are held not by men alone but by married couples. Not surprisingly, then, both the male and female lines of descent have long been important in Maya society.

Extended families and "houses" were also important to Maya social organization. Overall, documentary evidence shows that Maya society was stratified into a smaller elite group that controlled most of the wealth and advantages and a far larger nonelite group of producers. This division is reflected in the archaeological evidence, along with evidence for a middle class that emerged at the end of the Classic period. Through tribute in goods and labor, the nonelite supported the elite and constructed and maintained the infrastructure of Maya cities, great and small.

Before civilization developed, Maya society was basically egalitarian, without differences in status and authority except those based on age and gender. Maya communities today are also basically egalitarian. Many are organized around a system where positions of authority and status are rotated each year among members of the community. By holding a succession of offices, individuals advance with age in the community hierarchy, so that the elders hold positions of highest authority. All levels of status and authority are shared. There is no permanent ruling class. A similar system may have operated among the ancient Maya before social stratification developed and probably continued as the basic organization for small farming communities.

Stratified society emerged with Early Maya civilization. This may have begun as some individuals and groups gained more wealth and power and took measures to ensure that they kept their advantageous position. A small but permanent elite class along with its servants and retainers soon dominated the larger settlements. The nonelite have always made up the bulk of the population, living in the most humble dwellings located on the peripheries (except for the service personnel needed by the elite). The commoners supported the ruling class by paying tribute in both goods and labor. In return, the elite class provided leadership, direction, and security with its knowledge of calendrics and supernatural prophecy. This knowledge gave rulers control over the times for plant and harvesting crops, thus ensuring agricultural success for the benefit of all society.

In time, with continued growth in population and in the complexity of society, many more groups emerged that were defined by differences in wealth, authority and status. By the time of Middle Maya civilization, many Maya cities were populated by large numbers of nonagricultural specialists representing many occupational groups and divisions. The ruling elite was subdivided into many different ranks and specialties. The same process of differentiation took hold of the nonelite as well, although the basic producers of food, the farmers, were always the largest group within Maya society. In time, the gap between the ruling elite and commoner classes was filled by an emerging "middle" class, defined by a variety of occupational groups derived from higher ranking commoners and lower ranking elite, including full-time occupational groups such as administrators or bureaucrats, merchants, warriors, craftsmen, architects, and artists. Many of these people were clients of the kings and others in the powerful elite. Otherwise, the core of Maya cities continued to be inhabited by the ruler, his family, and other members of allied elite houses that held the major positions in the political, religious, and economic hierarchy of society.

FURTHER READING

Abrams 1994; Andrews 1975; Ardren 2002; Ashmore and Sabloff 2002; Canuto and Yaeger 2000; Chase and Chase 1992; Christie 2003; Dunning 1992; Edmonson 1982, 1986; Farriss 1984; Gillespie 2002; Hill and Monaghan 1987; Houston 1998; Lohse and Valdez 2004; Masson and Freidel 2002; McAnany 1995; Proskouriakoff 1963; Sabloff 1994; Sabloff and Henderson 1993; Sharer and Traxler 2006; Sheets 2006; Tedlock 1985; Tozzer 1941; Vogt 1969; Wilk and Ashmore 1988; Willey 1987.

10

MAYA GOVERNMENT

The foundations of Maya society lay in ties of kinship, class, and community. Most Maya communities were part of one of the many independent Maya polities that rose and fell during the pre-Columbian era. The supreme ruler of each polity in the southern lowlands, the *kuhul ajaw* ("holy lord"), was a member of a royal house and part of a dynasty of ancestral kings. Maya kings usually ruled with an advisory council, composed of the major elite lords within the state who also held title to specific offices within the upper levels of the state hierarchy.

Maya rulers were very concerned with advertising their achievements. The monuments, buildings, and texts they left behind provide the most explicit evidence for reconstructing the Maya political system, especially as it existed during Middle Maya civilization. But we must also remember that these sources were not unbiased, for they also contained political propaganda designed to impress others with the successes and power of the king.

BASES OF POLITICAL POWER

The foundations for the political power held by the Maya elite lay in the social and economic differences in the class structure of Maya society. Because these distinctions were common to all Maya polities, other factors must account for the different degrees of power and success enjoyed by some polities over others. One factor stemmed from differences in political organization itself. But, more basic, differences in the environmental and economic potentials of each Maya settlement help explain why some cities grew to be the capitals of powerful states while others were dominated by their more successful contemporaries.

The location and prosperity of all human settlements are conditioned by access to essential resources, such as water and food, trade routes, and security in times of conflict. Thus, it is no accident that the largest and most successful Maya cities were positioned to take advantage of good soils and dependable water sources. In addition, many Maya cities were located along major rivers (Yaxchilan, Piedras Negras, and Quirigua, to name only a few) that served as important communication and trade routes, in addition to providing water and productive alluvial soils for agriculture. El Mirador, Tikal, and Calakmul, all located on the divide between major lowland drainage basins, were able to control the heads of navigation and canoe portages for transport across the Petén. Most sites in this region are associated with *bajos,* the shallow seasonal lakes that provided water and yielded rich harvests when modified by raised fields. Other sites, such as Cerros, Lamanai, and Tulum, were located to control seacoast trade along the east coast of the Yucatan Peninsula.

Major resources with widespread demand influenced the location and prosperity of Maya cities. Examples include Kaminaljuyu, in the southern highlands (control of obsidian); Chunchucmil and Dzibilchaltun, in northern Yucatan (access to coastal salt); Colha, in Belize (control of good-quality flint); Guaytan, in the middle Motagua Valley (control of jade sources); and Quirigua, in the lower Motagua Valley (control of cacao production).

Yet, the location and prosperity of Maya settlement cannot be entirely explained by environmental and economic factors. Religious considerations were also critical. Cities enjoyed increased prestige from their cosmological and mythological associations, such as being an eastern capital associated with the rising sun. The locations of many Maya cities adjacent to bodies of water and caves were important because these landscape features were important in Maya cosmology, since both were associated with Xibalba, the watery underworld. Maya cosmological principles are also reflected in the ways Maya sites were planned and grew through time.

Factors such as these help explain why Maya cities varied in size, arrangement, and style. The smallest covered less than a square mile, whereas the largest, such as Tikal and Calakmul, extended over areas of some 130 square kilometers. The political and economic power these two cities commanded were also evident in their elaborate buildings, their myriad monuments and hieroglyphic inscriptions, and the numerous times each was mentioned by other cities in historical texts.

Differences in size and complexity indicate that some Maya cities exerted political dominance over others, and these relationships are often verified by texts that record one king's acknowledgment of his subordinate status to another. Economic and political alliances provided for varying degrees of control by more powerful cities over smaller centers. Dominant capitals such as Tikal sponsored the founding of colonial centers in outlying regions. Calakmul used alliances with smaller cities to nearly surround and finally defeat Tikal. The kings of many cities used raids and open warfare to defeat their neighbors, then extracted tribute to maintain their domination.

The distribution of Maya road (*sacbe*) systems is evidence of the degree to which political authority was centralized, as well as of the extent of past political realms. El Mirador's connections with its hinterland were defined by its radiating causeway system, constructed in the Late Preclassic. The Classic period capital of Caracol was connected to a series of satellite centers by causeways. The most extensive system was at Coba, where a network of roadways linked the site core with a series of outlying sites and subordinate cities, including Yaxuna some 100 kilometers distant, clearly reflecting the extent of Coba's ancient centralized authority.

MAYA POLITIES

The Maya were never politically unified, always being divided into numerous independent polities. Individual Maya polities rose and fell over a span of some 2,000 years (ca. 600 B.C.E.–1500 C.E.). Some of these states lasted only a few hundred years, but many, such as Tikal, endured for 600 or 800 years. A few, like Kaminaljuyu, adapted to changing conditions and survived almost 2,000 years.

Scholars have long been interested in the factors that contributed to the growth and decline of these independent states and, in particular, how large the most successful examples grew in both territory and population. Maya sources give little direct information; the best historical information comes from the period of the Spanish Conquest. These sources enable scholars to reconstruct a great deal about the relationships between kingdoms and the approximate number of ancient Maya political realms at the end of the pre-Columbian era (some 18 in Yucatan; to be discussed further later on) but offer little information about territorial boundaries and population size.

Territorial Size

Networks of radiating causeways help define the extent of political control exerted by some Maya capitals. However, determining the size of ancient Maya polities is difficult, especially when there are no records of actual boundaries. Yet, Maya polities were defined by their territory, which often expanded and contracted over time. Copan enjoyed its maximum size in the Early Classic, before losing its northern territory in the Late Classic when Quirigua broke free of its control. Other states, such as Calakmul and Dos Pilas, reached their greatest extent as the result of successful warfare in the Late Classic. On the other hand, the populations

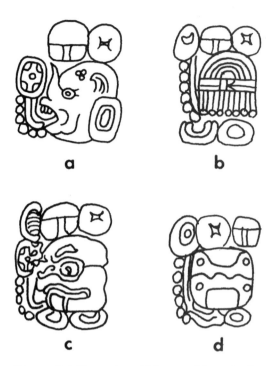

Figure 10.1 Examples of Maya emblem glyphs that represent major Classic-era polities: (a) Copan; (b) Tikal; (c) Calakmul; (d) Palenque. Each is a royal title that reads "holy ruler of [name of city]."

of most lowland polities reached their maximum at the end of the Classic period, before suffering a catastrophic decline in the Terminal Classic.

The reconstruction of ancient Maya political realms and relationships is based on different kinds of evidence. Emblem glyphs represent titles used by kings to proclaim their rule over a named realm, such as the holy lords of Tikal. Thus, emblem glyphs identify the seats of sovereign political power. However, not all capitals identified by emblem glyphs were equal in power and sovereignty; some kings recorded that they recognized the kings of larger, more powerful polities like Calakmul and Tikal as their overlords. So, use of an emblem glyph may represent a *claim* for a polity's sovereignty, although the relative power and degree of independence that polity enjoyed may have varied over time.

The size of ancient Maya polities has been estimated by various means, which produce generally consistent results. Differences in site patterning and locations define the polity boundary between Piedras Negras and Yaxchilan. The known extent of Late Preclassic causeways of El Mirador suggest a polity of between 5,000 and 6,000 square kilometers. Caracol's causeway network indicate that it controlled a Late Classic polity of about the same size. Calakmul's causeways cover a somewhat smaller area of about 4,000 square kilometers. The largest network, at Coba, suggests a polity that might have reached 20,000 square kilometers at its peak in the Terminal Classic period. Ethnohistoric accounts suggest that the sizes of Postclassic polities in the northern lowlands ranged from about 1,000 to more than 10,000 square kilometers.

Polity size can also be estimated from the maximum distance that military forces could be controlled from a capital. This appears to have been about 60 kilometers, to judge from logistic requirements and marching distance figures from Conquest-era central Mexico. The 60-kilometer optimum distance figure implies that Maya capitals could have controlled polities of up to about 11,000 square kilometers. However, the density of Late Classic capitals in the southern lowlands indicates that most polities were somewhat smaller, probably about 8,000–9,000 square kilometers. Yet, there is evidence that the most powerful Maya states extended their reach over far greater distances. Texts record that Calakmul twice successfully attacked Palenque over a distance far greater than 60 kilometers.

Incidentally, if we use an average polity size estimate of about 8,500 square kilometers, the total population of the Tikal polity could have approached a million people at its peak. This estimate is based on a Late Classic population of 92,000 for "greater Tikal" (chapter 9), plus an estimated 820,000 people for its rural hinterland of about 8,200 square kilometers inhabited by an average of 200 people per square kilometer (assuming that about one-half of this area was uninhabited), yielding a total of 942,000 people.

Economic and Social Relationships

Regardless of size, each independent Maya polity experienced growth and decline. A variety of events and circumstances contributed to both the successes and the failures of each kingdom. Some of these were internal and unique to each polity. For example, success often depended on the personal abilities and lifespans of individual kings. It also might be influenced by the efficiency of the king's administrators or by the occurrence of good weather that allowed local farmers to harvest enough food for the population. Other factors were external and involved a much wider network of relationships with other states. These included social and economic exchanges, competition, and warfare. And these were not only social, political, or economic relationships; as with most aspects of Maya culture; they were also imbued with levels of religious motivation and meaning.

Maya lowland states maintained many social and economic ties that reflected interactions between kingdoms. For example, there were visitations and marriage arrangements, exchanges of goods and services, and even payments of tribute between polities. It is likely that most social interaction, including visits and marriage alliances, occurred between people from the same or nearby communities, although some undoubtedly involved more distant regions. We know from the inscriptions that Maya kings used royal visits and marriage exchanges between royal houses to cement alliances between polities. There are records from the time of the Spanish Conquest of reciprocal arrangements between Maya communities—some separated by several days' travel by foot—whereby each town provided female marriage partners for the men living in the other town.

Warfare

Not all interaction between Maya kingdoms was peaceful. Warfare was an important determinant of the relative power and prestige of individual polities. Most conflicts were limited in scale and scope. The most common results recorded on monuments were the taking of sacrificial captives from neighbors, used to sanctify events such as the inauguration of a ruler or the dedication of a new temple. Often, this involved forces from a polity capital raiding a far smaller town within a neighboring kingdom. Successes in taking captives and gaining tribute were important for the prestige of Maya kings; therefore, warfare of this kind contributed to the growth of royal authority, especially in establishing the power of new dynasties as the number of Maya polities expanded.

Warfare also had religious meaning. The timing of war and the degree of success were believed to be determined by the will of the gods. Important conflicts between kingdoms were reenacted in ritual ball games, held in the victorious city, culminating in the sacrifice of captives after they had played out a preordained game scenario. The timing of raids and captive sacrifice rituals coincided with important anniversaries of past events or auspicious positions of the sky deities (planets), especially Venus, in keeping with Maya beliefs in predestiny and the cyclical nature of time (discussed further in chapter 11).

However, some conflicts were motivated by more practical concerns, such as commercial rivalries. It is quite probable that Quirigua attacked and gained its victory over its former master at Copan to secure independent control of the Motagua jade route. It is very likely that the war between Calakmul and Tikal that periodically raged for more than a century was fought to determine which power would control the major overland trade routes in the Maya lowlands. Warfare often ensured economic prosperity for the victor and also created tempting targets for rival powers. Thus, it is no surprise that several prominent Maya cities were fortified, including the greatest rivals of Middle Maya civilization: Tikal by earthworks and Calakmul by an encircling canal.

Figure 10.2 The most vivid representation of Maya warfare comes from the Bonampak murals; in the center of this scene the victorious ruler holds a spear and grasps a captive by the hair (Late Classic). From Ruppert, Thompson, and Proskouriakoff 1955. Reprinted by permission of the President and Fellows of Harvard College.

Wars between Maya kingdoms clearly had several purposes. The prevailing forms of warfare were ritualized conflicts or raids undertaken for religious, economic, and political purposes—to provide captives to sacrifice to the gods, while at the same time increasing the wealth and power of the victor and diminishing the wealth and power of the vanquished. But the aims and scale of warfare expanded over time. Some winners, such as the Petexbatun kingdom, increased their territory by conquest. Some victors succeeded in breaking away from older kingdoms and creating new polities, as when Quirigua gained its independence from Copan. Conflict also grew in intensity as competition for resources, prestige, and power increased, becoming even more frequent by the end of Middle Maya civilization. By then, warfare was endemic in some regions, like the Petexbatun. Wars of conquest and the scale of violence undoubtedly contributed to the decline of Middle Maya civilization, even as it became more common during Late Maya civilization.

The Cycles of Political Unity

Maya kingdoms experienced a constantly changing political landscape. Some Maya cities, obviously larger and more powerful than others, likely controlled larger territories and exercised dominance over their smaller neighbors. The careers of some southern lowland polities enjoyed one or more cycles of growth and prosperity, followed by decline and depression. El Mirador seems to have dominated much of the southern lowlands in the Late Preclassic. After its fall, a number of new polities developed during the Early Classic era. Some of these states expanded their realms through colonies and even conquest, as Tikal did in annexing Uaxactun. Calakmul came close to unifying much of the southern lowlands under its dominion through alliance and warfare. But, following Calakmul's failure to consolidate its victory and Tikal's eventual triumph over its adversary, the number of independent polities again expanded. New capitals were founded, and some formerly subordinate sites, like Quirigua and Xunantunich, broke away and, for a relatively brief time, became the capitals of independent polities.

During Middle and Late Maya civilization in the northern lowlands, there was a similar ebb and flow of fortunes. Yucatan was fragmented into many polities large and small until much of the northern lowland area was united under the rule of Chichen Itza. After that city's downfall, central Yucatan was dominated by a new capital at Mayapan, only to fragment again into at least 18 independent polities by the time of the Spanish Conquest. Collectively, these trends throughout the history of Maya civilization can be seen as fluctuations between times of political consolidation (fewer and larger polities), and times of political fragmentation (more numerous and smaller polities).

KING AND POLITIES

The earliest monuments and texts indicate that increasingly powerful individual rulers began using the title *ajaw* during the era of Early Maya civilization in both the southern area and the lowlands to the north. By the beginning of Middle Maya civilization, kings throughout the lowlands began to take on the more exalted title of *k'uhul ajaw,* holy lord. In the royal inscriptions, later kings often referred to the earliest ruler in each polity as a "founder" and in many cases counted the line of succession from this hallowed individual. Especially successful kings accumulated additional titles honoring their achievements in battle ("captor of..."), prestigious advanced age ("four *k'atun* lord"), and their identification with supernatural powers (*K'inich* or "radiant sun lord").

Some rulers, like the kings of Tikal, also took the title or *Kaloomte'*, which apparently refers to "supreme king." Less powerful rulers became subordinated to more powerful kings through alliances; although still referring to themselves as a *k'uhul ajaw,* they also recorded that they were a *Yajaw*

Figure 10.3 Stela D at Quirigua, Guatemala, portrays K'ak' Tiliw Chan Yopaat, who defeated Copan in 738; Maya kings were displayed to their subjects as majestic figures with symbols of political and religious power including costuming, headdresses, and scepters (Late Classic). After Maudslay 1889–1902.

(vassal lord) to another king, such as the king of Calakmul. When a subordinate king was inaugurated, the texts would record that he became king *u kabi* or "under the authority" of his overlord, the king of Calakmul.

At the same time, the elite class and the various secondary offices held by elite men grew in numbers. The hierarchy of authority continued to expand, and in some Maya states records tell us that the king's administrative subordinates had formal titles, such as *sajal* ("noble"). A number of these administrators were under the authority of a *baah sajal* ("head noble") or *baah ajaw* (head lord) who reported to the king.

The Basis of Royal Authority

These lines of authority were enforced by economic and religious factors. The ruler and his elite officials provided security and protection for their subjects, but people were also motivated to be obedient because they received economic and religious benefits as a result. From the king on down, officials rewarded good deeds with gifts of food and goods. State festivals and feasts distributed the bounty of successful king to their subjects. Religious belief reinforced the system by holding that everyone's success and health depended on staying in harmony with the Maya universe, an important part of which required obeying the king and his officials. The sanctions for disobedience were loss of economic benefits and the wrath of the gods, bringing misfortune and even death. Maya governmental authority relied on economic and religious sanctions, although, when all else failed, severe punishments were available for individuals who displeased the king. The lesson learned from watching captives being sacrificed was obviously a powerful incentive for people to obey the king and his officials.

By the same token, the authority and prestige of each Maya king depended on the economic and supernatural success of his polity. Power was transmitted by promoting economic benefits, agricultural success, and ready access to markets and religion, especially the sponsoring of public ceremonies that were believed to ensure favor from the gods. Agricultural failures could weaken a king's prestige and cripple his ability to bestow favors on his officials and subjects. A disaster such as a defeat in war could undermine royal authority because it was seen as a sign that the gods were angry with the defeated king and his polity. As a result, the Maya political landscape was composed of many competitive kingdoms that were dependent on each other since they shared the same cultural values, subsistence technology, economic system, and religious beliefs.

Each polity had a capital where the king, his court, and the advisory council lived. A loose hierarchy of subordinate centers surrounded the capital. The size of each kingdom and the number of its subordinate centers shifted through time, varying according to its success in war and in providing for its subjects. Aggressive and powerful kings attempted to expand their power. For example, for 50 years Yuknoom the Great dominated the southern lowlands after his kingdom of Calakmul used a network of alliances to defeat Tikal, its chief rival. Tikal's fortunes were at low ebb until an especially effective and powerful king, Jasaw Chan K'awiil, took power and defeated its former enemies.

A Maya ruler had to be a successful war leader, a successful diplomat to organize alliances, and a successful religious leader to conduct ceremonies. To be effective, a Maya king also had to personally control his subordinates, especially in the collection of tribute in goods and labor. A failure, whether caused by inability or by bad luck, could bring misfortune to the entire kingdom. Most critical of all, the capture and execution of a king by a rival could mean subjugation or even a complete takeover of the defeated polity. A case in point is the aggressive kings of the Petexbatun kingdom who conquered more and more territory by defeating their rivals—until the tables were turned. When Tikal and Palenque lost their kings to their enemies, even though they remained too powerful to be completely subjugated, both polities suffered declines—far more serious in the case of Tikal. In another case, when the former subordinate ruler of Quirigua captured and beheaded the king of Copan, the result was political independence for Quirigua and a severe blow to the prosperity and prestige of Copan. Even though the Copan kingdom eventually regained its prestige and power, the power of its kings never fully recovered from this defeat. The power vacuum was filled by elite nobles of the advisory council who assumed more power in the wake of the defeat.

The New Political Order

When an ever-increasing number of Maya kings failed to solve the problems of overpopulation, degradation of the environment, increasing violence, and drought, their prestige and power rapidly evaporated. When their subjects lost faith in the power and authority of their kings, they moved elsewhere. By the end of Middle Maya civilization, the problems in many areas of the southern lowlands were so severe that most of this area never recovered. But, even in less devastated regions, such as Yucatan and the highlands, the old system of dynastic rulers was discredited, and a new political order emerged. The new political system relied less on the personal achievements and power of the king and more on the collective wisdom of the *multepal* or elite council. The *multepal* proved to be far more flexible and responsive than the old royal system.

Kings did not completely disappear, but they ruled in conjunction with their councils and no longer promoted themselves as "holy lords." The most effective and powerful of the new lowland states ruled by a *multepal* system was Chichen Itza. This form of government allowed Chichen Itza to control far more territory and resources than its predecessors. Chichen Itza was succeeded by Mayapan, but when this capital was destroyed, the political landscape of Yucatan was fractured into the many small and diverse polities that the Spanish encountered and eventually conquered.

DYNASTIES AND ROYAL HOUSES

The power of Maya kings was based on connections to past rulers. The most obvious examples are royal successions from father to son that kept kingship within the same patriline. Yet, such father-to-son successions rarely lasted more than three or four generations. Although the long-term sequences of kings within each polity formed dynasties, these were interrupted by the loss of kings to capture and sacrifice, conquest, and usurpers. Royal succession was not always automatic, as the change in rulership at Tikal in 378 shows. Yet, Tikal's dynasty continued—when Yax Nuun Ayiin took the throne he was proclaimed the fifteenth successor to Tikal's dynastic founder, even though he was a usurper, perhaps even a foreigner. So Maya dynasties were not based on unbroken records of lineal descent but rather were proclaimed by royal titles that identified each ruler's place in a line of succession that began with a founding king. Each *k'uhul ajaw* was sanctioned by his predecessors, which ultimately led back to a dynastic founder or a deified ancestor who could be invoked by ritual.

Political stability often requires a flexible system for succession, especially if this prevents disastrous power struggles and allows the most talented individual to become king. Such flexibility is provided by a "house system," which in this case refers to a recognized residential group that is maintained through time by including members on the basis of flexible criteria, including kinship, marriage, ties to a common ancestor, and adoption. Examples include the ruling houses of Europe, maintained by rights to inheritance and succession that are often patrilineal, fictive kinship ties, and even appeals to mythic origins. Great Britain's royal House of Windsor is a case in point, both for its ability to maintain its substantial wealth and property and for its reliance on both patrilineal and matrilineal succession to the throne.

Evidence suggests that many of the same characteristics apply to Classic Maya ruling houses, which were composed of dynasties of rulers that clearly maintained wealth and power for many centuries and relied on both patrilineal and matrilineal succession. Maya ruling houses were associated with residential locations—royal palaces within polity capitals. They were also defined by reference to ancestral founding figures and exclusive patron deities, kinship, marriage, religious beliefs, and a commitment to maintain their power and status within society. The practice of many Maya ruling dynasties of tracing their succession to a single founder regardless of actual lineal descent is characteristic of a house-based organization.

Lesser versions of house-based organizations probably operated in elite Maya society. These houses would have occupied the range of elite residences, varying in size and elaborateness of construction, found within each Maya city. These probably represent a hierarchy of elite houses that held offices in Maya polities and maintained estates for their members over many generations. House-based groups allowed a flexible means to perpetuate power and wealth, especially for the elite and royal echelons of Maya society. This made it much easier for better-qualified individuals to inherit positions of power, including that of the king, especially when difficulties in succession arose. It smoothed over abrupt changes in succession as long as usurpers could demonstrate ability and legitimacy to rule and fits well with the records of ruling dynasties that dominated much of the Maya world for more than a thousand years.

GOVERNMENT IN A COMMONER COMMUNITY

Although Maya texts say nothing about how the thousands of rural settlements were governed, archaeological evidence from the extraordinarily preserved Classic period site of Cerén, El Salvador, gives us a glimpse of government in a small commoner community. Cerén was undoubtedly within the polity of San Andrés, a relatively small capital only about 5 kilometers away. One building at Cerén has been identified as a public building used for local governance. It is located on the west side of the plaza area and is the largest building at the site, measuring 8 by 5 meters and situated on a meter-high 10-by-8-meter platform. Its walls are thicker and higher than those of other Cerén buildings and were made of solid adobe rather than *bajareque,* finished by a smooth coat of mud plaster. Also unlike other buildings, it had a thatched roof supported by posts set outside the walls, although, like other Cerén buildings, its overhang covered an area twice the size of its interior. Entered from a roofed veranda on its eastern side, it had a doorway wider than any other at Cerén. The veranda floor preserves patterns of wear from foot traffic, indicating that the prevailing directions for people entering and leaving the building were to the east and west. The interior was divided into a front and a rear room by a medial wall and doorway. The front room had two wide adobe benches set against its sidewalls. Incised graffiti of lines and punctations were preserved on the south wall.

Its distinctive characteristics indicate this building was used for purposes different from those of Cerén's prevailing household structures. This is also obvious from the general lack of artifacts associated with household activities. A very large jar was found on the south bench, and a somewhat smaller storage jar was on the veranda. The only other notable artifacts discovered with the building were two perforated mortars, probably used to grind materials. The usual array of domestic implements and containers found in other Cerén buildings was absent. There were no obsidian blades or scrapers, no manos or metates, celts, or baskets. The full inventory of pottery cooking, serving, and storage vessels was also missing.

The evidence, therefore, points its purpose as a community meeting place. Members of the community may have assembled on the veranda, waiting to be summoned into the front room. The large benches in this room were likely used to seat people with authority—community elders and/or councilors—who would have met to discuss community affairs, make decisions, and settle local disputes. Drinks ladled from the great vessel on the south bench could have sealed these actions. These authorities probably also announced assignments of corvée labor obligations and other orders received from the nearby governing center of San Andrés.

POLITIES AT THE DAWN OF SPANISH CONQUEST

By the time of the Conquest, the many independent states in Yucatan and in the highlands were organized in different ways. But, overall, these systems continued the lessons learned from the failure of the earlier dynastic kings, balancing the concentration of power in the hands of individual rulers with power shared among elite councils and a multitude of office-holders.

What we know about the political systems in these areas comes from documentary sources. In Yucatan we have the Maya chronicles of the *Books of Chilam Balam* and the detailed account written by Bishop Diego de Landa in the sixteenth century. In the K'iche Maya area of the highlands we have the most remarkable Maya book, the *Popol Vuh*, and other Maya and Spanish chronicles.

The Northern Lowlands

At the time of the Spaniards' arrival, the 18 independent Maya states in Yucatan had three forms of government. In fact, these systems had a great many shared features, but all but a few were ruled from a capital city (*cah*) with a ruling lord and a council of nobles. The elite council met in the *popol nah* ("house of the mat") and functioned as an advisory body to the ruling lord. In the absence of a ruler, the council acted as supreme authority within the state. In addition, there were several polities without a central capital that relied on a loose confederation of allied cities, each controlled by elite houses.

Nine of the 18 polities were ruled by a single lord, called either *ajaw* or *halach winik* ("true man") in Yucatan. Although this system descended from the old dynastic rulers of Middle Maya civilization, it differed in important respects. The later ruling lords did not advertise themselves or their achievements on carved monuments. They possessed less personal power and shared more authority with their advisory councils. They did not link their personal prestige with the fate of their kingdom.

Landa reports that both civil and religious offices were hereditary and came from the elite class. However, there were important exceptions. The ruling lords of Yucatan were *usually* succeeded by their oldest sons, although Landa says that brothers or the best-qualified candidate could become king if there was no qualified son: "If, when the lord died, there were no sons [old enough] to reign...the priests and principal people [elite council] elected a man proper for the position" (Tozzer 1941: 100; trans. of Landa's original manuscript of ca. 1566).

The *halach winik* was the head of government. He was also likely the highest religious authority. He apparently formulated foreign and domestic policies with the aid of a council of the leading chiefs, priests, and town councilors (*aj kuch kabob*) who met in the *popol nah* to discuss public affairs. The elite council was an advisory body to the *halach winik,* or, if there was no single ruler, it acted as supreme authority for the polity.

Below the *halach winik* were the *batabob,* or subordinate lords. These were members of the hereditary nobility, the *almehenob,* appointed by the *halach winik* to administer the polity's towns and villages. Each *batab* presided over a local council, sentenced criminals, and decided civil suits.

If cases were unusually important, he consulted the *halach winik* before passing judgment. The *batab* was provided with food and other necessities by his subjects, and he ensured that his town or village paid its required tribute to the *halach winik*. In times of war, each *batab* also headed a unit of warriors under the authority of a supreme military commander (*nacom*). Below the *batab* were the town councilors. Each had a vote in the town government and was the head of a *nahlil,* or subdivision of the town.

The *holpopob* ("those at the head of the mat") assisted in governing their towns and served as intermediaries for townspeople seeking to speak with the *batab*. At least two towns in late Postclassic Yucatan were ruled by a *holpop*. Elsewhere the *holpopob* were advisers on foreign policy and masters of the *popol nah.*

The *kulelob* were assistants who carried out the orders issued by the *bata-bob* and accompanied their masters wherever they went. The *tupiles,* or town constables, were responsible for enforcing the laws and keeping the peace.

There were also *chilanes,* or "speakers," who reported to the people the replies of the gods. The *chilanes* were held in such high respect that the people carried them on their shoulders when they appeared in public. The most likely descendants of the *chilanes* today are the shamans (*ajmen,* or "he who understands") who still practice divination, cure disease by traditional methods, and conduct rituals.

The Maya Highlands

At the time of the Spanish Conquest, the highland Maya were organized in ways similar to those of the people of Yucatan. The best-documented Postclassic highland government is that of the K'iche Maya.

The *ajpop* ("lord of the mat") served as supreme ruler of Utatlan. He made political appointments, led the religious rituals held for the welfare of the population, and was the head of the army. The heir apparent, the *ajpop k'amja,* assisted the *ajpop* before assuming the ruling office. The *q'alel* was the supreme judge, and the *atzij winaq* was the speaker for the government. The *ajawab* elders, together with other specialists, including several high priests, formed a council that advised the ruler and helped formulate policy for all K'iche society.

Near Utatlan were two other K'iche centers, Chisalin and Ismachi, each with its own ruling elite and populations. Owing to marriage alliances and the military supremacy exercised by the ajpop in Utatlan, K'iche society functioned as a fairly unified kingdom at the time of the Conquest. Yet, allied groups could marshal sufficient military strength to challenge the power of the *ajpop*. This did indeed happen on several occasions and culminated in the revolt of the Kaqchikel and their subsequent establishment of an independent state with its capital at Iximche.

On the eve of the Conquest, there was a series of independent Maya polities in the highlands, many with political organizations similar to that of the K'iche. The K'iche state expanded to subdue some of its neighbors, such as the Mam Maya to the west. But the neighboring Kaqchikel and Tz'utujil Maya kingdoms, sworn enemies of the K'iche, remained independent. Despite these conflicts, the K'iche and the other highland polities maintained mutual relationships through peaceful commerce, religious pilgrimages, gift exchanges, and marriage alliances. Thus, though far from politically unified, the Postclassic Maya highlands were tied together by economic, religious, and kinship bonds.

FURTHER READING

Ardren 2002; Bell, Canuto, and Sharer 2004; Braswell 2003; Chase and Chase 1996; Culbert 1991; Demarest 2004; Farriss 1984; Fash 2001; Fox 1978, 1987; Golden and Borgstede 2004; Grube 2001; Hill 1996; Inomata and Houston 2001; Jones 1998; Lohse and Valdez 2004; Looper 2003; Marcus 1992b; Martin and Grube 1995, 2008; Sabloff 1994, 2003; Schele and Freidel 1990; Sharer and Traxler 2006; Tiesler and Cucina 2006; Tozzer 1941.

11

MAYA RELIGION

Maya religion was based on a body of beliefs and concepts about super-natural powers that explained life and the universe. These concepts rein-forced the social and political order and were the basis for the power held by kings and by the elite class. Indeed, the political system included priests who were in charge of the rituals and the knowledge that allowed them to communicate with the supernatural and to interpret events through the keeping of historical chronicles. Maya religious beliefs were held by all levels of society—commoner, elite, priest, and king.

By the time of the Spanish Conquest, changes in Maya religion had oc-curred as new customs were introduced from other parts of Mesoamerica. It relied less on huge public spectacles like those once conducted at Tikal or Chichen Itza, although the practice of human sacrifice increased. Family rituals became more prominent—every household included large incense burners and other deity figures. There was more emphasis on pilgrim-ages to sacred locations, such as Chichen Itza's famous sacred cenote, and shrines. But Maya religion was changed much more drastically in the sixteenth century by the imposition of Christianity, sometimes forcibly. To the Spaniards, Maya priests were agents of the devil and accordingly were converted, killed, or driven underground.

The disappearance of the Maya priesthood, the most visible aspect of "paganism," produced great changes in Maya religion. Public shrines and their "idols" were destroyed, and public ceremonies were banned. With the disappearance of Maya priests and the public aspects of Maya reli-gion, much of Maya learning, including the writing system, disappeared also. Maya books were confiscated and burned. Fortunately, a few native accounts survived, preserving a fragmentary record of ancient Maya religion and recorded knowledge.

The less public elements of the Maya belief system often escaped detection and managed to be perpetuated within Maya family and village life down to the present. When Spanish pressure for conversion was intense, Maya beliefs and rituals were kept secret and apart from Christianity. Although baptized and officially "converted," many Maya people learned to accept the public aspects of the new religion inside the Catholic Church but continued the old family rituals in their houses and the agricultural rituals in their fields. Some Christian and Maya symbols were similar, making it easier for the Maya to accommodate the new religion by seeming to accept Christian concepts, while preserving their old beliefs under a new guise. For instance, the cross existed as an ancient Maya symbol for the tree of life, the sacred ceiba supporting the heavens; thus, the Christian cross was accepted, although it was often venerated for its traditional Maya meaning.

In the sixteenth century, the Spanish Inquisition was brought to Yucatan to extinguish all vestiges of "paganism." Many Maya people fled from Spanish oppression, establishing refugee settlements deep in the forests of southeastern Yucatan. Under the leadership of their shamans, the Maya preserved their religious traditions in these communities amid a fierce tradition of Maya independence. These included the veneration of a Maya "talking cross" that served as an oracle. In the nineteenth century, the Mexican government tried to gain control over these independent Maya communities, resulting in the "War of the Castes." Although peace came early in the twentieth century, many of these communities remained isolated and independent of outside control until the mid-twentieth century.

Another group that remained isolated until recently is the Lacandon Maya in the southern lowlands of the state of Chiapas, Mexico. Many vestiges of ancient Maya religion survived in their beliefs and rituals. For instance, the Lacandon continued to make and use pottery incensarios, similar in form and use to those of the pre-Columbian era. Lacandon rituals are still held in sacred caves and in the ruined temples of several lowland Maya cities.

In other areas, Christianity was peacefully introduced—largely thanks to the efforts of Father Bartolomé de Las Casas, who defended the Maya against exploitation by Europeans wherever he could. One such area was the Alta Verapaz, in the highlands of Guatemala, where Maya and Christian elements have blended into a religion that preserves both traditions. Over the years, in the remote communities of the highlands, Maya shamans, in the absence of Catholic priests, assumed control of public ceremonies, such as baptisms and masses held in churches, while continuing their traditional practices of divining and curing illnesses. Maya highland shamans have also preserved elements of the ancient calendrical system,

Figure 11.1 As in ancient times, Maya shamans continue to conduct curing rituals, burning copal incense and making blood offerings,
as in this case from the Maya highlands.

such as the 260-day almanac, used to determine the birthday names of
infants and the proper days for ceremonies.

Thus, although 500 years of European efforts have profoundly changed
the more public aspects of Maya religion, many traditional beliefs have
been passed down from generation to generation within Maya families
and from generation to generation of Maya shamans. In Maya communities today there are shamans and many other people who continue to hold
concepts and beliefs that come from the pre-Columbian past. In fact, over
the past few decades, there has been a resurgence of Maya religion. This
has led to a great increase in the number of Maya rituals and ceremonies
conducted at sacred locations, including many archaeological sites.

Ancient Maya religion can be reconstructed in part from these present-
day Maya beliefs and practices, supplemented by archaeological evidence and accounts from the time of the Conquest. This chapter explores
some of these reconstructed aspects of Maya religion as it existed before
the Conquest.

COSMOLOGY

The basic Maya concepts of life and the universe are quite different from Western views, which see the world as being composed of separate natural and supernatural realms. Westerners use science to study and understand the natural world, defined by everything that can be observed, including both the living realm of creatures on the earth and the physical realm of our planet Earth, the solar system, the Milky Way galaxy, and the entire universe. Western science is not concerned with the supernatural realm, defined by everything that is unobservable, including the beliefs held by codified religions.

Maya cosmology, the concepts that described and explained their world, did not distinguish between natural and supernatural realms. For the Maya, all things animate or inanimate were part of a single existence that is both visible and invisible. Everything in the Maya world was imbued in different degrees with an unseen power or sacred quality. Rocks, trees, mountains, sun, moon, stars, and all living creatures—including humans— were animated by this sacred essence. The Mayan word for this essence is *k'uh*, meaning divine or sacredness. *K'uh* can refer to a sacred entity or "god." It is the root for *k'uhul ajaw*, the "holy lord" title of Maya kings. The Maya believed this sacred quality was part of a life force in humans associated with blood, the heart, and breath (*ch'ulel* in many modern Maya languages) that continued on after death, somewhat like the Western concept of the soul. This is reflected in depictions of human breath as a flower or jade bead in Classic period art and in the importance of offerings of blood in Maya rituals.

Sacredness was also manifested in the concept of the *way* (pronounced "why"), an invisible co-essence or spirit companion associated with living and divine beings. Every person had a *way* or spirit companion whose destiny was intertwined with that person. The most powerful *wayib* were embodied in what we call "gods" or deities, best defined as beings that controlled aspects of the universe. Maya deities had different manifestations, sometimes very visible (such as the sun or lightning), sometimes heard but not seen (such as thunder or earthquakes). Both gods and *wayib* could be represented by forms that were animal-like (zoomorphic) or human-like (anthropomorphic). The Maya today continue to believe that each person has a spirit companion, often called the *nagual*—a word of Mexica (Aztec) origin—whose life and destiny parallel those of every individual.

The Maya Universe

The universe of the ancient Maya was composed of *kab*, or Earth (the visible domain of the Maya people), *kan*, or the sky above (the invisible realm of celestial deities), and *xibalba*, or the watery underworld below (the invisible realm of the underworld deities). The Earth was the back of a huge reptile, represented as a caiman or a turtle that swam in the primordial sea. Mountains (*witz*) were seen as the ridges on the back of this giant reptile. The celestial realm had 13 layers, each presided over by one of the *Oxlahuntik'uh* gods (*oxlahun* "13," *ti* "of," *k'uh* "god" in Yucatec Mayan). Xibalba had nine layers, each presided over by one of the *Bolontik'uh* gods (*bolon*, "nine").

There were five directions in the Maya world. Center was the direction of the great sacred tree of life, a giant ceiba that supported the sky, symbolized by a cross. East was the direction of the sun being reborn each morning. West was the direction of the dying sun falling into Xibalba at dusk. North was straight up: the zenith, the direction of the sun in the fullness of life in the sky each day at noon. South was straight down, the nadir: the direction of the underworld, where the dead sun battled the lords of Xibalba in order to be reborn at dawn.

The caves (*ch'een*) found throughout much of the Maya area were considered entrances to Xibalba. These were especially sacred and dangerous places where the dead were buried and special rituals for the ancestors were conducted. Doorways in some of the great Maya temples were symbolic cave entrances that allowed kings and priests to enter the *witz*, or sacred mountain (the temple platform), and communicate with the lords of the underworld.

Many powerful celestial deities dwelt in the sky. During the day (*k'in*) the all-powerful sun (*K'inich ajaw*) dominated the sky. At night the sky was filled with countless deities, the moon, the "sky wanderers" (the visible planets), and the stars. Itzamnaj was the great celestial reptilian god who extended across the entire sky (the Milky Way), seen as a great two-headed beast. In their Classic period portraits, many Maya kings carry a representation of this cosmic deity in their arms, known as the double-headed serpent bar.

On earth, buildings and entire cities were imbued with unseen power and constructed as symbolic reflections of the Maya universe. Individual buildings were "born" with dedication rituals, had a span of life, then died and were buried with termination rituals. Some arrangements of ritual buildings replicated the Maya concept of the universe; for example, Twin Pyramid Groups at Tikal were built for cyclical calendrical ceremonies (held at each *k'atun*, or the end of each 7,200-day period). Four structures, one on each side, were built around a central plaza that represented the center of the world. Twin pyramids, one on the east side and one on the west side, marked the birth and death of the sun. A building with nine doorways on the south represented the nine-layered underworld. The celestial domain was represented by a walled enclosure on the north, open to the sky, which contained a paired stela and throne dedicated to the king who sponsored the *k'atun* ceremonies.

Although Maya cities were not laid out according to a single master plan, their arrangements also reflected the Maya cosmos. Each city grew

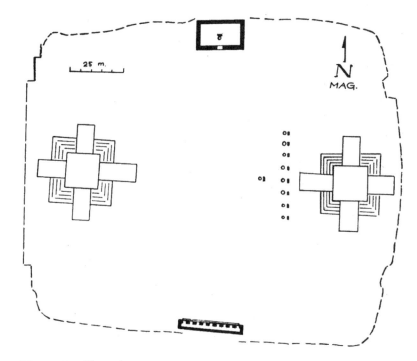

Figure 11.2 Plan of a Twin Pyramid Group at Tikal, Guatemala; used for calendrical ceremonies, it replicated the Maya universe with four buildings (four directions) built around a plaza (center of the world). Courtesy of Tikal Project, University of Pennsylvania Museum.

over time, but the positions of buildings remained properly aligned with the primary directions of the Maya world. These symbolic associations provided the inhabitants of Maya cities with the security of living in a sacred and properly ordered place, protected by a powerful king and even more powerful deities. The earthly realm at the center of the world was represented by the palaces of the living ruler in the center of the city. Often the funerary shrines and tombs of dead kings were to the north, associated with the celestial realm where the royal ancestors dwelt after their apotheosis (rebirth from Xibalba as deities). The intervening threshold between this world and the celestial realm was often the location of the ritual ball court, where the sacred ball game and sacrifices celebrating the creation myth were conducted.

The Maya believed that there had been several worlds before the present one and that a great flood had destroyed each. The Maya of Yucatan today believe that there have been three worlds previous to this one. The first world was inhabited by dwarfs, the second world was inhabited by people called "offenders," the third world was populated by the ancient Maya, and the fourth or present world is peopled by a mixture of all the previous inhabitants of the Peninsula. Eventually, a flood will also destroy this world.

The Origin Myth

The most complete and beautifully written record of Maya myth and history is preserved in the *Popol Vuh*, the sacred book of the highland K'iche Maya. This account also relates that there were multiple creations before the present world. The people of the present world were created out of maize, and the saga of the first humans, the Maya Hero Twins, is the central drama of the creation myth in the *Popol Vuh*. Their names in K'iche are Hunapu and Xbalanque (or Hun Ajaw and Yax Balam in Yucatec). These names have contrasting associations, recalling both sun and Venus and life and death. Hunapu ("First Lord") is associated with Venus and celestial life. Xbalanque ("Sacred Jaguar") is associated with the jaguar sun and death in the underworld.

The father of the Hero Twins was Hun Hunapu, the maize god, who had played ball in Xibalba and then was decapitated by the gods of death. After he was sacrificed, his head was hung in a calabash tree. From the tree, Hun Hunapu's head impregnated one of the daughters of the death gods by spitting into her hand. Fleeing her angry father, the pregnant girl came to the earthly realm. There she gave birth to the first humans, the Hero Twins, who grew up and found their father's old ball game equipment. Realizing their heritage, they followed their father by becoming such famous ball players that they were invited to play ball in Xibalba with the lords of the underworld.

In Xibalba, the gods of death subjected the Hero Twins to a series of daily ball games and nightly trials, but they outwitted the death gods each time. However, the only way they could escape Xibalba was by jumping into a pit of fire. After the death gods ground their bones into powder and threw them into a river, the Hero Twins were reborn and returned to Xibalba seeking revenge. They succeeded by showing the death gods an amazing feat. One twin decapitated the other and then brought him back to life. The death gods were so amazed by this they demanded that the Hero Twins perform the trick on them. This is what the Hero Twins were waiting for, so they decapitated the gods of death but of course refused to bring them back to life. Following their victory over death, the Hero Twins escaped from Xibalba and were transformed in the sky as the sun and Venus, destined to reenact their descent into Xibalba and their escape and rebirth forevermore.

The central themes of Maya creation myth were replicated in religious rituals and the lives of individuals. The account of the Hero Twins entering Xibalba, outwitting the gods of death, and returning to life was a metaphor for the sun, the greatest power in the universe. It also showed that rebirth came through sacrifice. The rebirth of the Hero Twins after being sacrificed is a metaphor for human rebirth after death, a theme celebrated by Maya ritual of human sacrifice. The ball court was the setting for the confrontation between the Hero Twins from this world and the death gods of Xibalba. In many Maya cities, the ball court symbolized the threshold between the earthly realm and Xibalba. The ritualized ball game played in this arena reenacted the original confrontation between the Hero Twins and the death gods. Maya kings had the closest associations with the Hero Twins. Kings had the power to enter Xibalba and confront the death gods, play the sacred ball game, and perform human sacrifice. When a Maya king captured another ruler in war, the captive king could be taken to the ball court to be ritually defeated a second time and then sacrificed by decapitation. Thus, he was sent to Xibalba to be born again in the sky in a ritual that reenacted the myth of the Hero Twins.

Dualistic symbolism is an obvious feature of the Maya creation myth, where twins struggled with the lords of death. The struggle was between the forces of good (life) and evil (death). The Maya conceived of their world as an eternal replication of these two forces in conflict. For example, benevolent forces bring rain to make their fields grow to ensure that the people will have food. But evil forces cause drought, hurricanes, and plagues that destroy the crops and bring famine and death. Other obvious dualistic themes permeated the Maya view of their world, such as male-female and day-night. In fact, Maya deities had many contrasting sets of attributes.

Life after Death

The underworld was the dwelling place of the dead. The nine levels of Xibalba may have been associated with differences in life. After the Conquest, Bishop Landa reported that the Maya believed that the underworld was divided into places of rest and places of suffering, although there may be European influence in this account. Priests and kings were said to go to the place of rest after death. Women who died in childbirth, warriors killed in battle, and suicides also went there. All those who went to the place of rest could dwell in the shade and be free from labor. There was an abundance of food and drink and no pain or suffering. Those who led evil lives went to the place of suffering in the ninth and lowest underworld.

The *Popol Vuh* creation myth also refers to a Maya concept of rebirth after death. Evidence from inscriptions and the excavations of royal tombs at Palenque, Tikal, and other cities suggests that, after death and journeying to Xibalba, Maya kings were believed to be transformed into deities. This royal apotheosis replicated the myth of the rebirth of the Hero Twins and the daily rebirth of the sun rising out of the underworld. It was believed that Maya kings, after their rebirth, were transformed into stars that dwell in the sky. But there is no evidence that any other people were believed to have escaped Xibalba after death.

The Concept of Time

The Maya universe was both a living and an ordered place. Order could be seen in the predictable movements of the great celestial deities—the sun, moon, planets, and stars—that marked the passage of time. Their movements represented repeated cycles of life, death (setting or disappearance), and rebirth (rising or reappearance). In the Maya universe, time itself was alive, expressed by a series of deities that governed each recurring cycle.

The sun, or *k'in* (also "day"), established the basic order of the Maya universe. The *k'in* life cycle was the interval in which this deity passed out of the underworld to be reborn at dawn and moved across the sky, only to be swallowed in death at dusk by the underworld once again. Another cycle was 20 *k'ins* that formed another anthropomorphic deity known as *winal*. The word derives from the word for human, *winik* in Yucatec Mayan, because humans with their 20 digits (fingers and toes) are beings who are imbued with the rhythm of the sun, according to the *Book of Chilam (Balam of Chumayel)*. The ever-greater cycles of *k'ins* formed the solar calendar, while the various cycles of the other sky wanderers formed calendars based on the moon and visible planets (discussed further in chapter 12).

The Maya held a series of ceremonies associated with the solar calendar. One of the most important of these centered on the Maya New Year. These ceremonies began in the closing five days of the preceding year (which were unlucky days, when everyone was concerned about misfortune) and culminated on the first day of the New Year. Another important calendrical ceremony was held at the end of each *k'atun*, a period of 20 *tuns* (360-day "years") or 7,200 days, which was marked by the dedication of a new stone monument. There were 13 differently named *k'atuns*, each with its own patron deity and its special rites. *K'atun*-ending ceremonies were celebrated for nearly 12 centuries (ca. 350–1520). The most elaborate version was celebrated at Tikal and was marked not only by carved monuments but also by the construction of a Twin Pyramid Group. At some lowland cities, a ritual was celebrated twice each *k'atun*, or every 3,600 days. At Quirigua and Piedras Negras, carved monuments also commemorated the end of each quarter-*k'atun* (1,800-day period).

MAYA DEITIES

According to Maya belief, the most powerful supernatural beings controlled aspects of the universe. The Maya referred to these beings as *k'uh*, "sacred or divine entity." The Maya saw the beings we call "gods" as the

Figure 11.3 Maya deities as shown on Classic period pottery vessels (left to right, top to bottom): Itzamnaaj, sky deity; Chaak, rain deity; K'inich Ajaw, sun deity; underworld jaguar deity; K'awiil, lightning deity; underworld deity; Chak Chel, rainbow deity; Ix Sak Un, moon goddess. Drawings by Simon Martin, University of Pennsylvania Museum.

most powerful embodiments of this sacred quality in the universe, but it would be a mistake to assume these beings had distinct or anthropomorphic (human-like) qualities like the gods of ancient Greece or Rome.

Maya deities were not finite. They were complex and sometimes contradictory beings. Each possessed multiple aspects that blended together, often making precise identification difficult. Several deities could merge into one being. Some aspects were visible; for example, the sun god was seen in the sky each day. But other aspects of the same deity were invisible, like the sun after being transformed when it entered Xibalba at night. In this aspect, the sun took on the attributes of the most powerful nocturnal animal of the tropical forest and became the jaguar sun of the underworld. Any Maya representation of the sun god, whether carved on a stone monument or painted on a vessel, might emphasize any one of these multiple aspects, so that any given depiction can appear to us as being very different from other images of the same god. Moreover, the portraits of Maya rulers are often shown wearing costumes, masks, and headdresses with attributes of one or more of the gods.

Maya deities had different aspects based on sex (male or female), direction (east, west, north, south, and center), age (old or youthful), color, and so forth. Direction and color were usually linked, so that one aspect of the rain god (Chaak) was referred to as Chak Xib Chaak, the Red Chaak of the East. Gods also could possess one or more inner essences or *wayib*, adding more possibilities to their variability. Because of these diffuse qualities, there is general agreement about the identity some Maya deities but disagreement about the remainder. The total number of such deities is unknown, but we can briefly describe several of the most important.

Itzamnaaj was the central deity of ancient Maya religion. One famous Maya scholar, Sir Eric Thompson, proposed that all other deities were but aspects of Itzamnaaj, making Maya religion in a sense monotheistic. In his various aspects, Itzamnaaj was the lord over the most fundamental opposing forces in the universe—life and death, day and night, sky and earth. As lord of the celestial realm, he was the Milky Way, usually depicted as a two-headed reptile or serpent, his body representing the sky, from which other sky deities (stars) were suspended. He was also the first priest, the inventor of writing, and a curer of disease.

K'inich Ajaw was the sun god who possessed several aspects corresponding to the different phases of the sun's daily journey. During the day, the face of K'inich Ajaw was represented with crossed eyes and a distinctive curl at the corners of his mouth. At dusk, he was the dying sun. In his night aspect, he became the jaguar sun of the underworld in his journey through Xibalba. These aspects were closely associated with the concepts of life, death, and rebirth. Maya kings associated themselves with K'inich Ajaw and his power. His name often appears in the titles and names of rulers, and his face is often found on the headdresses and shields borne by kings in their carved portraits.

Chaak, the rain and storm deity, is also represented with a reptilian features. Many aspects of Chaak have been identified, including four associated with colors and directions: Chak Xib Chaak (Red Chaak of the East), Ek Xib Chaak (Black Chaak of the West), Sak Xib Chaak (White Chaak of the North), and Kan Xib Chaak (Yellow Chaak of the South). The benevolent aspect of Chaak was associated with creation and life. For Maya farmers, Chaak was an all-important deity who nourished the fields and made life possible.

K'awiil, the lightning deity, was depicted with an ax or smoking tube in his forehead, an upturned snout, and a serpent leg. Images of K'awiil adorn the scepters held by Maya kings. Eccentric flints depicting K'awiil were probably once part of these scepters. Taking the K'awiil scepter symbolized the act of becoming a Maya king.

Hun Hunapu, the maize deity, was the father of the Hero Twins. A benevolent deity representing life, prosperity, and abundance, he was represented in the Classic period as a youth. His death and rebirth from the underworld were central metaphors for the belief in the apotheosis of Maya kings. One Late Classic scene shows Hun Hunapu reborn and rising out of a spilt tortoise shell (the earth), flanked by his sons, the Hero Twins. Like maize itself, he had many enemies, and his destiny was controlled by rain, wind, drought, famine, and death.

Kimi, the death deity, was depicted as a skeletal or bloated figure, often wearing bells. One of his aspects in Classic and Postclassic times has a black band across his eyes and an *ak'bal* ("darkness") glyph on his brow. This deity probably combines a god of war and the usual consequence of war, death by human sacrifice.

Ek Chuaj, the merchant deity, or "black scorpion," was usually shown painted black and having a large, drooping lower lip. He was also the patron of cacao, one of the most important products traded by Maya merchants.

Chak Chel or *Ix Chel*, the rainbow deity, was an aged goddess with a serpent headdress and jaguar claw hands. She is known as both Chak Chel (Great or Red Rainbow) and Ix Chel (Lady Rainbow) from her shrines on Isla de Mujeres and Cozumel, where women made pilgrimages to venerate her as goddess of fertility, childbirth, and weaving. The Maya believed that rainbows came from the underworld and were dreaded omens of illness or even death.

K'uk'ulcan, the Feathered Serpent, known in Mexico as Quetzalcoatl, was the patron of rulers, learning, and merchants. In one aspect he was also the wind god. K'uk'ulcan became prominent in the Terminal Classic religion of Chichen Itza and later at Postclassic Mayapan.

Ix Sak Un, the moon goddess, is portrayed as a young and beautiful woman, often seated in the crescent moon holding a rabbit. The Maya see the figure of a rabbit, rather than the "man in the moon," in the face of the full moon. She was associated with fertility and maize and was often paired with the sun god.

There were numerous other gods, such as the paddler gods who transport the dead into the watery underworld in their canoe. Some gods had localized associations and were believed to have lived in specific places across the Maya landscape. Each Maya capital and its ruler had special patron deities, often depicted as *wayib*. For example, Calakmul is associated with a deer-serpent patron. Copan's texts suggest that its local patron deities were seated in rulership along with the king at his inauguration. Quirigua's accounts of its defeat of Copan record the capture of its thirteenth ruler and its patron gods. Several of Tikal's carved wooden lintels depict triumphal processions that displayed giant figures of the patron deities of Naranjo and El Peru-Waka, who were captured when these rival cities were defeated.

SHAMANS AND PRIESTS

Maya religion was guided and controlled by two kinds of specialists, shamans and priests. These were specialists with powers to communicate with the deities and thereby understand the universe.

Shamans represent a far older tradition, with origins long before the development of Maya civilization. Most were commoners who looked after peoples' well-being in local communities throughout the Maya area. Shamans, on the basis of their knowledge of plants and their effects, provided medicines to cure illness. They performed divination rituals to determine the meanings of events, foretell the future, and cure the sick. These skills gave shamans prestige and a measure of power over other members of society. Shamans undoubtedly helped establish the basics of the Maya calendar and were seen as essential to the world order because they knew how to track the cycles of time reckoned by the movements of the "sky wanderers." With this knowledge, the annual coming of the rains could be predicted and the proper time to plant the crops determined.

Priests who were full-time specialists in religious matters emerged as Maya society became larger and more complex. The Maya priesthood undoubtedly evolved from the older tradition of shamanism, which was primarily associated with the nonelite farming population. In contrast, Maya priests were associated with the elite class and the management of religious matters that reinforced and supported their elevated status. Thus, those aspects of Maya religion that involved social and political concerns beyond the local level were taken over by elite-class priests. They managed the calendar, divination, the books of history and prophecy, and public ceremonies—all of which ensured success and prosperity for the king and his polity.

The Maya priesthood was a self-contained group of specialists that formed an important part of the elite class. The priesthood was perpetuated through the recruitment and training of acolytes. Since there were not enough political offices for every member of the elite class, the priesthood served an important function as an alternative occupation for the increasing number of younger sons of elite families, including the many children of royal families.

Over time, Maya priests developed a considerable amount of esoteric knowledge that was codified and recorded in books (known as codices; see chapter 12). This body of knowledge—records of myth, history, prophecy, ritual, and astronomical observations—had both practical and religious purposes. Some of this information was used to develop an increasingly complex calendrical system to record events and cycles of time. These calendrical cycles were used for astrological purposes, that is, to predict events and determine the destiny of the king, his polity, and, ultimately, the entire Maya world.

Elaborately costumed Maya priests conducted spectacular public ceremonies calculated to inspire awe and obedience on the part of the king's subjects. These religious ceremonies included music, processions, dancing, incense burning, and offerings to the gods. Offerings were made of food and drink, sacrificed birds and animals, and the blood of the priests and even the king, drawn by sharp obsidian blood letters for the occasion. For especially important occasions, human sacrifices were made. Maya kings often served as chief priest for their subjects, conducting rituals to protect them from disease and misfortune, divining the future and the will of the gods to ensure the success of the state, and maintaining the harmony of the Maya universe by their own blood sacrifices.

CEREMONIES

To keep the universe harmonious and to prevent disasters or the end of the world, the deities had to be placated by rituals and offerings. The Maya concept for this was "feeding" the gods. Nourishment came directly from offerings or indirectly from devoting time and energy to the deities. When something did go wrong, it was believed to be a reflection of the anger of the gods who had not been properly nourished. Thus, a drought was explained as the anger of an offended rain god.

The Maya conducted a variety of private rituals and public ceremonies intended to secure individual and collective success. Religious rituals were a part of everyday life: a mother would offer a bit of tortilla to Ix Chel for the health of her child, or a farmer would make a quick prayer to Chaak to begin his day in the fields. As head of Maya families, fathers would conduct rituals on behalf of all family members to communicate with the gods and to help secure benefits and prevent ill fortune. Such rituals were performed in relation to critical events, such as the planting or harvesting of crops, the construction of new household buildings, travel, or the undertaking of crucial steps in craft manufacture. Family rituals centered on presenting offerings and burning incense (usually copal). For example, the Maya would end their house-building rituals by placing offerings beneath the new house foundations. Farmers would make an offering to the gods of the earth and rain at planting time to ask for a successful crop. Women potters made offerings prior to firing their vessels as insurance against breakage.

At Cerén, pottery incensarios were found inside almost every household building, indicating that each was the setting for some kind of ritual. Just as in present-day Maya ritual, copal placed on hot coals produced a fragrant white smoke, which, drifting skyward, was believed to transport prayers to the gods. The incensarios found at Cerén suggest that rituals involving the burning of incense were conducted in domiciles, kitchens, and storerooms. In other words, religious rituals were very much part of the daily round of activities within each family household.

Community Ceremonies at Cerén

One building excavated at Cerén, El Salvador, was used for religious purposes, indicated by its unusual design and its distinctive decoration with white and red paint. Archaeological evidence recovered from the building's excavation shows that it was used to prepare and dispense food for communal feasts and to store ritual paraphernalia used at community festivals. Owing to its proximity to one of Cerén's residential compounds (Household 1), we may assume that the family that occupied the compound was involved in the maintenance or operation of these religious events.

This ceremonial structure departed from the usual orientation of Cerén's buildings (30 degrees east of north) and faced almost due east, the direction of the rising sun. The entrance was at the end of a roofed veranda on its northern side, which wrapped around the building's front on the east. The eastern veranda had a wide opening to its front, formed by a half-wall that allowed communication and interaction but not access. On its opposite side, there was a full opening that stepped up into the building's interior, which was divided into a front and a rear room by a medial wall and doorway.

The veranda contained two hearths and areas for food storage and meal preparation. Excavation has revealed that a feast was in progress when the eruption struck. A large cooking vessel filled with maize was still on one hearth. Nearby, several corncobs lay discarded, and a mano and a metate were in use grinding maize. A variety of storage and serving vessels was also present. Once prepared, feast food was served over the eastern half-wall to participants assembled on the heavily compacted ground surface east of the building. This area was kept swept and clear, undoubtedly for feasts as well as ritual dances and performances.

The more elevated eastern room was marked as a sacred place. Its eastern interior wall was painted red, as were its doorjambs and the cornice that embellished the room's perimeter. It was used to store sacred paraphernalia for religious dances and rituals. Excavation revealed several sacred items still in place, the most important of which was a headdress made from the antlers and cranium of a deer, painted red with blue accents. When found on a wooden shelf in the room, the deer headdress still had agave fiber string used to secure it to the head of a dancer or celebrant. Deer were and still are especially important to the Maya as symbols of the natural world's fertility. Adornments from ceremonial costumes, such as tubular bone beads, a jade axe, and two obsidian blades, were also found in this eastern room. The blades were undoubtedly used in bloodletting rituals, for tests on one revealed the presence of human hemoglobin. Several jars were found on the room floor, including one adorned with a modeled caiman head. The caiman was revered by the Maya as an earth deity. The jar was filled with achiote seeds, which when ground provide a bright red powder used to transform food by the sacred color of blood.

Public Ceremonies

In contrast to community rituals at Cerén, the larger public ceremonies sponsored by king and state involved hundreds or thousands of people and might extend over several days and nights. Whether small or large, most ceremonies included offerings to the gods. The most potent offering was life itself, or the divine or sacred essence represented by blood. The Bonampak murals depict a public ceremony marking the designation of the heir to the throne; the ceremony involved sacrifices, music, and dancing. Kings performed many rituals while costumed as a god, probably because it was believed that they assumed the identity of a supernatural power at these times. But a whole range of ceremonies involved people at every level of Maya society, not only the king and his court but merchants, craftsmen, farmers, and the individual members of families.

Whether conducted by farmer or king, most Maya religious ceremonies included similar rituals. Divination determined the auspicious day for the ceremony in advance, and one of several means of divining the will of the gods might also be included in the actual ceremony. Fasting and abstinence, symbolizing spiritual purification, also preceded most ceremonies. Most ceremonies included rituals to expel evil powers, music and processions, the burning of incense, the offering of food, and some sort of sacrifice. If blood was offered, it could be burned like incense. At the time of the Conquest, blood was smeared on the idol of the god being appealed to in the ceremony. According to the Spanish, the priests were also smeared with blood, their hair becoming clotted and gory mops. Usually, celebrations with music, dancing, feasting, and drinking brought the ceremonies to a close.

Fasting, burning of copal, offerings of food and blood, feasting, and ritual drinking all survive in Maya rituals conducted today. Today, however, if offerings of blood are called for, the blood of sacrificed chickens is used instead of human blood.

Divination

The Maya used divination to communicate directly with the supernatural and to determine future events. In addition to being used to determine an auspicious day for a ceremony, divination was also used to ascertain the causes for events, such as why crops failed. Because it was a means of communicating with the supernatural, divination ritual might be included within a larger public ceremony.

In the past, the Maya used a variety of divination methods, and some of these are still used today. For example, in the Maya highlands, shamans still interpret events according to ancient 260-day almanac and the random casting of sacred red beans (sortilege). In the past, the many permutations of the complex Maya calendar foretold future events, and there are depictions of Maya kings in the "scattering gesture."

Divination at Cerén

A building for divination was identified at Cerén, located east of the ceremonial building. This function is reflected in its distinctive design, its unusual orientation, and its decoration by white and red paint. The divination structure is the only building at Cerén with windows, the only one with no artifacts stored on the tops of wall or in its thatched roof (a "child-proofing" measure to secure sharp obsidian blades and other dangerous or fragile items). It is also the only building with practically no roof overhang, indicating that all of its activities were practiced inside the building. Its central doorway is so low that one has to stoop or crawl to enter its extra-wide north room, which was painted red with vegetative designs. In the wall to the west of the entrance, there is a waist-high window covered by latticework. Access from this room to the two back rooms was by small low doorways that led to progressively higher floor levels, first to a smaller east room and then to a larger west room. The west room had a small latticed window that faced west.

A small adobe bench at the rear of the northern room contained a storage niche. This held a variety of sacred items, among them a deer antler perforated for feather adornments, a female figurine, and a cluster of beans. The beans may have been used for sortilege by Maya shamans to reveal patterns or counts that are "read" as answers to specific questions. Another cluster of beans was found inside the building, along with a cluster of mineral fragments. Otherwise, the artifacts found with this building do not form specific functional assemblages, and none are associated with male activities, so the shaman who conducted divinations here may have been a woman.

The evidence allows a reconstruction of the performance of divinatory rituals at Cerén. Members of the community desiring to know why a family member was sick or looking for information about the future would come to the front latticed window to consult the shaman. There a small object would be left as payment for the shaman's services; some of the small artifacts found inside the building—an antler tine or an obsidian blade—may represent such payments. The shaman would then collect the needed ritual items and go into the larger rear room to conduct the appropriate divination ceremony to answer the supplicant's question. The supplicant would then go back to the small window on the west side of the building to receive the results of the divination.

Altered States of Consciousness

The Maya also used various substances that altered normal states of consciousness as a part of rituals in the past. The shamans saw the taking of narcotics, hallucinogens, and other psychotropic substances as a way to transform themselves and to communicate with the supernatural realm. Experiences in these altered states were understood as messages from the gods and were interpreted to answer questions and determine future events. The general populace consumed some active substances—especially alcohol and tobacco—but most of the more potent hallucinogens and psychotropic agents were reserved for specialists and for ritual divination.

Fermented alcoholic beverages were most often used to alter states of consciousness. One important ritual beverage was balche, made from fermented honey and the bark of the balche tree (*Lonchocarpus longistylis*). Wild tobacco (*Nicotiana rustica*) was also used; it is more potent than today's domestic varieties, and, when rolled into cigars and smoked, it can produce a trance-like state. Several mushroom species that contain hallucinogens were probably used in divination. Stone replicas of mushrooms are found in the Maya highlands, often accompanying burials. The names of several mushrooms in highland Mayan languages clearly indicate their use in divination; for example, *xibalbaj okox,* "underworld mushroom," was believed to transport the taker to Xibalba.

Ritual Purification

Bishop Landa recorded that most important ceremonies in Yucatan began with fasts and sexual abstinence for various periods before the event. These rituals were scrupulously observed by the priests and those who assisted them but were voluntary for other participants and observers. For some ceremonies, new equipment and clothing were made. Water used in ceremonies had to be pure; virgin water collected from caves was the most important. Incense made from the resin of the copal tree (*pom*) or, less frequently, of rubber, chicle, or other substances was burned and used to purify objects such as images of the gods. Incense was burned in specially shaped pottery incense burners adorned with modeled heads or figures of deities; plain versions are called *incensarios* today. The smoke rising from the incensario was believed to convey requests directly to the gods in the sky.

Music and Processions

The Maya made music from a variety of instruments, not as a means of entertainment but as a fundamental part of religious ritual. Archaeologists have found a variety of musical instruments, usually made from pottery. Others are depicted in Maya art, the most famous being the painted scene of musicians on the Bonampak murals. Percussion instruments predominated and included wooden drums, two-toned *tunkul* drums (made from hollowed-out logs), turtle shell drums, bone rasps, and gourd rattles. Wind instruments included trumpets made from conch shells and whistles, ocarinas, and flutes made from either fired clay or wood.

Figure 11.4 Scene from the Bonampak murals showing musicians accompanying a public ceremony by playing a variety of instruments; in the lower procession (left to right) are large trumpets, turtle shell rasps, a large drum, and rattles (Late Classic). From Ruppert, Thompson, and Proskouriakoff 1955. Reprinted by permission of the President and Fellows of Harvard College.

We can assume that music was believed to be pleasing to the gods and thus facilitated the success of the ceremonies. Music undoubtedly accompanied the impressive processions of priests that opened most public ceremonies and punctuated the steps in each important ritual. It was also was part of the ritual dances and the general celebration that closed most ceremonies.

Offerings for the Gods

Sacrifices varied according to the urgency of the occasion. They included offerings of food, small birds, animals, and precious substances, including human blood. Sacrifices used to cure illness or solve a minor problem might require offerings of food or the sacrifice of birds or small animals. Larger ceremonies might require the sacrifice of a deer, which would also provide an important contribution to the feast that followed. The dedication of Altar Q by the sixteenth king of Copan included the sacrifice of 15 jaguars, each symbolizing the powerful spirit essences (wayib) of the 15 predecessors of the king, Yax Pasaj Chan Yopaat. For especially important ceremonies, conducted to bring rain or to end a drought for the common good, one or more human sacrifices might be required.

The sacred essence or *ch'ulel* was in the blood of living things. Blood from animals was, and still is, one of the most important offerings used by the Maya in their rituals. In the past, human blood drawn from sharp obsidian blades was the most important personal offering that could be made to the gods. Several scenes carved on monuments show the wives of kings and other elite women drawing blood, often from the tongue. Maya kings offered sacrifices of their own blood to ensure the continuity of the cosmos. Rulers are sometimes depicted holding implements identified as blood letters, made from stingray spines, that were used to draw blood from the penis, a ritual of obvious symbolic meaning for human fertility. Drawn blood was absorbed by strips of bark paper in pottery vessels and then burned as an offering to the gods. In 1sixteenth-century Yucatan, the Spaniards recorded that blood was sprinkled over idols of gods inside temples. An offering found at the base of the Hieroglyphic Staircase at Copan included a Spondylus shell containing a residue identified as human blood by chemical tests.

Human Sacrifice

The ultimate offering of the sacred *ch'ulel* essence came from human sacrifices. This was the practice that most horrified the Spaniards. It was used not only by the Maya but also by most other peoples of the Americas as the offering appropriate for the most crucial of their ceremonies. (Ironically, in

Figure 11.5 This bone engraving from Tikal, Guatemala, depicts a bound captive lord from Calakmul, stripped of all vestiges of power and prestige, destined to be sacrificed (Late Classic). Courtesy of Tikal Project, University of Pennsylvania Museum.

their claims of horror, the Spaniards overlooked their own human sacrifices by burning people alive in the name of religious orthodoxy.)

Among the Maya, human sacrifice was not an everyday event but was essential to sanctify certain rituals, such as the inauguration of a new ruler, the designation of a new heir to the throne, or the dedication of an important new temple or ball court. Warfare usually provided the victims. After all, captives were a major goal of warfare; whereas those of low status might be adopted or enslaved, elite captives were usually sacrificed. In Early Maya civilization, heads of decapitated captives were worn as trophies by Maya kings or buried with dead rulers in their tombs, but these practices had largely died out by the Classic period. By Late Maya civilization, public displays of captive heads ("skull racks") were in use, following the custom established in central Mexico.

The most prized of all sacrifices was another king. Although rare, the sacrifice of a Maya ruler by another king required a special ceremony and ritual decapitation, apparently performed at the climax of a ritual ball game. This was seen as a reenactment of both the victory and capture of the defeated king and the Hero Twins' defeat and decapitation of the lords of Xibalba in Maya mythology.

Other than the ritual ball court, the place of sacrifice was usually either the summit of a temple platform or a courtyard in front of a temple. Human sacrifices were performed in several different ways, as illustrated in a number of painted and sculptured scenes and in ancient graffiti found on abandoned building walls. A famous graffito at Tikal depicts the ritual of scaffold sacrifice in which the captive was tied to a wooden framework and shot through by a cluster of arrows. In the excavations of Group G at Tikal, graffiti vividly depict a disemboweled captive, his hands tied to a post behind his back.

One of the most famous places for these rituals was the Well of Sacrifice at Chichen Itza, sacred to the gods of rain. When there was drought or famine, pilgrimages were made from all over the Maya lowlands to make offerings and sacrifices to appease the angry rain gods. To divine the will of the gods, at daybreak both children and adults were thrown from the rim of this great cenote into the water some 20 meters below. Those that survived the plunge were pulled out at midday and asked by the priests for any messages from the gods they had heard while in the cenote. Those witnessing the ceremony also hurled offerings of jade, gold, and other precious materials into the well. At the end of the nineteenth century, the cenote was dredged, bringing to the surface about 50 human skulls and numerous human long bones. Also found were sacrificial knives made of flint; masks, bells, jewelry, cups, and plates made of gold and copper; and pendants and beads made of jade and shell. The most numerous items were blue-painted cakes of pom incense, many found still inside pottery incense burners.

By the Postclassic, the custom of heart removal, probably imported from central Mexico, had become prevalent for human sacrifices. The victim

Figure 11.6 Scene from the Bonampak murals showing a ceremony accompanied by elaborately clad dancers on a stairway, a festive occasion probably witnessed by a large public assembly (Late Classic). From Ruppert, Thompson, and Proskouriakoff 1955. Reprinted by permission of the President and Fellows of Harvard College.

was painted blue (the sacrificial color), wore a special peaked headdress, and was led a stone altar. There, after ritual purifications, four assistant priests, also painted blue, grasped the victim by the arms and legs and held him on his back on the altar. The priest plunged the sacrificial flint knife into the victim's ribs just below the left breast, thrust his hand into the opening, and pulled out the still-beating heart. The heart was handed to another priest, who smeared the blood on the idol to whom the sacrifice was being made. If the sacrifice had been a valiant and brave warrior, parts of his body might be prepared and eaten by elite warriors to gain his strength. Later, as a mark of prowess, his captor would wear some of his bones.

Celebration

Religious ceremonies provided one of the few occasions for the general population to experience celebration. The Maya did not have leisure time, as we know it, so religious celebrations provided an important break from the hard work and routine of most people's lives. The throngs of people who attended and witnessed such ceremonies undoubtedly believed that these events would deeply influence their lives, but they also sought enjoyment and festive celebration. Indeed, the finale of most ceremonies that included dancing, feasting, and drinking was an important release of pent-up emotion. Music and dancing provided a physical means of expressing this emotional release. There were separate dances for men and women, and only rarely did they dance together. Various dances required great skill. The dancing and general enjoyment of these celebrations was certainly enhanced by the many festive foods and fermented beverages that brought most ceremonies to a close.

FURTHER READING

Ardren 2002; Aveni 2001; Benson and Boone 1984; Demarest 2004; Farriss 1984; Grube 2001; Houston 2000; Jones 1998; McAnany 1995; Schele and Freidel 1990; Sharer and Traxler 2006; Sheets 2006; Stuart 2005; Taube 1992; Tedlock 1982, 1985; Tozzer 1941; Vogt 1969.

12

MAYA WRITING AND CALENDARS

Written records kept by the Maya give us vital historical information about past events and people, without which our knowledge of Maya civilization would be much less complete. There are records from the time of the Conquest, accounts written by both Spaniards and the Maya themselves. But the Maya are unique in the Americas for the amount of pre-Columbian historical records that we can draw upon for information. There are inscriptions found on stone monuments, buildings, and artifacts, along with three or four surviving Maya books (codices). These accounts were rendered in a sophisticated writing system that recorded a spoken Mayan language, and included references to one or more calendars the Maya used to place events in time. This chapter examines both pre-Columbian information systems: Maya writing and calendars.

WRITING

Writing allows information to be stored for future use. This greatly increases the accumulation of knowledge and ensures its preservation from generation to generation. Maya kings used texts to proclaim their achievements. Priests recorded accumulated knowledge about their world. Historical records for the Maya were used not only to remember the past but also as a means of divination—a way to see into the future. The Maya believed that events were repeated over cycles of time, so they kept detailed histories, anchored in time by their calendars, to understand the present and to predict future events. By deciphering these accounts, scholars today have a unique and crucial means to better understand Maya civilization.

By keeping records of the rainy and dry seasons, the Maya could determine the best times to plant and harvest their crops. By recording the movements of the sky deities (sun, moon, planets, and stars), they developed accurate calendars that could be used for prophecy. With long-term records, the Maya were able to predict planetary cycles—the phases of the moon and Venus, even eclipses. This knowledge was used to determine when these deities would be in favorable positions for a variety of activities such as holding ceremonies, inaugurating kings, starting trading expeditions, or conducting wars.

The Maya writing system was one of the greatest achievements of Maya civilization. With a set of symbols, they could record every sound and every word of their language. This was the culmination of a long tradition of using notations and symbols that originated with the earliest civilizations in Mesoamerica. By the time of Early Maya civilization, the basic features of Maya writing were in use from the southern Maya area to the Preclassic cities of the lowlands. This system included a means of recording numbers used to keep track of both time and economic activities.

Numbers

The Maya, like all Mesoamerican peoples, used a *vigesimal* (base 20) numbering system, and their numeral expressions reflect this. Mayan languages use new words at the vigesimal multiples (20, 400, 8,000, and so on). The first 19 numerals were structured like our English terms, with unique names for the numerals from 1 through 10 and the names for 11 through 19 combining the words for 1 through 9 with the word for 10.

The basic bar and dot symbols for writing numbers were used by the Maya and other Mesoamerican peoples. A single dot has a value of 1, and a bar has a value of 5. Bar and dot symbols were used for the numbers 1 to 19. Above 19, numbers were indicated by position. From early times the Maya used a positional numeration system, based on the mathematical concept of zero. Scholars believe this is the earliest known example of this concept anywhere in the world. The symbol for zero value, or completion, was an elliptical shell.

In Maya calculations, the values of the positions increase by powers of 20 in rows from bottom to top. The bottom row represents numbers from 1 to 19, the second row the "20s," third row the "400s," and so on. Thus, a number such as 999 would be rendered by two dots in the third row (2 × 400 = 800), a bar and four dots in the second row (5 × 20 = 100 + 4 × 20 = 80), and three bars and four dots (19 × 1 = 19) in the bottom row. The number 980 would be rendered in the same way, except that a shell (zero) would replace the number 19 in the bottom row. Maya merchants used this system to keep track of their transactions, and used counters, such as

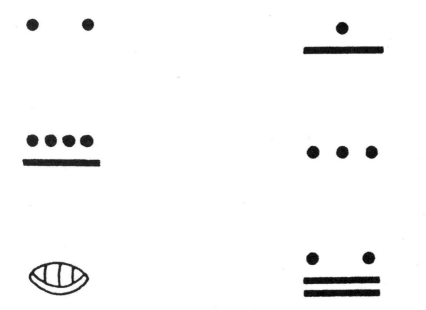

Figure 12.1 Bar (5) and dot (1) numerals, and the shell (0) were the basis of Maya mathematics; the examples illustrate the Maya vigesimal positional system: The left column records the number 980 by two dots in the upper row (2 "400s"), a bar and four dots in the middle row (9 "20s"), and a shell in the bottom row (0 "1s"); the right column records the number 2,472.

cacao beans, to make computations on any available flat surface or on the ground. Addition and subtraction is a straightforward process of simply adding or subtracting counters from the appropriate row. Modern studies have shown how more complex functions (multiplication and division) could also be done with this numerical system.

Glyphs

Symbols known as *glyphs* were used to record nonnumerical information. The earliest glyphs stood for entire words (logographic symbols). We use some logographs in our modern writing system, as when we write "&" instead of "and" or "15" instead of "fifteen." Logographs are essentially shorthand symbols that the Maya used for several hundred common words—many more than we use.

Another class of glyphs, which probably developed somewhat later, stood for the sounds that make up words (phonetic symbols). We use phonetic symbols for our writing system—each of the symbols printed here ("letters") stands for a sound unit in each word. Our phonetic system is alphabetic: there are different symbols for the sounds of each vowel and consonant in our words. The Maya phonetic system was syllabic: there were different symbols for the sounds of each syllable that make up Maya words. Since Maya writing used both logographic and phonetic-syllabic symbols, it is an example of a *logosyllabic* script.

Mayan words are generally regular in their sound structure—much more so than English. Most syllables consist of two or three sounds, namely a consonant (C) followed by a vowel (V), with or without a final consonant (C), producing the shape CV, as in *mo'* (macaw), CVC, as in *k'uk'* (quetzal), or in multiple syllables, CVCVC, as in *K'uk'ob* (quetzals). The prevailing sound system used by Mayan languages includes 5 vowels and about 20 consonants, divided into nonglottalized and glottalized (as in our expression "oh-oh"), indicated by an apostrophe, as in *kan* (snake) versus *k'an* (yellow). Thus, there are about 100 potential CV syllables, but the actual number is about 85, since not all potential CV combinations are present in Mayan languages. So the Maya writing system needed at least 85 phonetic symbols. There are actually more, since most CV syllables are represented by more than one glyph. There are about 850 known Maya glyphs, of which about 700 are logographs and about 160 are phonetic symbols—far fewer than in a purely logographic system like Chinese, which has well over 12,000 characters. Generally speaking, the most commonly used Mayan words were represented by

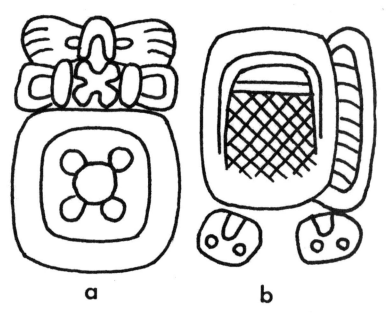

a   b

Figure 12.2 Example of two Maya glyphs: (a) logograph meaning *pakal* (shield) composed of a main sign (below) and prefixes (above); (b) phonetic spelling of the same word with the main sign pronounced *pa*, the postfix (to the right) pronounced *ka*, and the subfix (below) pronounced *la*, together spelling *pakal(a)*.

logographs, whereas all other words were "spelled out" by using phonetic symbols for their syllables.

Maya glyphs usually contain several elements that are combined to give individual glyphs a generally oval appearance. One element is often a larger than the others and is called the *main sign*. The other elements joined to the main sign are *affixes*. If the main sign is a logograph, it may have phonetic affixes. When a word is spelled out phonetically, both the main sign and the affixes are usually phonetic glyphs.

Maya glyphs appear complicated to our eyes. While some are recognizable as a picture of natural objects, others are unrecognizable, even though their meaning was clear to the Maya. But even a glyphic symbol recognizable to us may carry a meaning very different from the object it portrays. Thus, a glyph portraying a monkey head is a logograph meaning *sacred* or *divine*, either as a noun, *k'uh*, or as an adjective, *k'uhul*.

The appearance of Maya glyphs is often quite variable. The shape and meanings of some glyphs changed over time. Moreover, glyphs carved in stone usually have a more regular and uniform appearance than those painted on walls or in books. Scribes recorded texts in murals and books with fine brushes, which gave them more freedom to embellish their work. Two examples of same glyph may be rendered differently in the same text. Of course, ancient Maya scribes expressed their individual writing styles in their texts in much the same way that handwriting varies from person to person today.

Texts

Glyphs for various parts of speech in Mayan—verbs, nouns, adjectives, and particles—have been identified, as well as glyphs for various grammatical prefixes and suffixes. The general pattern of Mayan word order is verb-object-subject in transitive sentences, verb-subject in intransitive sentences. In written examples, glyphs are normally organized into rows and columns, and rows are usually read in pairs from left to right, while columns are read top to bottom, as follows:

1	2	7	8
3	4	9	10
5	6	11	12

Most surviving texts from Early or Middle Maya civilization are royal accounts of mythical and historical events. Like the records of early states in the Old World, ancient Egypt, and Mesopotamia, they deal with the histories of cities and the reigns of their rulers, their gods, rituals, genealogy, births, marriages, deaths, alliances, wars, and conquests. Also like early Old World histories, these accounts must be critically evaluated, because some contain propaganda intended to boost the prestige of their royal sponsors. There are also more mundane texts on a variety of personal objects like pottery and jewelry that label their use and ownership ("This is the chocolate cup of X"). Most of the texts from the later period of Maya civilization survive in a handful of books or codices (discussed later) and deal more with astronomy, divination, calendars, and other esoteric matters. In addition, some pre-Columbian historical accounts were transcribed into European script after the Conquest (discussed in chapter 1).

THE END OF MAYA WRITING

The Spanish Conquest ended the use of Maya writing. Church and civil officials saw Maya writing as "pagan" and did everything in their power to stamp it out. The Spaniards systematically destroyed the most visible expressions of "paganism," the ancient writings found in Maya books. In Yucatan, Bishop Landa vividly described this campaign of destruction: "We found a large number of books...and, as they contained...superstition and lies of the devil, we burned them all, which they regretted to an amazing degree, and which caused them much affliction" (Tozzer 1941: 78; trans. of Landa's original manuscript of ca. 1566).

Maya scribes were taught to use European script to write Mayan translations of the Bible and other European works. Because the new script offered a more efficient means of record keeping, the ancient knowledge of Maya writing soon disappeared. However, unbeknownst to the Spanish authorities, Maya scribes also copied many ancient Maya books using the newly learned European script. In this way, many priceless examples of Maya literature, such as the *Popol Vuh* (see chapter 11), avoided destruction.

SOURCES

Most of the surviving records in Maya script come from the era of Middle Maya civilization and are either carved or painted on durable surfaces (usually stone and pottery) or captions on murals inside buildings. These often accompany carved or painted scenes, so they are usually brief abstracts—outlines of mythical and historical events, including royal life histories, dynastic successions, alliances, and wars.

Codices

The ancient Maya wrote much more detailed records on perishable materials, such as paper made from the soft inner bark from the amate tree (tropical fig). Most important records were kept in books (or *codices*) like those destroyed by the Spaniards. These were long sheets of bark paper folded like a screen. Both sides of each page were coated with a smooth white material made of fine lime plaster. Columns of texts were painted on these surfaces in black and red inks with a fine brush. Painted pictures often illustrated the glyphic text.

But bark paper and codices are not durable; even before the Spanish authorities had a chance to burn all the Maya books they could find, over time entire libraries of information gradually decayed in the wet climate of the Maya lowlands. Archaeologists have found the decayed remains of Maya books in Classic period tombs, but all had disintegrated and no written information could be recovered.

Up to the time of the Conquest, the Maya kept pace with the forces of natural destruction by periodically recopying their books, much like the medieval monks did in Europe. Thus, most of the books burned by the Spaniards represented relatively fresh copies of far older books, containing irreplaceable records extending back hundreds or even thousands of years into the past. A few codices survived because they were sent back to Europe as mementos by Spanish authorities. Three of these pre-Columbian Maya books—the Dresden, Madrid, and Paris codices—are known from the cities where they were sent and later rediscovered. A fourth example has dubious origins but is named after the Grolier Club in New York City, where it was first publicly displayed; it now is in Mexico City.

The Dresden Codex was purchased in 1739 from a private library in Vienna. Its earlier history is unknown. It suffered water damage after

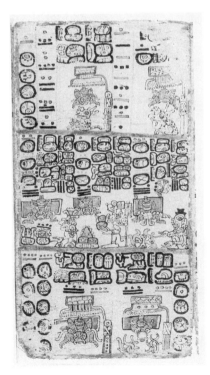

Figure 12.3 Page 103 of the Madrid Codex, a surviving pre-Columbian Maya book, with text and drawings dealing with beekeeping and honey. The three seated figures in the middle of the page are images of the gods (left to right) Itzamnaaj, Chaak, and Kimi (Postclassic). Courtesy of the University of Pennsylvania Museum Library.

bombing during World War II but has been restored. Today it is in the Sächsische Landesbibliothek in Dresden, Germany. The Paris Codex was rediscovered in 1859 at the Bibliothèque Nationale, Paris. It is only a fragment of the original book, and the lime coating has disintegrated at its margins, so only the text and pictures in the middle of the pages remain. The Madrid Codex was found in Spain in the 1860s in two unequal parts. These were rejoined, and the codex is now in the Museo Arqueológico in Madrid. How the Grolier Codex was discovered has remained a secret; it was presumably looted or stolen from its place of origin. Tests indicate that the bark paper is pre-Columbian, yet it could be a forgery, since ancient-appearing glyphs can be painted on blank ancient pages.

While the Grolier Codex's secret origins make its date uncertain, the other three codices clearly date to the last century or two before the Spanish Conquest. All four are concerned with divination and deities more than historical events. The Dresden Codex is probably the oldest and is our best record of divination and astronomical calculations, including amazingly accurate records for the cycles of Venus as morning and evening star. The Madrid Codex is similar but has fewer astronomical tables. Both were probably used by Maya priests in their divination rituals. The fragmentary Paris Codex records a sequence of *k'atuns* with their patron deities and ceremonies and a depiction of sky deities (often referred to as the Maya zodiac). The entire Grolier Codex is a simplistic Venus almanac that adds little to the more sophisticated Venus calculations in the Dresden Codex.

DECIPHERMENT OF MAYA WRITING

Because the knowledge of Maya writing was lost after the Spanish Conquest, the system had to be deciphered by later scholars. Vital clues for decipherment comes from the *Relación de las cosas de Yucatán*, written about 1566 by the Bishop of Yucatan, Diego de Landa. In this history and description of the Yucatec Maya, Landa included information about Maya writing that was based on interviews with at least one Maya scribe. Landa recorded important accounts of the Maya calendar and a listing of glyphs often called the Maya alphabet. This was a record of the Maya glyphs that Landa thought corresponded to the letters of the Spanish alphabet. We now know that the Maya scribe who provided these glyphs responded to the Spanish pronunciation of each letter by providing the closest glyph for the sound he heard. Thus, upon hearing the Spanish letter "q" (pronounced "cu"), he provided the Maya glyph for the CV syllable *ku*.

Decipherment gained momentum with the discovery of an abridged copy of Landa's book in 1863 by a Flemish monk named Brasseur de Bourbourg. A few years later, part of the Madrid Codex was found, and Brasseur, recognizing that the glyphs were similar to those in Landa's book, realized that the Codex was a Maya book. Although most of his ideas about how to read Maya glyphs were wrong, he did recognize

Figure 12.4 The glyphs recorded in Bishop Landa's *Relación de las cosas de Yucatan* as given by a Maya scribe for the sounds of the Spanish alphabet. Note that the comb-like symbol for CA is equivalent to the phonetic symbol for *ka* in the spelling of *pakal*. Source: Alfred M. Tozzer, ed., *Landa's Relación de las Cosas de Yucatan: A Translation*, Papers of the Peabody Museum of American Archaeology and Ethnology, Harvard University, col. 18, 1941. Reprinted courtesy of the Peabody Museum, Harvard University.

Maya numerals, the *k'in* glyph for "sun" or "day," and the glyph for *u*, the Yucatec Mayan third-person pronoun. Other early scholars attempted to use Landa's "alphabet" as a phonetic solution to decipher Maya writing but failed because they assumed the Maya used an alphabetical system, rather than a syllabic system. By the beginning of the twentieth century, the astronomical and calendrical portions of Maya texts were well understood, but there was so little progress in reading other glyphs that attempts at phonetic decipherment were abandoned.

By the mid-twentieth century, most Maya glyphs had been catalogued. Sir Eric Thompson established a referencing system for glyphs in both the codices and the inscriptions. But, thanks largely to the work of Thompson and several other influential scholars, the prevailing view held that the system was logographic, not phonetic. Since there was no key to the meaning of most logographic glyphs, it was assumed that the vast majority of Maya texts outside calendrical dates could never be read. This pessimistic prospect was tempered by the belief that Maya texts were not that important anyway since they recorded only the endless cycles of time and had nothing to do with the lives of kings or the mundane events of history.

The Discovery of History

In the late 1950s, two major discoveries changed these views. These came from the work of a Russian-born American scholar, Tatiana Proskouriakoff, and a German-born Mexican scholar, Heinrich Berlin. They deciphered the meanings of several key glyphs and thereby proved that many Maya texts were very important indeed, since they recorded historical information.

Proskouriakoff's study was based on a 200-year span of Late Classic stelae at the lowland city of Piedras Negras. These monuments were clustered in six groups at the site. Because the individual monuments had readable dates, she could see that none of the six groups exceeded a span of about 60 years, a normal human lifetime. As discussed in chapter 5, the earliest stela in each group depicted a male figure seated in an elevated niche, often accompanied by a figure of a woman. Proskouriakoff proposed that a particular glyph and its associated date on these initial monuments referred to the carved scene: the inauguration of the male figure as ruler, overseen by a woman, probably his mother. Noting the inclusion of a date in the texts that was always more than a decade before this inauguration date, Proskouriakoff reasoned this must refer to the ruler's birth, thereby also identifying the Maya glyph for *birth*. She concluded that intermediate dates in the group referred to events in the ruler's career, such as marriages. The last date prior to the next inauguration date obviously marked the ruler's death. As a result of her detective work, Proskouriakoff concluded that these groupings of monuments recorded the lives and reigns of a sequence of six Piedras Negras kings. Later research has shown that her breakthrough conclusions were correct.

This research revolutionized Maya studies. Before Proskouriakoff's work, the figures on Maya stelae were assumed to be gods and anonymous priests. Many dates in the texts were thought to be calendrical corrections. Proskouriakoff showed that these were portraits of actual men and women—kings and their mothers in this case—and that the dates represented historical events. After her initial discoveries from the Piedras Negras monuments, Proskouriakoff studied the Yaxchilan inscriptions and identified new glyphs for *capture, captor,* and *death.*

At about the same time, Berlin noticed a patterned distribution of a glyph that always had the same prefixes but a variable main sign. The specific main sign tended to be unique to a specific site. From this, he concluded that these glyphs identified individual cities, either as a place name or as the name of its ruling dynasty, so he called them *emblem glyphs.* The use of one site's emblem glyph at another site was evidence of relationships between Maya cities resulting from alliances, marriages, or wars. This again indicated that Maya texts included historical information and that the prevailing interpretations were wrong.

The Phonetic Code

The breakthroughs made by Proskouriakoff and Berlin did not provide actual *readings* of the Mayan words represented by glyphs. They were able to decipher the meaning of specific logographs without reading Mayan words from phonetic symbols. The second breakthrough in decipherment followed soon afterward. This was the recognition of a phonetic code, which then could be used to read actual Mayan words represented by phonetic glyphs. It began with the work of the Russian scholar Yurii V. Knorozov. Although his arguments were not as carefully made as Proskouriakoff's, Knorozov used the old Landa "alphabet" as the basis for deciphering a set of phonetic signs—not for individual consonants and vowels but for the CV syllables that formed most Maya words.

However, under such a system, the spelling of common Mayan CVC words, those ending in a consonant, not a vowel, presented a problem—how did the Maya record the final vowel if their phonetic symbols stood for CV syllables? Knorozov's solution was to propose that the final consonant was written with a second CV sign that agreed with the vowel of the first syllable but that this final vowel remained silent. He called this the rule of *synharmony*. By such a rule, a Mayan CVC word like *kutz* would be spelled by two phonetic glyphs, *ku* and *tzu*, yielding *kutz(u)*, with the understanding that the final vowel was not pronounced.

We can better understand the phonetic system and see how glyphs are deciphered by looking at a series of Mayan words that share certain CV sounds. We can start with glyphs whose meaning is established, those for *kutz*, or "turkey" (often associated with pictures of turkeys in the codices). The first glyph that should stand for the sound *ku* can be found in Landa's "alphabet," where it represents the sound of the Spanish letter "q." This works, so now we can propose that the second glyph stands for *tzu*, by the rule of synharmony. We can test this proposal by looking at glyphs

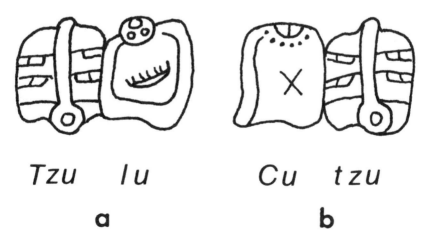

Figure 12.5 Phonetic spellings of two Mayan words: (a) *tzul* (dog); (b) *cutz* (*kutz*; turkey), both illustrating the rule of synharmony (see text).

for another word that has this same *tzu* syllable: *tzul,* or "dog." Indeed, the glyph associated with pictures of dogs in the codices begins with the same sign as the second glyph in *kutz.* Because the dog glyph must end with the glyph for the syllable *l(u),* we can continue by looking for examples of this symbol.

Phonetic decipherment proceeds this way from one proposed reading to another. But this procedure does not always lead to a complete reading of a Maya text, because Maya writing is a complex mixture of phonetic and logographic glyphs. And the phonetic component is not always consistent (any more than our English system of pronunciation is!). Not all phonetic spellings follow the rule of synharmony; for example, the word for "vulture" (*kuch*) is spelled *ku-ch(i),* not *ku-ch(u).* (We should expect that a writing system used for some 2,000 years would have some antiquated spellings that, as in English, did not keep up with changes in the language over time.) Some words are spelled phonetically, other words only partially so, and more are purely logographic. Many Maya glyphs were *polyvalent* (had two or more meanings), and two or more different glyphs may refer to the same word.

Despite these difficulties, the phonetic breakthrough has allowed scholars to read 80 or 90 percent of Maya texts, and more progress is being made with each passing year. It is now clear that the language recorded by Classic period texts was a Ch'olan dialect, ancestral to Ch'orti' Mayan still spoken in the vicinity of Copan in western Honduras and eastern Guatemala.

Results of Decipherment

We now know that the constant prefix on emblem glyphs is an antiquated version of the royal title *ajaw.* It is a combined logographic and phonetic element read *ajpo* (from the ancient title *ajpop,* "lord of the mat") but is accompanied by the suffix *wa* as a phonetic complement to indicate the end of the word *ajaw* (lord or ruler). The other constant prefix is the *k'uhul* logograph, "holy, or divine." We can decipher some emblem glyph main signs. The main sign of the Yaxha emblem glyph reads phonetically *yax ha,* an example of an ancient Maya city name that has survived to the present day. The reading of the Yaxha emblem glyph would be *k'uhul yaxha ajaw,* "holy Yaxha ruler." Tikal's ancient name was *Mutul.* The glyph for the site of Aguateca reads *K'inich pan witz,* "sunny split mountain." The *witz* glyph in this case is split, just like the mountain (or escarpment) on which Aguateca sits, which is split by a deep fissure in the limestone bedrock.

Beginning with the emblem glyphs and glyphs for "birth," "accession," "death," titles, "capture," and "captor" identified by Berlin and Proskouriakoff, deciphered glyphs have greatly increased our understanding of past social and political matters. There are deciphered glyphs for "captive," "marriage," and "parentage," including forms that read "child of man" (*unen*) and "child of woman" (*yal*). One glyph identifies the founder of many royal lineages, and another gives the numerical position for kings in the line of succession. The glyph for royal birth dates identified by Proskouriakoff is now read as the verb "to be born" (*siyaj*). The glyph for "inauguration to rulership," also identified by Proskouriakoff, can be read as *hok'* (tied knot, referring to the wearing of the royal headband). Texts refer to royal inauguration as *ch'am K'awiil* ("receiving the K'awiil scepter") or as *chum-wan-i ti-ajawel* ("he sits in kingship"). Many personal names and titles have been identified, and some of these can be read phonetically. Part of the glyphic name of the Palenque king K'inich Janaab Pakal, for example, often combines the logograph for shield (*pakal*) and the phonetic spelling *pa-ka-l(a)*.

Kings were transformed into sacred beings upon accession, recorded by their taking a new name that identified them with deities. When a noble named K'uk' Mo' ("Quetzal Macaw") received the K'awiil scepter, he became K'inich Yax K'uk' Mo' ("Radiant Sun First Quetzal Macaw"), Copan's dynastic founder. Many Maya kings incorporated the names of the sun god (K'inich), the creator deity (Itzamnaaj), the lightening god (K'awiil), or the rain god (Chaak) in their royal names.

Important events in the reigns of kings were recorded by "planting" (*ts'ap*) a carved stela or great stone (*lakamtuun*) at the end of a *k'atun* cycle, sometimes marked by "stone binding" (*k'al tuun*). Ceremonies performed by kings included fasting and blood letting (*ch'ab*) and scattering (*chok*) incense or blood offerings (*ch'aaj*) to conjure (*tsak*) a god or to take on the god's image (*u baah*) by wearing a deity mask and performing a dance (*ak'taj*).

Kings acquired additional titles to honor reaching a prestigious age, as in *Ox K'atun Ajaw* ("Three K'atun Lord"). Some kings took the title *Aj Pitzal* ("He of the Ballgame"). A king's victory over another was expressed by the phrase *jubuy u-took' pakal*, "they fall, his flint (and) shield." The measure of success in war was recorded by the taking of captives, as in the title *aj* (number 20) *baak* ("He of 20 captives").

Many objects have painted or carved glyphs, and many of these are now being read as "name tags" that often accompany the owner's name. The glyphs on a jade ear spool excavated at Altun Ha, Belize, reads *u tup*, "his ear spool." Glyphs on incised bone offerings in Jasaw Chan K'awiil's tomb at Tikal include the phrase *u bak*, "his bone." Pottery vessels are often tagged with *u lak*, "his bowl." The function of the tagged object may also be given, as in the glyphs on an Early Classic bowl from Rio Azul that is labeled as a pot for *kakaw* (chocolate). A painted vase owned by Tikal's twenty-seventh king has a text stating that it is the "chocolate pot of Yik'in Chan K'awiil, 3 *k'atun* holy Tikal ruler." The scene on the vessel shows Yik'in Chan K'awiil seated on a cushioned throne, accompanied by a small pot decorated with the Naranjo emblem glyph, identifying this as tribute or booty taken from Naranjo.

Decipherment has increased our understanding of ancient Maya religion. The glyph that reads *way*, spirit companion or "co-essence," is fairly common in Classic period texts. It is now clear that some representations once identified as gods or kings are in fact supernatural companions. References to actual gods can now be identified from the glyph *k'uh*, sacred entity or "deity." *K'uh* is used to refer to the patron gods "owned" by specific Maya kings. This concept of sacredness, also seen in the adjectival form (*k'uhul*) used in the emblem glyph title for kings, designates the special divine status claimed by Maya kings that set them apart from the rest of society. Maya writing was used for far more than recording time; it was used to reinforce the sacred authority and prestige of kings and their polities.

CALENDARS

The Maya accurately recorded the cyclic movements of their sky deities—sun, moon, and planets—by sophisticated arithmetical and writing systems. Of course, the Maya had to rely upon observations without benefit of the instruments of modern astronomy. They probably used a pair of crossed sticks or similar sighting devices from high observation points such as temple summits. With long lines of sight to the horizon, the Maya could fix positions for the rising or setting of sun, moon, or planets, to within less than a day's error. When any of these celestial bodies rose or set at the same point a second time, one cycle was completed.

Yet, it must be remembered that the Maya did not understand these movements as we do, on the basis of modern astronomy. The movements were observed and recorded by the Maya to prophesy events these celestial deities were believed to control. Like Babylonian and medieval sky watchers, the Maya used the results of their observations for both mystical and practical purposes. Indeed, they believed that supernatural forces ruled numbers, time, and the entire universe. By recording the cycles of these forces, the Maya created a series of calendars used to understand events and to predict the future. These calendars were matched with the stuff of history, the reigns of rulers, their conquests and achievements, and other events. For the Maya, each passing cycle produced the possibility of repeated destiny.

One of the oldest and important calendars was an almanac of 260 days that operated without regard to any celestial cycle. There were several Maya calendars based on the recurring cycles of movements of the sun, moon, and the planets. The first two form the basis for our 365-day calendar year and our 30-day (on average) month. The Maya marked the sun's cycle with a solar calendar and the moon's cycle with a lunar calendar, but they also recorded the cyclic movements of the visible planets, such as Venus, Mars, and Jupiter. There was also a purely mathematical count of 819 days associated with each of the four quadrants of the universe, each ruled over by one of the four color and directional aspects of the deity K'awiil—a red aspect for east, black for west, white for north, and yellow for south.

Counts of days in these cycles were recorded by the bar and dot and vigesimal positional notation we have already discussed. To record the numbers 1 to 10 in calendrical texts, the Maya sometimes used alternative symbols known as *head-variant* numerals. The numbers 1 to 13 and zero were represented by images of the heads of the deities for these numbers. The head-variant glyph for 19 is a skull. The head-variant numbers from 14 to 18 were formed by combining the appropriate head variant (numbers 4 to 9) with the skeletal lower jaw from the head variant for 10. For example, the number 17 combined the skeletal lower jaw with the head-variant glyph for the number 7.

The most common cyclic counts used by the ancient Maya—the 30-day lunar period, the 260-day almanac, the 365-day solar year, and the calendar round cycle of 52 years (discussed later)—were very old concepts, shared by all Mesoamerican peoples. Most of the populace was familiar with these calendars, for they were believed to guide the daily lives and destinies of rich and poor alike. But the more complex calendars, such as those based on planetary cycles and the 819-day count, involved knowledge that must have been guarded by the ruling elite as a source of great power. Possessing knowledge of the sky deities and being able to predict their movements demonstrated to the common people that their kings and priests were in close communion with the supernatural forces that governed the universe.

The Lunar Cycle

Like all peoples, the Maya observed the phases of the moon, which they believed helped control human destiny. By recording the length of the lunar cycle—the time span between new moons, for example—they soon realized this period is a little over 29.5 days. Because Maya arithmetic did not use fractions, they used another method to keep track of the lunar cycle. It is similar to the way in which we keep our calendar year in harmony with the true solar year. Because the actual length of the solar year is between 365 and 366 days, we make a slight overcorrection every four years, by adding a day to create leap year. This overcorrection is compensated for by a slight undercorrection by skipping one leap year once every century. This system of successive adjustments keeps our 365-day calendar in harmony with the sun's annual cycle.

Initially, the Maya seem to have alternated lunations (the period between successive new moons) of 29 and 30 days, producing an average lunation of 29.5 days. But a lunar calendar based on a 29.5-day lunation would gain an entire day every two and two-thirds years. To be more accurate, the Maya figured that 149 lunar cycles was equivalent to 4,400 days. This yields an average lunation of 29.53020 days, extremely close to the modern calculated period.

The Sacred Almanac

The basis of prophecy and much of the pattern of daily life for all Maya people was governed by the "count of days," a sacred almanac that repeated itself every 260 days. The origin and significance of the 260-day count are unknown but probably derive from the span of human gestation, which is about the same length of time. In fact, one of the prime uses of the sacred almanac was to determine the destiny of each person's life, which was established by the characteristics of the patron god governing each birth date. Many highland Maya people today continue to use the 260-day almanac for this and other means of divination, even assigning children's names according to the date of their birth.

Each day (*k'in*) was designated by combining a number from 1 to 13 with one of the 20 day names. Since the 13 numbers and 20 days were actually deities, the attributes of each day reflect the characteristics of each number and day combination. The names of the 20 day deities in Yucatec Mayan are:

Imix	Kimi	Chuwen	Kib
Ik'	Manik'	Eb	Kaban
Ak'bal	Lamat	Ben	Ets'nab
K'an	Muluk	Ix	Kawak
Chikchan	Ok	Men	Ajaw

A given day in the sacred almanac would be named 1 Ak'bal. This was followed by 2 K'an, 3 Chikchan, 4 Kimi, and so on. After reaching the day 13 Men, the next day would be 1 Kib as the number cycle started over. This was followed by 2 Kaban and so on. The next time the starting day deity was reached, it would be combined with a new number deity (8 Ak'bal). A sacred almanac cycle was completed when all 13 numbers had been combined with all 20 day names (13 × 20 = 260).

The Solar Year

The calendar based on the solar year of 365 days was called the *haab*. The solar year was divided into 18 months of 20 days each (the *winal*), with an additional period of 5 days (the *wayeb*). Each of these months began with a *k'in* that was referred to as the "seating of the month." We designate the first day of the first *winal*, "the seating of Pop," as "0 Pop," followed by the day 1 Pop, 2 Pop, and so on until the last day of the *winal*, 19 Pop.

This is followed by "the seating of Wo" (0 Wo). The names of the *winals* in Yucatec are:

Pop	Xul	Sak	Pax
Wo	Yaxk'in	Keh	K'ayab
Sip	Mol	Mak	Kumk'u
Sots'	Ch'en	K'ank'in	(Wayeb)
Sek	Yax	Muwan	

The Calendar Round

The complete designation of each *k'in* referred to both the position in the sacred almanac and the Haab, as in "1 Imix 4 Wayeb," followed the next day by "2 Ik 0 Pop," then by "3 Ak'bal 1 Pop," and so on. Any given day designation does not reoccur for 18,980 days, or 52 years. This 52-year cycle is called the Calendar Round, which was used by most peoples of Mesoamerica, although the names of their days and months varied according to their languages. The Mexica saw time as an endless succession of 52-year cycles, which they called *xiuhmolpilli* ("year bundles"). But the Maya conceived and used time periods longer than the Calendar Round.

The Long Count

The Maya were unique in Mesoamerica in recording a series of far longer cycles of time. Of these, the Long Count was the most prominent. It was closely associated with the political system based on dynastic kings. Both the Long Count and holy kings came into use during the Late Preclassic period (Early Maya civilization) and disappeared at the end of the Classic period (Middle Maya civilization). In essence, kings used the Long Count dates to fix the events of their reigns in the great cycles of time. As we have seen, most kings of Middle Maya civilization dedicated monuments with Long Count dates at the end of each *k'atun* as part of the important ceremonies marking these occasions.

The Long Count recorded Calendar Round dates within a larger cycle of 13 *bak'tuns* (1,872,000 days, or some 5,128 years). This anchored any given date within a great cycle of time, which began in 3114 B.C.E. This beginning date probably refers to an important mythical event such as the creation of the current world. It precedes the earliest known use of the Long Count by some 3,000 years. The current great cycle will end on December 21, 2012, and a new great cycle of 5,128 years will begin the following day.

Long Count dates record the number of days elapsed from the beginning date. To make this calculation, a modified vigesimal system was used to record (in reverse order) the number of elapsed *k'ins* (days), *winals*

Figure 12.6 Long Count date from Stela E, Quirigua, Guatemala: After the large introductory glyph, the first three rows of glyphs read 9.14.12.4.17 12 Caban (260-day almanac), followed by a glyphic passage identifying this as the date of the inauguration of K'ak' Tiliw Chan Yopaat under the authority of the king of Copan (the crescents in some of the numerals are space-fillers) (Late Classic). After Maudslay 1889–1902.

(20 k'ins), *tuns* (18 winals, or 360 days), *k'atuns* (20 tuns, or 7,200 days), and *bak'tuns* (20 *k'atuns*, or 144,000 days). In a pure vigesimal system, the third order would be 400 (20 × 20 × 1), but the Maya used 18 *winals*, or 360 (instead of 400) *k'ins*, to create a closer approximation to the length of the solar year (365 days). We now express Long Count dates in Arabic numerals, as in 9.15.10.0.0, referring to 9 *bak'tuns* (1,296,000 days), 15 *k'atuns* (108,000 days), 10 *tuns* (3,600 days), zero *winals*, and zero *k'ins* to reach the Calendar Round date 3 Ajaw 3 Mol (June 30, 741).

A Long Count date was recorded by a standardized sequence of glyphs that was announced by an oversized introductory glyph. The only variable part of this introductory glyph was the central element, used for the patron deity of the *haab* month of the day being recorded. Following the introductory glyph, three rows of glyphs recorded the number of *bak'tuns*, *k'atuns*, *tuns*, *winals*, and *k'ins* that had elapsed since the beginning date. After this tally of days, the first part of the Calendar Round date, the sacred almanac day, was recorded. It was followed by a series of glyphs that recorded the appropriate *Bolontik'uh*, or underworld patron of the date, and the lunar cycle—the age of the moon on the date recorded, the length of the lunar month in which the Long Count date fell (29 or 30 days), and other information. Long Count inscriptions closed by recording the second part of the Calendar Round date, the *haab* day and month glyphs.

Distance Numbers

Long Count dates were precise but cumbersome, requiring more than 10 glyphs and a great deal of space in a typical inscription. In many texts, the Long Count date is the starting point for recording other dates and events by using a less lengthy format. These derived dates are called Distance Numbers because they calculate the distance (in the number of days) forward or backward from the Long Count date. The distance numbers were usually recorded in ascending order (*k'ins, winals, tuns,* and so forth). For example, a Long-Count date of 9.16.0.0.0 2 Ajaw 13 Sek might be followed later in the text by reference to an event that occurred 11 *k'ins* and 8 *winals* (171 days) later on the day 4 Chuwen 4 K'ank'in (corresponding to a Long Count date of 9.16.0.8.11).

Later Replacements for the Long Count

As Middle Maya civilization began to wane, the Long Count was often replaced by a less bulky count called period ending dating. This was used to record the days on which each *k'atun* fell, as in K'atun 16, 2 Ajaw 13 Sek, equivalent to 9.16.0.0.0. As we saw in chapter 11, each of the 13 *k'atuns* had its patron deity, its prophecies, and its special ceremonies. Monuments and entire assemblages of buildings (such as Tikal's Twin Pyramid Groups) were erected for ceremonies to celebrate the end of the auspicious *k'atun* cycle. Once recorded, *k'atun*-ending notations were used as base dates for dating other events, just like the Long Count.

During Late Maya civilization, historical recording was abbreviated further. Dates were recorded in the *u k'ahlay k'atunob,* or "count of the *k'atuns,*" of Yucatan. This method referred only to the day of a *k'atun* ending in the sacred almanac but did not give the number of the *k'atun* or the *haab* date. The period-ending date mentioned earlier, K'atun 16, 2 Ajaw 13 Sek, would be recorded as "K'atun 2 Ajaw" in the *u k'ahlay k'atunob.* It was assumed that the reader would know the information (the *k'atun* number) necessary to understand the date.

Because every *k'atun* ended on a day Ajaw, there were 13 differently designated *k'atuns* in this method of dating (1 Ajaw, 2 Ajaw, 3 Ajaw, and so on). But the number of the day Ajaw on each successive *k'atun* ending was two less than that of the previous *k'atun,* so the sequence through time was K'atun 13 Ajaw, K'atun 11 Ajaw, K'atun 9 Ajaw, and so on. After K'atun 1 Ajaw, the next ending date was K'atun 12 Ajaw, followed by K'atun 10 Ajaw, and so forth. The same Ajaw day repeated every 260 *tuns* (256¼ solar years). One occurrence of the date K'atun 13 Ajaw ended in 771, another K'atun 2 Ajaw ended in 1027, another in 1283, and another in 1539, during the Spanish Conquest. The *u kahlay k'atunob* was a historical abstract that was useful as long as the sequence remained unbroken. By the time of the Conquest, this record covered 62 *k'atuns* from 9.0.0.0.0 (435), a span of 11 centuries.

The Venus Cycle

Known to the Maya as *Noh Ek*, "Great star," or *Xux Ek*, "Wasp star," Venus was Hunapu, one of the Hero Twins, the most important of the sky wanderers (see chapter 11). The average interval for Venus to make one synodical revolution—the time for it to repeat its cyclic movement in the sky—is 583.92 days. These actually run in a cycle of five synodical revolutions of approximately 580, 587, 583, 583, and 587 days each.

The Venus cycle is divided into four parts. For about 240 days, Venus is the morning star. Then, for about 90 days, it disappears, obscured by the sun. Then, for another 240 days, it reappears as the evening star; it then vanishes again for 14 days before reappearing as the morning star. The Maya figured slightly different spans for these four phases, calculating that Venus was the morning star for 236 days; invisible for 90 days; the evening star for 250 days; and invisible a second time for 8 days. The total span of this cycle, 584 days, was too long by 8/100 of a day. To correct the error, the Maya used their knowledge of the variations in the cycle of five synodical revolutions. In fact, they discovered that five synodical revolutions of Venus (2,920 days), which they commemorated as an important ceremonial cycle, are equal to eight solar years ($8 \times 365 = 2{,}920$ days). Their discovery of this link between solar years and Venus cycles allowed the Maya to check and correct their Venus calendar.

Other Cycles

The Maya observed and recorded the movements of other planets. Mars has a synodical cycle of about 780 days, and there are tables in the Dresden Codex that record multiples of 78 that probably refer to the movements of Mars. The Maya also tracked the other visible planets, Mercury, Jupiter, and Saturn. References to days corresponding to the cycles of both Jupiter and Saturn have been deciphered from several inscriptions of Middle Maya civilization.

CORRELATING MAYA AND EUROPEAN CALENDARS

Because the Long Count system was no longer used when the Spaniards arrived, the Maya Long Count cannot be directly correlated with the European calendar. But there are sixteenth-century references to *u kahlay k'atunob* dates and their corresponding dates in the European calendar. From this we know that K'atun 13 Ajaw ended sometime during the year 1539. But, because this same date repeated every 256 ¼ years, to correlate this with the older Long Count, we have to know which K'atun 13 Ajaw this date corresponds to in the Long Count.

The accepted solution is called the GMT correlation, which equates the end of K'atun 13 Ajaw in the *u kahlay k'atunob* with the Long Count *k'atun* ending of 11.16.0.0.0 13 Ajaw 8 Xul with November 12, 1539. This correlation agrees best with the evidence from both archaeology and history. It has also been supported by results of radiocarbon dating of wooden lintels from Tikal that are directly associated with carved Long Count dates. The dates given in this book are based on the GMT correlation.

FURTHER READING

Aveni 2001; Bricker 1986; Coe and Van Stone 2001; Edmonson 1982, 1986; Fash and Sharer 1991; Grube 2001; Houston 2000; Houston, Chinchilla, and Stuart 2001; Houston, Robertson, and Stuart 1996; Justeson and Campbell 1984; Kelley 1976; Marcus 1992a; Martin and Grube 2008; Schele and Freidel 1990; Sharer and Traxler 2006; Stuart 2005; Stuart and Houston 1989; Tedlock 1985; Tozzer 1941.

13

THE MEANING OF MAYA CIVILIZATION

It is often remarked that those who do not learn from the past are likely to repeat the problems and tragedies suffered by our forebears. But the past can teach us both to avoid the failures and to adopt the successes experienced by people of long ago. Maya civilization is no exception. Provided we heed the lessons of the past, history offers a number of ways we can better our lives today and in the future.

LEARNING FROM SUCCESSES IN THE MAYA PAST

Over the long course of their history, the Maya people learned many things about their environment that improved their lives and contributed to the success of their civilization. The Maya have given us a long list of plants and foods that have benefited people all over the world. Along with their neighbors in Mesoamerica, the Maya spent thousands of years of effort to domesticate and improve maize. Today, by most measures, the many varieties of maize grown throughout the world produce the largest yields of any single food crop. In fact, maize is now being promoted as one of the plants that, once converted to ethanol, can help relieve the world's dependence on fossil fuels. The Maya have also given us chocolate, one of the greatest pleasure foods enjoyed by people the world over. The list also includes several varieties of beans, squashes, pumpkins, papayas, pineapples, manioc, chili peppers, and vanilla, to name only the most familiar food plants.

An even greater benefit for both agriculture and our environment may be realized if we learn a valuable lesson from the Maya before it is too late. We are all aware of the tragic loss of tropical forests throughout the world. The habitat with the greatest biological diversity on our planet is being destroyed for short-term profits by a few timber and cattle interests. Once the great trees are cut and the soils exhausted by overgrazing, this fundamental resource will be destroyed. The Maya succeeded in utilizing the tropical forest within their area to produce a tremendous harvest of food and other products without destroying it. They culled the nonproductive trees and plants in the forest, allowing the many productive trees to prosper and to yield huge harvests of fruits, nuts, and other products. They also made the lowland lakes and swamps into renewable agricultural breadbaskets by building canals and raised fields. In a few places, modern farmers are being taught these ancient techniques we have learned from the Maya and other Native Americans in Central and South America. If they succeed—more to the point, if they are *allowed* to succeed in the face of the threat posed by the timber and cattle exploiters—the entire world will benefit from a new and renewable source of food that preserves, rather than destroys, most of the natural environment of the world's tropical forests.

Finally, the Maya certainly have taught us the value of tradition and family life. The Maya people have preserved their languages and culture in the face of oppression and violence over a span of thousands of years. When their own kings failed them, the Maya people left the overpopulated southern lowlands to find peace and prosperity in new areas. When the Spaniards conquered their land and established 500 years of economic and social exploitation, the Maya people took refuge in the strengths of their family life and ensured that their traditions were preserved from generation to generation. For the most part, their resistance to exploitation and persecution has been passive. In some cases, they have been forced to meet the violence directed against them with violence for self-preservation. But they have usually responded to direct attacks by moving away from the forces of oppression. Of course, the doctrine of nonviolence has had many other proven successes; Mohandas Gandhi in India and Martin Luther King Jr. in the United States both led their people toward freedom by this philosophy. We can hope that the Maya people will yet succeed in finding their freedom by their traditional path of nonviolence.

LEARNING FROM FAILURES IN THE MAYA PAST

The Maya achieved great things during their long history. But, like all human societies, they also made mistakes, and at times their very successes brought about failures. The Maya were so successful in producing food from their forest gardens and raised fields that in time they created two problems that are all too familiar to us today—environmental destruction and overpopulation—and were impacted by climate change. The success the Maya enjoyed in harvesting great quantities of food allowed their population to grow unchecked until the environment reached the limit of its ability to support people. Ultimately, the demands of overpopulation damaged the environment as forests were cut down and fertile soils were exhausted. Erosion overwhelmed formerly productive lakes and wetlands. Warfare and climate change (droughts) likely accelerated the decline as malnutrition, disease, and starvation fostered disillusionment with the leaders of society.

Most of the Maya people survived by moving away from the centers of disaster to continue their lives in new settings. But the lessons for us in today's world should be clear. What happened to the Maya is a relatively small-scale example of what is happening on a far larger scale to our world today. If we do not heed the lesson of the Maya and solve the problems of environmental destruction, overpopulation, and climate change, the disaster that awaits us will be far more profound and will affect our entire planet. The Maya were able to move from the lowland disaster areas to adjacent undamaged regions. Where will we be able to find such undamaged refuges in today's world?

FURTHER READING

Farriss 1984; Fischer and Brown 1996; Harrison and Turner 1978; Jones 1989; Montejo 1999; Sabloff 1994; Sharer and Traxler 2006; Sullivan 1989; Warren and Jackson 2002.

BIBLIOGRAPHY

NONPRINT SOURCES

DVDs

Dawn of the Maya. National Geographic Television (2004)
Lost King of the Maya. A NOVA Production by Providence Pictures, Inc. WGBH/
    Boston (2001)
Lost Kingdom of the Maya. National Geographic Television (1993)
Mayan Mystery. National Geographic Television (2008)

Web Sites

Foundation for the Advancement of Mesoamerican Studies: www.famsi.org
Institute of Maya Studies: www.mayastudies.org
Maya Exploration Center: www.mayaexploration.org
Mesoweb: www.mesoweb.com
Wayeb (European Maya Association): www.wayeb.org

PUBLISHED SOURCES

Abrams, E. M. 1994. *How the Maya Built Their World: Energetics and Ancient Archi-
tecture.* Austin: University of Texas Press.
Alvarado, P. de. 1924. *An Account of the Conquest of Guatemala in 1524.* Trans.
S. J. Mackie. New York: Cortés Society.
Andrews, G. F. 1975. *Maya Cities: Placemaking and Urbanization.* Norman: University
of Oklahoma Press.

Andrews, A. P. 1983. *Maya Salt Production and Trade*. Tucson: University of Arizona Press.

Andrews, A. P., E. W. Andrews, and F. Robles C. 2003. The Northern Maya Collapse and Its Aftermath. *Ancient Mesoamerica*14: 151–156.

Andrews, E. W., and W. L. Fash, eds. 2005. *Early Classic Royal Power in Copan: The Origins and Development of the Acropolis (ca. AD 250–650)*. Santa Fe, NM: School of American Research Press.

Ardren, T., ed. 2002. *Ancient Maya Women*. Walnut Creek, CA: Alta Mira Press.

Ashmore, W. A., and J. A. Sabloff. 2002. Spatial Orders of Maya Civic Plans. *Latin American Antiquity* 13: 201–216.

Ashmore, W. A., and R. J. Sharer. 2005. *Discovering Our Past*. New York: McGraw-Hill.

Aveni, A. F. 2001. *Skywatchers: A Revised and Updated Version of Skywatchers of Ancient Mexico*. Austin: University of Texas Press.

Barrera Vásquez, A. 1980. *Diccionario Maya Cordemex, Maya-Español, Español-Maya*. Mérida: Ediciones Cordemex.

Bell, E. E., M. A. Canuto, and R. J. Sharer, eds. 2004. *Understanding Early Classic Copan*. Philadelphia: University of Pennsylvania Museum.

Benson, E. P., and E. H. Boone, eds. 1984. *Ritual Human Sacrifice in Mesoamerica*. Washington, DC: Dumbarton Oaks.

Bove, F. J., and L. Heller, eds. 1989. *New Frontiers in the Archaeology of the Pacific Coast of Southern Mesoamerica*. Tempe: Arizona State University Anthropological Research Papers.

Braswell, G. E., ed. 2003. *The Maya and Teotihuacan: Reinterpreting Early Classic Interaction*. Austin: University of Texas Press.

Bricker, V. R. 1986. *A Grammar of Mayan Hieroglyphs*. New Orleans: Middle American Research Institute, Tulane University.

Canuto, M., and J. Yaeger, eds. 2000. *The Archaeology of Communities: A New World Perspective*. London: Routledge Press.

Chamberlain, R. S. 1948. *The Conquest and Colonization of Yucatan, 1517–1550*. Publication 582. Washington, DC: Carnegie Institution of Washington.

Chase, A. F., and D. Z. Chase. 1996. More Than Kin and King: Centralized Political Organization among the Late Classic Maya. *Current Anthropology* 37: 803–830.

Chase, D. Z., and A. F. Chase, eds. 1992. *Mesoamerican Elites: An Archaeological Assessment*. Norman: University of Oklahoma Press.

Chase, A. F., and P. M. Rice, eds. 1985. *The Lowland Maya Postclassic*. Austin: University of Texas Press.

Chiappelli, F. ed. 1976. *First Images of America*. Berkeley: University of California Press.

Christenson, A. J. 2003. *Popol Vuh: The Sacred Book of the Maya*. New York: O Books.

Christie, J. J., ed. 2003. *Maya Palaces and Elite Residences: An Interdisciplinary Approach*. Austin: University of Texas Press.

Clark, J. E., R. L. Carneiro, and R. de Los Angeles Montaño P., eds. In press. *The Evolution of Olmec Societies*. Cambridge: Cambridge University Press.

Coe, M. D., and M. Van Stone. 2001. *Reading the Maya Glyphs*. London: Thames and Hudson.

Culbert, T. P., ed. 1973. *The Classic Maya Collapse*. Albuquerque: University of New Mexico Press.

———, ed. 1991. *Classic Maya Political History*. Cambridge: Cambridge University Press.

Dahlin, B. H. 2000. The Barricade and Abandonment of Chunchucmil: Implications for Northern Maya Warfare. *Latin American Antiquity* 11(3): 283–298.

———. 2003. Climate Change and the End of the Classic Period in Yucatan: Resolving a Paradox. *Ancient Mesoamerica* 13: 327–340

Demarest, A. A. 2004. *Ancient Maya: The Rise and Fall of a Rainforest Civilization*. Cambridge: Cambridge University Press.

Demarest, A. A., P. M. Rice, and D. S. Rice, eds. 2004. *The Terminal Classic in the Maya Lowlands: Collapse, Transition, and Transformation*. Boulder: University Press of Colorado.

Díaz del Castillo, B. 1956. *The Discovery and Conquest of Mexico, 1517–1521*. Trans. A. P. Maudslay (original published 1632). New York: Grove Press.

Dillehay, T. D. 2000. *The Settlement of the Americas: A New History*. New York: Basic Books.

Drennan, R. D., and C. A. Uribe, eds. 1987. *Chiefdoms in the Americas*. Lanham: University Press of America.

Dunning, N. P. 1992. *Lords of the Hills: Ancient Maya Settlement in the Puuc region, Yucatan, Mexico*. Madison, WI: Prehistory Press.

Edmonson, M. S., ed. and trans. 1982. *The Ancient Future of the Itza: The Book of Chilam Balam of Tizimin*. Austin: University of Texas Press.

———, trans. 1986. *Heaven Born Mérida and Its Destiny: The Book of Chilam Balam of Chumayel*. Austin: University of Texas Press.

England, N. C. 2003. Maya Language Revival and Revitalization Politics: Linguists and Linguistic Ideologies. *American Anthropologist* 105: 733–743.

Farriss, N. M. 1984. *Maya Society under Colonial Rule: The Collective Enterprise of Survival*. Princeton: Princeton University Press.

Fash, W. L. 2001. *Scribes, Warriors, and Kings: The City of Copan and the Ancient Maya*. Revised edition. New York: Thames and Hudson.

Fash, W. L., and R. J. Sharer. 1991. Sociopolitical Developments and Methodological Issues at Copán, Honduras: A Conjunctive Perspective. *Latin American Antiquity* 2: 166–187.

Fedick, S. L., ed. 1996. *The Managed Mosaic: Ancient Maya Agriculture and Resource Use*. Salt Lake City: University of Utah Press.

Feinman, G. M., and J. Marcus, eds. 1998. *Archaic States*. Santa Fe, NM: School of American Research Press.

Fischer, E. F., and R. McKenna Brown, eds. 1996. *Maya Cultural Activism in Guatemala*. Austin: University of Texas Press.

Flannery, K. V., ed. 1976. *The Early Mesoamerican Village*. New York: Academic Press.

———, ed. 1982. *Maya Subsistence: Studies in Memory of Dennis E. Puleston*. New York: Academic Press.

Flannery, K. V., and J. Marcus. 1983. *The Cloud People: Divergent Evolution of the Zapotec and Mixtec Civilizations*. New York: Academic Press.

Fox, J. W. 1978. *Quiché Conquest*. Albuquerque: University of New Mexico Press.

———. 1987. *Maya Postclassic State Formation*. Cambridge: Cambridge University Press.

Freidel, D. A., and J. A. Sabloff. 1984. *Cozumel: Late Maya Settlement Patterns*. New York: Academic Press.

Garber, J. F., ed. 2004. *The Ancient Maya of the Belize Valley: Half a Century of Archaeological Research*. Gainesville: University Press of Florida.

Gill, R. B. 2000. *The Great Maya Droughts: Water, Life, and Death*. Albuquerque: University of New Mexico Press.

Gillespie, S. D. 2002. Rethinking Ancient Maya Social Organization: Replacing "Lineage" with "House." *American Anthropologist* 102: 467–484.

Golden, C. W., and G. Borgstede, eds. 2004. *Continuity and Change in Maya Archaeology: Perspectives at the Millennium*. New York and London: Routledge.

Grove, D. C. 1984. *Chalcatzingo*. New York: Thames and Hudson.

Grove, D. C., and R. A. Joyce, eds. 1999. *Social Patterns in Preclassic Mesoamerica*. Washington, DC: Dumbarton Oaks.

Grube, N., ed. 2001. *Maya: Divine Kings of the Rain Forest*. Cologne: Könemann.

Hanks, W. F., and D. S. Rice, eds. 1989. *Word and Image in Maya Culture: Explorations in Language, Writing and Representation*. Salt Lake City: University of Utah Press.

Harrison, P. D., and B. L. Turner, eds. 1978. *Pre-Hispanic Maya Agriculture*. Austin: University of Texas Press.

Haug, G. H., D. Gunther, L. C. Peterson, D. M. Sigman, K. A. Hugden, and B. Aeschlimann. 2003. Climate and the Collapse of Maya Civilization *Science* 299: 1731–1735.

Helms, M. W. 1975. *Middle America: A Cultural History of Heartland and Frontiers*. Englewood Cliffs, NJ: Prentice Hall.

———. 1993. *Craft and Kingly Ideal: Art, Trade, and Power*. Austin: University of Texas Press.

Hill, R. M. 1996. Eastern Chajoma Political Geography: Ethnohistorical and Archaeological Contributions to the Study of a Late Postclassic Maya Polity. *Ancient Mesoamerica* 7: 63–87.

Hill, R. M., and J. Monaghan. 1987. *Continuities in Highland Maya Social Organization: Ethnohistory in Sacapulas, Guatemala*. Philadelphia: University of Pennsylvania Press.

Hirth, K. G., ed. 1984. *Trade and Exchange in Early Mesoamerica*. Albuquerque: University of New Mexico Press.

Houston, S. D. 2000. Into the Minds of Ancients: Advances in Maya Glyph Studies. *Journal of World Prehistory* 14: 291–201.

———, ed. 1998. *Function and Meaning in Maya Architecture*. Washington, DC: Dumbarton Oaks.

Houston, S. H., O. Chinchilla M., and D. Stuart, eds. 2001. *The Decipherment of Ancient Maya Writing*. Norman: University of Oklahoma Press.

Houston, S. D., J. Robertson, and D. Stuart. 1996. The Language of Classic Maya Inscriptions. *Current Anthropology* 41: 321–356.

Innes, H. 1969. *The Conquistadors*. New York: Knopf.

Inomata, T., and S. D. Houston, eds. 2001. *Royal Courts of the Ancient Maya. Vol. 1: Theory, Comparison, and Synthesis. Vol. 2: Data and Case Studies*. Boulder: Westview Press.

Johnson, A. W., and T. K. Earle. 2001. *The Evolution of Human Societies: From Foraging Groups to Agrarian State*. Stanford, CA: Stanford University Press.

Jones, G. D. 1989. *Maya Resistance to Spanish Rule: Time and History on a Colonial Frontier*. Albuquerque: University of New Mexico Press.

———. 1998. *The Conquest of the Last Maya Kingdom.* Stanford: Stanford University Press.

Jones, G. D., and R. R. Kautz, eds. 1981. *The Transition to Statehood in the New World.* Cambridge: Cambridge University Press.

Justeson, J. S., and L. Campbell, eds. 1984. *Phoneticism in Mayan Hieroglyphic Writing.* Albany: State University of New York Press, Institute of Mesoamerican Studies.

Kaufman, T. S. 1974. Mesoamerican Indian Languages. *Encyclopaedia Britannica* (fifteenth edition) 11: 959–963.

Kelley, D. H. 1976. *Deciphering the Maya Script.* Austin: University of Texas Press.

Kowalski, J. K. 1987. *The House of the Governor: A Maya Palace of Uxmal, Yucatan, Mexico.* Norman: University of Oklahoma Press.

Las Casas, B. de. 1957. *Historia de las Indias.* Madrid: Ediciones Atlas.

Lohse, J. C., and F. Valdez, Jr., eds. 2004. *Ancient Maya Commoners.* Austin: University of Texas Press.

Looper, M. 2003. *Lightening Warrior: Maya Art and Kingship at Quirigua.* Austin: University of Texas Press.

Love, M. W., M. Poponoe de Hatch, and H. L. Escobedo, eds. 2002. *Incidents of Archaeology in Central America and Yucatan: Essays in Honor of Edwin M. Shook.* Lanham, MD: University Press of America.

Lowe, J.G.W. 1985. *The Dynamics of Apocalypse: A Systems Simulation of the Classic Maya Collapse.* Albuquerque: University of New Mexico Press.

Marcus, J. 1992a. *Mesoamerican Writing Systems: Propaganda, Myth, and History in Four Ancient Civilizations.* Princeton: Princeton University Press.

———. 1992b. Dynamic Cycles of Mesoamerican States. *National Geographic Research and Exploration* 8: 392–411.

Martin, S., and N. Grube. 1995. Maya Superstates. *Archaeology* 48(6): 41–46.

———. 2008. *Chronicle of the Maya Kings and Queens.* Second Edition. London: Thames and Hudson.

Masson, M. A., and D, A, Freidel, eds. 2002. *Ancient Maya Political Economies.* Walnut Creek, CA: Altamira Press.

Maudslay, A. P. 1889–1902. *Biología Centrali-Americana: Archaeology.* 5 vols. London: R. H. Porter and Dulau.

McAnany, P. A. 1995. *Living with Ancestors: Kinship and Kingship in Ancient Maya Society.* Austin: University of Texas Press.

———, ed. 2004. *K'axob: Ritual, Work, and Family in an Ancient Maya Village.* Los Angeles: Cotsen Institute of Archaeology, University of California at Los Angeles.

Meyer, K. E. 1977. *The Plundered Past.* New York: Atheneum.

Milbrath, S., and C. Peraza L. 2003. Revisiting Mayapan: Mexico's Last Maya Capital. *Ancient Mesoamerica* 14: 1–46.

Miller, M. E. 1986. *The Murals of Bonampak.* Princeton: Princeton University Press.

Montejo, V. 1999. *Voices from Exile: Violence and Survival in Modern Maya History.* Norman: University of Oklahoma Press.

Osborne, L. de Jongh. 1965. *Indian Crafts of Guatemala and El Salvador.* Norman: University of Oklahoma Press.

Pool, Christopher A. 2007. *Olmec Archaeology and Early Mesoamerica.* Cambridge: Cambridge University Press.

Proskouriakoff, T. 1963. *An Album of Maya Architecture.* Norman: University of Oklahoma Press.

Recinos, A., and D. Goetz. 1953. *The Annals of the Cakchiquels.* Norman: University of Oklahoma Press.

Richards, M. 2003. *Atlas Lingüístico de Guatemala.* Guatemala City: Universidad Rafael Landívar.

Roys, R. L. 1967. *The Book of Chilam Balam of Chumayel.* Reprint of the original edition (1933). Norman: University of Oklahoma Press.

Ruppert, K. J., J.E.S. Thompson, and T. Proskouriakoff. 1955. *Bonampak, Chiapas, Mexico.* Publication 602. Washington, DC: Carnegie Institution of Washington.

Sabloff, J. A. 1994. *The New Archaeology and the Ancient Maya.* Second edition. New York: W. H. Freeman.

———, ed. 2003. *Tikal: Dynasties, Foreigners, and Affairs of State: Advancing Maya Archaeology.* Santa Fe: School of American Research.

Sabloff, J. A., and E. W. Andrews, eds. 1986. *Late Lowland Maya Civilization: Classic to Postclassic.* Albuquerque: University of New Mexico Press.

Sabloff, J. A., and J. S. Henderson, eds. 1993. *Lowland Maya Civilization in the Eighth Century A.D.* Washington, DC: Dumbarton Oaks.

Saturno, W. 2002. Archaeological Investigations and Conservation at San Bartolo, Guatemala. Foundation for the Advancement of Mesoamerican Studies (FAMSI) Web site Research Report, available at www.famsi.org.

Schele, L., and D. A. Freidel. 1990. *A Forest of Kings.* New York: Morrow.

Sharer, R. J., and D. C. Grove, eds. 1989. *Regional Perspectives on the Olmec.* Cambridge: Cambridge University Press.

Sharer, R. J., and D. W. Sedat. 1987. *Archaeological Investigations in the Northern Maya Highlands, Guatemala.* Philadelphia: University of Pennsylvania Museum.

Sharer, R. J., and L. P. Traxler. 2006. *The Ancient Maya.* Sixth edition, revised. Stanford: Stanford University Press.

Sharer, R. J., and L. P. Traxler, eds. In press. *Origins of Maya States.* Philadelphia: University of Pennsylvania Museum.

Sheets, P. 2006. *The Cerén Site: An Ancient Village Buried by Volcanic Ash in Central El Salvador.* Second edition. Belmont CA: Thompson Wadsworth.

Stephens, J. L. 1841. *Incidents of Travel in Central America, Chiapas, and Yucatan.* 2 vols. New York: Harper. Reprinted by Dover, 1962.

———. 1843. *Incidents of Travel in Yucatan.* 2 vols. New York: Harper. Reprinted by Dover, 1963.

Stuart, D. 2005. *The Inscriptions from Temple XIX at Palenque.* San Francisco: Pre-Columbian Art Research Institute

Stuart, D., and S. D. Houston. 1989. Maya Writing. *Scientific American* 261(2): 82–89.

Sullivan, P. 1989. *Unfinished Conversations: Mayas and Foreigners between Two Wars.* New York: Knopf.

Tate, C. 1992. *Yaxchilan: The Design of a Maya Ceremonial City.* Austin: University of Texas Press.

Taube, K. 1992. *The Major Gods of Ancient Yucatan.* Dumbarton Oaks Studies in Pre-Columbian Art and Archaeology no. 32. Washington, DC: Dumbarton Oaks.

Tedlock, B. 1982. *Time and the Highland Maya.* Albuquerque: University of New Mexico Press.

Tedlock, D. 1985. *Popol Vuh: The Mayan Book of the Dawn of Life.* New York: Simon and Schuster.

Tiesler, V., and A. Cucina., eds. 2006. *Janaab' Pakal of Palenque: Reconstructing the Life and Death of a Maya Ruler.* Tucson: University of Arizona Press.

Tozzer, A. M. 1941. *Landa's Relación de las cosas de Yucatán.* Cambridge, MA: Peabody Museum of Archaeology and Ethnology, Harvard University.

Turner, B. L., and P. D. Harrison. 1981. Prehistoric Ridged-Field Agriculture in the Maya Lowlands. *Science* 213 (4506): 399–405.

Turner, B. L., and P. D. Harrison, eds. 1983. *Pulltrouser Swamp: Ancient Maya Habitat, Agriculture, and Settlement in Northern Belize.* Austin: University of Texas press.

Urban, P. A., and E. M. Schortman, eds. 1986. *The Southeast Maya Periphery.* Austin: University of Texas Press.

Vogt, E. Z. 1969. *Zinacantan: A Maya Community in the Highlands of Chiapas.* Cambridge, MA: Harvard University Press.

Warren, K. B., and J. E. Jackson, eds. 2002. *Indigenous Movements, Self-Representation, and the State in Latin America.* Austin: University of Texas Press.

Wilk, R. R., and W. Ashmore, eds. 1988. *Household and Community in the Mesoamerican Past.* Albuquerque: University of New Mexico Press.

Willey, G. R. 1987. *Essays in Maya Archaeology.* Albuquerque: University of New Mexico Press.

Wolf, E. R. 1959. *Sons of the Shaking Earth.* Chicago: University of Chicago Press.

INDEX

About the Author

ROBERT J. SHARER is Sally and Alvin Shoemaker Professor in Anthropology at the University of Pennsylvania. He is the author of *The Ancient Maya* (revised and expanded edition, 2006) and *Quirigua: A Classic Maya Center and Its Sculpture* (1990), has published more than 100 scholarly articles, and has cowritten two archaeology textbooks and several monographs reporting the results of his archaeological research. He has also coedited five books, including *Understanding Early Classic Copán* (2004), and *Regional Perspectives on the Olmec* (1989). He has conducted research in Central America for more than 40 years.